Deerland is an inquisitive and eye-opening tour through the history, science, politics, economics, and cultural quirks of our uniquely American relationship with the white-tailed deer. From ecologists and foresters to farmers, hunters, homeowners, and business owners, Cambronne introduces us to a fascinating cast of characters whose lives, like yours and mine, are inextricably linked to whitetails.

—Tovar Cerulli, author of *The Mindful Carnivore:*
A Vegetarian's Hunt for Sustenance

Whether you hunt them or watch them, love them or loathe them, you need to understand that deer are not just another wild species on the rural and suburban landscape but the single most economically important and problematic wild creature in our midst. This book tells you why in fascinating detail.

With *Deerland: America's Hunt For Ecological Balance and the Essence of Wildness,* Al Cambronne takes us deep inside what he calls "the deer-industrial complex" and the many billions of dollars spent annually not only growing and pursuing whitetails but also fixing the damage their overabundance causes. He takes us to auto body shops that thrive on deer-vehicle crashes and shows us crops, forests, and entire eco-systems stunted by whitetail over-browsing. He explains the whitetail's magical allure for hunters and watchers alike, but how the small fortunes they spend on supplemental food to keep deer around makes things worse.

Cambronne offers up a tour de force on deer history, biology, ecology, economics, and politics, and how the quest for deer and their antlers largely built America's outdoor industry. He's a good reporter, taking the reader along to learn from experts, then putting down what he learns in a wonderfully-written, comprehensive, balanced, often funny and important book.

—Jim Sterba, author of *Nature Wars: The Incredible Story of How*
Wildlife Comebacks Turned Backyards into Battlegrounds

D0778432

Deerland is an absorbing survey of both the depth and breadth of America's obsession with deer, and of the biological, economic, and sometimes lethal consequences of that obsession. From the multi-billion dollar deer hunting industry's antler-mania to the surge in "adult-onset" meat hunters to the bizarre way we have transformed our landscape into ecologically unbalanced deer preserves, after reading this book you will never look at Bambi in quite the same way again.

—Hank Shaw, author of *Hunt, Gather, Cook:*
Finding the Forgotten Feast

Fair-minded to a fault. . . . Even if you do not care about deer, deer hunting, or deer hunters, *Deerland* is a book well worth reading. Deer have become a major force in shaping the landscape. They also impact our economy: crop damage, collisions with deer, and treatment for Lyme disease add up to several billions of dollars annually. Al Cambronne has written a lively, thoroughly researched book on the way deer have shaped us and we have shaped deer.

—Jan Dizard, author of *Going Wild: Hunting, Animal Rights,*
and the Contested Meaning of Nature

DEERLAND

*America's Hunt for Ecological Balance
and the Essence of Wildness*

AL CAMBRONNE

LYONS PRESS
Guilford, Connecticut

An imprint of Globe Pequot Press

For Jean

Lyons Press is an imprint of Globe Pequot Press.

Project editor: David Legere
Text design: Sheryl P. Kober
Layout artist: Melissa Evarts

Library of Congress Cataloging-in-Publication Data is available on file.

ISBN 978-0-7627-8027-3

Printed in the United States of America
10 9 8 7 6 5 4 3 2 1

Contents

Foreword: Welcome to Deerland

We live in Deerland.

The United States now has over thirty million deer, a hundred times more than just a century ago. They routinely disrupt entire ecosystems. They ravage our gardens and suburban landscaping, and every year they kill and injure hundreds of us on our highways. No wild animal larger than a skunk or raccoon is anywhere near so numerous and widespread.

Still, deer are magical. Their mere existence makes the woods feel wilder. They signify far more to us than just meat, antlers, or a graceful, mysterious creature slipping through the shadows. In our collective imaginations they've become an archetypal symbol of the wilderness experience—or at least of a gentrified country lifestyle.

Love them or hate them, we've all come under their spell. We name suburban housing developments after them. We commute farther and borrow more so that we can live beside them. If money remains, we buy vacation homes where we'll see even more of them. A few of us happily spend two or three years' salary for a small piece of untillable land on which we can hunt them. In much of America, deer are now the single greatest driver of the rural real estate market.

More American hunters pursue deer than any other quarry, and this inevitably makes hunting part of our story. Rest assured, however, that hunting is only one part of a much larger environmental, social, and cultural story. And regardless of how you may feel about hunting, in many parts of America we now have a very real problem with too many deer. In some of those places, hunting is a big part of the solution. It's also, some would argue, a big part of the problem.

All too often we manipulate entire ecosystems in ways that benefit deer. When forced to choose between whitetails and all other wildlife, we almost invariably choose deer. As a result most of us, even if we spend a fair amount of time in the woods, have never once seen a forest that's not shaped by deer.

Still, for venison-loving hunters and vegan wildlife watchers alike, the very phrase "overabundant deer" can seem a puzzling oxymoron. And by the time we finally comprehend the choices we've made, there's no going back. Yes, it definitely is possible to have too many deer. The only question is: How many is too many?

Deer are one of the most charismatic of the charismatic megafauna. All too often their charisma prevents us from thinking clearly and rationally about questions like this one. Every time that happens, it has consequences for us, our deer, the environment, and the American landscape.

Indeed, our complex relationship with deer makes for a twisted tale of love, obsession, and consequences. First come love and obsession. Then come the consequences. At first glance these might seem like stories for two different books. In one, wildlife watchers lure deer to their backyard feeders, locavore foodies trade gourmet venison recipes, antler-obsessed bowhunters perch in treestands, and millions more hunters spend big bucks in the pursuit of big bucks. In the other are car crashes, Lyme disease, agricultural losses, environmental devastation, and endless hordes of deer invading America's suburbs.

But in the end these two stories are inseparable. They're two sides of the same coin, and it's impossible to tell one story without the other. Indeed, it's impossible to understand either story without fully understanding the other.

You're about to begin a journey through America's forests, farms, and suburbs. We'll peer inside America's deer-industrial complex, explore hidden subcultures, and learn how the effects of a gluttonous deer's dinner echo and reverberate through an entire ecosystem. It's time to take a long, hard look at our love, our obsession, and their unintended but inevitable consequences. By doing so we'll be better able to restore the balance we've disrupted. It's time to tame the charismatic mega-fawn.

Along the way our complex relationship with deer makes for a fascinating story that reveals much about America—and also about Americans. Yes, this is a story about deer. Most of all, however, it's a story about us.

Welcome to Deerland.

I. Love and Obsession

CHAPTER 1

Darwin's Deer

Let us suppose that the fleetest prey, a deer for instance, had from any change in the country increased in numbers, or that other prey had decreased in numbers, during that season of the year when the wolf was hardest pressed for food. Under such circumstances the swiftest and slimmest wolves would have the best chance of surviving and so be preserved or selected.

—CHARLES DARWIN IN *THE ORIGIN OF SPECIES*

Today we remember Aldo Leopold and John James Audubon for other reasons. Both, however, were avid deer hunters. Remarkably, so was Charles Darwin.

Now, just a few years past the 200th anniversary of Darwin's birth, few remember that he often enjoyed stalking deer at Maer Hall, the country estate owned by his uncle, Josiah Wedgwood II. As a boy, Darwin spent a great deal of time with his cousins at Maer. One of them quite took his fancy, and in 1839 he finally married his cousin Emma.

It was also at Maer Hall that Darwin drafted *The Origin of Species*. As he tentatively advances the ideas for which he'd later become famous, he repeatedly uses deer and deerhounds as examples of natural and unnatural selection. Earlier, in *The Voyage of the* Beagle, Darwin describes at length his excursions ashore to hunt deer in northern Patagonia. Sailors aboard the *Beagle* must have been glad for the fresh venison he brought back to the ship. In one passage he writes:

If a person crawling close along the ground, slowly advances towards a herd, the deer frequently, out of curiosity, approach to reconnoitre him.

*I have by this means, killed from one spot, three out of the same herd.
Although so tame and inquisitive, yet when approached on horseback,
they are exceedingly wary. In this country nobody goes on foot, and
the deer knows man as its enemy only when he is mounted and armed
with the bolas.*[1]

Today this species of Patagonian deer is far more wary and less abundant. Back home, however, much of Britain is plagued by overabundant deer of six different species: red deer, roe deer, fallow deer, Sika deer, muntjac deer, and Chinese water deer. All but the first two are nonnative invasives that were brought to Britain and then either escaped or were released intentionally.[2]

The area of North Staffordshire near Maer Hall has been especially troubled by overly abundant deer. In the 1980s the area's frequent deer-vehicle crashes led to the formation of the Deer Study & Resource Centre in nearby Stoke-on-Trent. Its mission was to develop educational materials that would help teachers, students, and the public become better informed about deer—and maybe even save a few motorists' lives.[3]

The center's director, Jeanette Lawton, told me these hordes of deer are still a problem locally. Few, however, actually make their home on the grounds of Maer Hall. They're mostly just passing through. That's because Copeland Cottage at Maer is now one of the most popular camps in Britain's Girl Guide (Girl Scout) system. Apparently all those Girl Guides romping through the woods and singing around the campfire were a bit much. The deer have moved on to greener and quieter pastures.

But if there were no calmer estates nearby, the deer of North Staffordshire would have surely adapted to the presence of all those Girl Guides. After all, their close relatives have happily adapted to similar levels of activity in the suburbs of Connecticut, New York, and Pennsylvania. Other deer have adapted and thrived in a wide variety of ecosystems all over the world. Darwin's deer are survivors.

THE CERVID FAMILY TREE

Within the class Mammalia are twenty-six orders, two of which walk on hooves and are called ungulates. In the odd way these categories sometimes work, horses and rhinos both belong to the order of ungulates that has an odd number of toes—either one or three. The other order, Artiodactyla, has an even number of toes. This catchall category includes hoofed mammals like cattle, bison, pigs, goats, and, best of all, deer.

Next, within the order Artiodactyla, the family Cervidae includes eighteen genera of deerlike animals that together include around fifty species. (Taxonomists sometimes disagree on the boundaries between certain species and subspecies.) These distant cousins within the deer family range in size from the ten-pound South American pudu to Alaskan moose that weigh nearly a ton.[4]

The main defining characteristic of cervids is that they shed their antlers every year. Except for caribou and reindeer, only the males have antlers. (Despite the existence of various subspecies in Canada, Scandinavia, and Siberia, it's simplest to just think of caribou as the North American term for reindeer.) Although the Chinese water deer doesn't have antlers, it's still considered a cervid by virtue of certain other anatomical features. Instead of antlers, males of this species have large upper canines. Even though these three-inch tusks may not strike terror in the hearts of humans, they're more than adequate for raging, rutting bucks that weigh thirty pounds and stand eighteen inches at the shoulder. Muntjacs, a separate genus of small deer that's native to Southern Asia, are fortunate enough to be equipped with both tusks *and* antlers.

The earliest known artiodactyl was Diacodexis, a rabbit-size ungulate that lived around forty to fifty million years ago. The first artiodactyls resembling modern deer were the saber-toothed Blastomeryx and Dremotherium, both of which lived around twenty-five to thirty million years ago. Over the millennia, with rare exceptions like the muntjacs and Chinese water deer, tusks shrank and antlers grew.

The oldest fossils of North American deer are from an animal that might have looked very similar to modern roe deer or Chinese water deer; they were found in five-million-year-old deposits in Florida. The first deer that would look familiar to most of us lived four million years ago in Kansas. Even to a scientist who specializes in such things, its fossil remains are indistinguishable from those of a modern whitetail. The quarter-ton dire wolves and saber-tooth cats that pursued these deer are long gone. So are the giant sloths and mastodons that once browsed beside them. Deer are survivors.

During the late Pleistocene, at least three distinct genera of deer wandered North America. Of the three, only Odocoileus remains. It's the genus that includes our modern mule deer (*Odocoileus hemionus*) and whitetails (*Odocoileus virginianus*). (Moose, elk, and caribou are all more recent arrivals that migrated across the Bering land bridge sometime later.) The next chapter of this story gets more complicated as glaciers advanced, receded, paused for a few millennia, and advanced again. It's a story of recurring migrations, separations, reunions, and hybridizations.

Noted deer biologist Jim Heffelfinger explains how the fossil record tells only part of the story.[5] For one thing, he writes, "repeated glaciations . . . scoured the land for thousands of years, destroying most evidence of early North American deer evolution." For another, even experts have a hard time differentiating skeletal remains of whitetail and mule deer unless they have certain leg bones, antlers from a mature male, or the tiny lacrimal bone, which is a part of the skull located on the inner sides of the eye socket. And although mule deer are on average slightly larger, both species come in a wide range of sizes.

During just the past few years, however, geneticists have begun tackling problems like this one by analyzing nuclear DNA, mitochondrial DNA, genetic microsatellites, molecular clocks, and genetic drift rates. Although these techniques have called into question previously held theories, they haven't yet led to a new consensus. When I got in touch with Heffelfinger for an update in 2012, he said our best estimate of the date when whitetails and mule deer became separate species still ranges from 750,000 to 3.7 million years ago. Exactly how and where that happened is also still open to debate.

As you might guess from their names, mule deer have large, mulish ears and whitetails have a large tail whose white underside serves as a warning flag when trouble arises. Mule deer have smaller tails that are black at the tip; hence their two subspecies are called blacktails. The average mule deer is also larger and chunkier than a whitetail, and males tend to have larger antlers that are a slightly different shape. Unlike whitetails, mule deer run with a bounding, stiff-legged gait called stotting. Although perhaps slower and less efficient, their gait helps them leap over obstacles that a pursuing predator will need to go around.

Even when their ranges overlap, the two species tend to seek out different habitats. In the foothills of Wyoming, for example, you're more likely to see whitetails in the river bottoms and mule deer on nearby hillsides. If you do see both species mingling in the same farmer's alfalfa field, you'll be able to tell them apart with little difficulty.

Of America's roughly thirty million deer, just under five million are mule deer or blacktails. All the rest are whitetails. Mule deer live only in the open spaces of the West; blacktails only in the Pacific Northwest. Whitetails are five times more numerous, and they're found in every state except Alaska, Hawaii, and for all practical purposes Nevada, California, and Utah. That leaves forty-five states with significant whitetail populations. They're also present in much of Central and South America, plus every province in Canada except Nunavut. In recent years their range has extended northward into the Canadian Yukon and the Mackenzie River valley. So far they've reached latitudes just south of the Arctic Circle.[6]

What's more, whitetails live in places where they're likely to interact with large numbers of humans—and not just hunters. When most Americans think of deer, they think of whitetails. True, when I tell of cervids invading our suburbs, perhaps I should mention mule deer in Boulder, elk in Estes Park, or moose in Anchorage. They're all members of the deer family, and locally they've all become a nuisance at times. But from here on we'll mostly be talking whitetails.

Like mule deer, whitetails have two generally recognized subspecies—possibly, depending on whom you ask, a few more besides. There was a time, in fact, when eager taxonomists had identified as many as thirty-eight subspecies. In 1984 one massive, 872-page reference work stated unequivocally that there were thirty subspecies in North and Central America, with at least sixteen here in the United States.[7] It's a remarkable coincidence that boundaries between subspecies so often corresponded to the boundaries between states. Somehow members of the northern subspecies *O. v. borealis* living in Indiana and Ohio must have known to keep their distance from members of the southern subspecies *O. v. virginianus* wandering the opposite bank in Kentucky and West Virginia. And vice versa.

Minnesotans, on the other hand, were supposedly fortunate enough to have three distinct whitetail subspecies living in their state. Intersecting lines on a map of the period suggest that in one small patch of woods at the edge of a cornfield somewhere due west of Minneapolis, an especially lucky hunter might have been able to bag all three. The truth, however, is that with very few exceptions there are no clear-cut genetic or pheno-typic differences that would allow even a trained biologist to differentiate between any of these thirty or more subspecies.

This long list of subspecies becomes even more suspect when we remember the role of human intervention. A century ago whitetails were nearly extirpated across most of America. To help bring them back from the brink, wildlife agencies and private citizens conducted hundreds of long-distance restocking operations over a period of decades. As with the more recent reintroduction of wild turkeys, it's a remarkable conservation success story.

Although it's likely there were many amateur efforts of question-able legality that are long forgotten, Heffelfinger cites these sanctioned and documented instances for starters: "Virginia was stocked with deer from 11 states. . . . Florida, Georgia, Arkansas, Kentucky, Louisiana, Mississippi, North Carolina, Tennessee, Virginia, and West Virginia each received hundreds of deer from Wisconsin. Mississippi received at least 72 deer from Mexico. . . . In addition to Wisconsin deer, deer from Texas were released in Florida (437), Louisiana (>167), and Georgia (1,058)."[8]

Today biologists still disagree about the precise number of distinct whitetail subspecies. But in its system for scoring trophy antlers, the Boone & Crockett Club recognizes only two, one of which is no longer hunted. The coues deer (pronounced "cows") is found in southeastern Arizona, southwestern New Mexico, and the area immediately across the border in Mexico. It's a smaller, daintier desert version of the usual whitetail. Even smaller, however, are the key deer of the Florida Keys. Mature does weigh around sixty pounds, and bucks rarely top eighty pounds. If their mainland counterparts are often described as "majestic," these bucks will have to settle for "cute." The population of key deer, which dipped as low as fifty in the 1940s, has now rebounded to around six hundred. They've been on the endangered species list since 1967, and no new trophy antlers from key deer will be entered into the record books anytime soon.[9]

THE FITTEST SURVIVOR

The same stealth, speed, and instinctive behaviors that once helped deer elude dire wolves and saber-toothed tigers just happen to be perfect for eluding humans too. I know of only one exception. When a deer sprints off and doesn't hear a pursuer behind it, it may pause and look back to verify the position of the original threat. As it does, it instinctively turns sideways so it will be less vulnerable to a predator attacking its hindquarters or hamstrings. For extra protection it may try to put a tree or other obstacle between it and any pursuing attacker.

Even then, however, running off a short distance, pausing, and turning sideways for a moment is probably not the best response to humans with rifles. Personally I've rarely seen deer do this—never when I was prepared to take advantage of it. It could be that in my neighborhood all the deer exhibiting this instinctive behavior are quickly being removed from the gene pool. And once their surviving relatives start running, they don't stop. They are, after all, survivors.

Deer have had four million years to evolve and get ready for us. Their senses are far more acute than ours, they're faster and more agile than we are, and they're perfectly comfortable sleeping naked in the snow for months on end. Every fall they shed their summer coats in favor of a thicker winter coat made of highly insulative hollow hairs. We not only can't grow hairs like this, we weren't able to manufacture enough of a synthetic substitute to insulate backpackers' sleeping bags until quite late in the twentieth century. (The first, developed in the 1970s, was DuPont's Hollofil. It's been largely superseded by a new version called Hollofil II.)[10]

True, deer aren't at the top of the food chain; even in summer, when it's not yet hunting season, they're always looking over their shoulder. And when they do, nearly everything they see is food. Even a deer's stomach is part of its survival strategy.

Strictly speaking, deer have four stomachs: reticulum, rumen, omasum, and abomasum. Each performs a specific function, and together they do a lot of digesting. After all those stomachs have done their work, deer still have up to sixty feet of small and large intestine.[11] Very few nutrients escape undigested. Nor is moisture wasted. When deer are browsing on succulent or dew-covered vegetation, they can easily survive in areas with little or no standing water.

From the name of that second stomach, the rumen, you may have guessed that deer are ruminants like cattle. This allows them to digest many foods we couldn't. For a prey species it has the added benefit of allowing them to quickly eat their fill and then go chew their cud while hiding in relative safety. But as a smaller ruminant with a smaller rumen, deer don't possess a giant bovine fermentation vat that breaks down huge quantities of less-digestible browse. They're selective browsers, preferring foods that are more digestible and nutritious.

As bystanders, we humans might look out into the woods and divide everything we see into two mental categories: wood and twigs, and grass and leaves. For deer it's not nearly as simple. Even delicacies like corn and alfalfa have woody stems containing a higher percentage of hard-to-digest lignin and cellulose. In response, deer make careful choices about what to eat and when to eat it. Younger plants are more succulent and digestible. Once the stems grow more fibrous, deer carefully select the terminal buds and outermost leaves.

Cattle graze; deer browse. If you look closely, you can see it in their faces. Cows have broad lawnmower noses, wide jaws, and a mouthful of teeth shaped for scissored, side-to-side grinding. Although moose and caribou share some of these same facial features, deer have long, slender noses and narrow jaws that end almost in a point.

Even a deer's teeth are made for choosing as much as chewing. Deer have lower incisors but none at the front of their upper jaw. On their upper jaw they have no teeth at all for the first few inches. On the lower jaw they have a correspondingly long gap between the front incisors and the rear molars. Although deer dentition is poorly suited for grinding large quantities of low-quality browse, it's ideal for plucking the perfect morsel and sending it back to the molars for a quick chew before it goes down the hatch.

With no upper incisors deer can only tear and pull at their food. If you awaken to find that some nocturnal creature has mown your hostas flat or snipped the stem of every single perennial you've worked so hard to grow, take a close look at what's left. If the cut is ragged, torn, and fibrous, the culprit was definitely a deer.

During a harsh Northern winter or a dry Southern summer, deer eat what they can get. The rest of the year, they can be surprisingly picky eaters. It's fascinating to watch them explore, sample, and browse. Although I've often "browsed" at libraries and bookstores, it was only after I spent a fair amount of time spying on deer that I truly understood the word's literal origins.

Deer don't carefully analyze the lignin and cellulose content of their dinner, any more than you do when you avoid the thickest romaine ribs in your Caesar salad or push aside the last two fibrous inches of those late-season asparagus stalks. Deer probably just eat what tastes good and feels good in their mouths. Like us, they crave foods that are sweet, salty, and unusually high in protein, carbohydrates, or fat. And like us, once they've finished sampling a buffet of these foods, they may decide to go hide somewhere and take a nap.

Deer prefer to hide when they can and run when they must. Even when they flee, they usually slip away slowly and silently. These are deer you'll never see. Others wait just a little too long before fleeing. It's common to almost step on them before they leap from hiding and crash off through the brush. Far more deer remain unseen, holding their ground as we stroll by ten or twenty yards away.

When deer do bolt, they may first give a warning signal in the form of a loud, snorting exhalation that even humans can hear from a quarter mile away. When you hear this "huff," you'll know you've been busted. If you see the deer at all, you may only glimpse the upraised tail that gives whitetails their name.

This may be the last you ever see of that particular deer. When deer do decide to run, they move fast. On open ground they can reach speeds of thirty-six miles per hour and leap over an eight-foot fence. Although other animals might be faster, few are more agile. What's most amazing is how fast deer can move through thick woods over uneven ground. Strong swimmers, they've colonized far-flung chains of islands from Alaska and British Columbia to the Florida Keys, Cuba, and the Virgin Islands.[12]

Deer almost always see us before we see them. Their eyesight, although very different from ours, is everything a deer could ever want. But more about that later. Beginning with vision would be a very human way of viewing the world. While we'll never know the small, alien mind of a deer, its thoughts are guided by sensory inputs very different from our own. Scent and sound give it important information about threats that aren't yet visible.

A deer's smelling equipment fills up a third of its head. The space above its jaw, from the tip of its nostrils all the way back to its eyes and its brain, is filled with pleats and folds of olfactory tissue that have over three hundred million scent receptors. Bloodhounds have around 220 million, humans fewer than five million.[13] To process all that information, a deer's brain has much larger olfactory bulbs than ours does.[14]

Even with my human nose, I've often smelled other hikers or hunters from a hundred yards away. Sweat. Aftershave. Perfume. A cigarette. A few times, mostly on warm, still summer days, I've even smelled unseen deer. A little like a horse only different. Sweeter. Although these claims might sound almost boastful coming from a human, no deer would be impressed.

Deer can smell food, water, or danger from a mile downwind. When we walk through the woods, we leave an invisible scent trail with every step. Deer know how fresh the trail is, when caution is still warranted, and when a scent is stale enough to be only a curiosity.

Long before we arrive they hear our approaching footsteps. An adult deer has cupped ears about three inches wide and six inches tall that rotate independently through a full 180 degrees.[15] When a deer hears something suspicious, or when it sees or smells something out of the ordinary, both ears swivel in that direction to pick up as much sound as possible. The rest of the time, the ears are constantly swiveling like a pair of radar dishes. Deer are especially good at pinpointing a sound's source. If one hears you make the slightest sound, a millisecond later it will be staring straight at you.

The one weakness of a deer's hearing might be that it's almost too sensitive and can be overwhelmed by an unusually loud noise, like a rifle shot. If a hunter misses but remains undetected by any of the deer's other senses, a confused deer may pause for the briefest moment while deciding the best direction in which to flee. It may pause just long enough to give the hunter a second shot.

Deer also have extraordinary vision. To frustrated hunters it can seem as though deer have eyes in the back of their head. They don't. But their enormous eyes do protrude from the sides of the head. That, combined with wide horizontal pupils, allows them to see distant objects through a 310-degree field of view. With the slightest movement of their heads, they can see everything in a full 360 degrees all around them.[16] And although deer see with single vision on the periphery, they still have binocular vision through a range nearly as wide as ours.

A deer's gigantic oval pupil lets in roughly nine times more light than our small round one. But that's only the beginning. Deer also have a tapetum lucidum, a reflective layer behind the retina that essentially allows them to use the same light twice. At night it's what gives deer eyes that reflective greenish glow in your headlights. On the retina itself we find even more differences. All mammalian retinas have two types of photoreceptors: rods for night vision in shades of gray; cones for daytime color vision. Compared with humans, deer have a much higher concentration of rods. This allows them to see in near-total darkness.[17]

In exchange, we have much better color vision than deer. Except for those with certain types of color blindness, humans have three types of cones that roughly correspond to red, blue, and green wavelengths. Deer have only the cones that sense blues and greens. Thanks to research done in the early 1990s, biologists now know precisely which colors deer are able to see, even the wavelengths to which they're most sensitive. By placing tiny electrodes on the eye of an anesthetized deer and then targeting its retina with pulses of monochromatic light, biologists verified that deer see blues and greens much better than we do. Fortunately for hunters, however, deer lack cones that sense light in red and orange wavelengths. This means their eyes are much less sensitive than ours to the 595- to 605-nanometer wavelength of blaze orange.[18]

Less fortunately for hunters there's another complication: Deer are extremely sensitive to certain wavelengths that are nearly invisible to humans. Unlike deer, we have a filtering layer that blocks about 99 percent of all ultraviolet (UV) light. Deer, however, are especially sensitive to these wavelengths, which excite their blue-sensing cones the same way blaze orange excites our red-sensing cones.[19]

Today most laundry detergents contain UV brighteners. To the human eye, they make our wash look brighter and cleaner. To the cervid eye, they make us glow like bright blue lightbulbs. Most fabrics, including the camouflage material used to make hunting clothing, are now treated with these brighteners right at the mill. Unless hunters use special detergents and UV blockers, their modern camo can put them at a decided disadvantage. One researcher has suggested that if Native Americans had been forced to wear modern hunting clothing, they would have starved.

Deer Die Young

Despite their agility, speed, stealth, and incredibly acute senses, very few deer die of old age. They meet their fates early, and in ways that are nearly countless. In the South, deer die from heat stress and starvation during hot, dry summers. In the North, they freeze and starve during long, cold winters. Some winters 80 to 90 percent of the casualties are fawns.[20] Most of the fawns born every spring, however, never live long enough to see their first snowflake.

Here in the woods of northern Wisconsin, a 2012 study found that only 27 percent of fawns survived their first seven months. A full 64 percent of that mortality was due to predators that included bears, bobcats, and coyotes. (Although none of the fawns in this study were taken by wolves, a few of the adult deer were.) Another 14 percent of fawns were harvested by hunters, and 9 percent starved. In a more agricultural area to the southeast, predators and starvation each accounted for 33 percent of fawn mortality. The next leading cause of mortality, at 17 percent, was vehicle collisions. In the northern study area, hunters accounted for 38 percent of adult mortality, with another 26 percent due to predation. Farther south, hunters accounted for 61 percent of adult mortality, vehicle collisions 24 percent.[21]

The more heavily populated corners of states like Connecticut, New York, and Pennsylvania are likely to see less predation from wolves, bears, and bobcats, but still lose deer to the occasional coyote. Within the city limits, deer are generally safe from hunters. They may even get an extra nutritional boost from well-meaning wildlife lovers who put out grain for them. These deer are most likely to die when they succumb to disease or are hit by a car. Or, after ingesting large amounts of carbohydrate-rich feed to which they're unaccustomed, they may fall victim to acidosis, enterotoxemia, or aflatoxin.

Small, statistically insignificant numbers of deer meet their fate in random freak accidents. They entangle their legs in barbwire fences, strangle themselves in children's swing sets, and freeze or drown after falling through thin lake ice. When the ice is thicker, other deer slip and fall, tearing ligaments and dislocating joints so severely that they never arise. They remain on the ice, legs splayed out, until they freeze, starve, or are discovered by predators.[22]

Whatever the mortality numbers, and however they might vary locally, one thing is certain: It's not easy being a deer. They're infected by viral diseases that include epizootic hemorrhagic disease (EHD), cutaneous fibromas and pappilomas, and arboviruses like West Nile virus and eastern equine encephalitis. Their bacterial diseases include anthrax, bovine tuberculosis (TB), salmonella, and various skin conditions and brain abscesses. As primary hosts of adult blacklegged deer ticks, they play an important role in spreading the bacteria that causes Lyme disease. Deer themselves appear to be unaffected by it.[23]

Deer are also tormented by several other species of ticks, plus ear mites, mange mites, lice, nasal bots, and of course deerflies. They host protozoan parasites that include toxoplasmosis, babesiosis, and theileriosis, and they're often infested with liver flukes, lungworms, stomach worms, meningeal worms, arterial worms, abdominal worms, and tapeworms.

The deer affliction most in the news recently, however, is not a parasite. Nor is it a disease caused by viruses or bacteria. Called chronic wasting disease (CWD), it's caused by prions, which are tiny scraps of malformed protein. Smaller than a virus, they contain no DNA or RNA. By some definitions, they're not even alive. They're difficult to destroy with ultraviolet light, freezing, or cooking. They're unfazed by a trip through an autoclave used to disinfect surgical instruments, and in the soil they can remain infectious for a minimum of two years, possibly much longer.[24]

As you might guess, chronic wasting disease is named for its most visible symptom. Infected cervids, most commonly deer or elk, eventually become emaciated and weakened. They often salivate excessively and may behave oddly. Typically they lose all fear of humans.

CWD appears to be 100 percent fatal, and there's no known treatment. It's a transmissible spongiform encephelopathy (TSE) that attacks the brain and central nervous system, and its incubation period lasts from a minimum of sixteen months to a maximum that far exceeds the typical deer's lifespan. If all this sounds familiar, it's because CWD is closely related to other, more well-known TSEs, including sheep scrapie, bovine spongiform encephalopathy (BSE, also known as mad cow disease), and Creutzfeldt-Jakob disease.

Just to be safe, state and provincial wildlife agencies caution hunters to not eat meat from an animal that's obviously infected and to take commonsense precautions when field-dressing or butchering animals from an area where CWD is known to be present. Typically they're advised to wear rubber or latex gloves, avoid sawing through bone, minimize the handling of brain and spinal tissues, and not consume the brain, spinal cord, spleen, tonsils, eyes, or lymph tissues.[25] So far, the prions that cause CWD don't seem able to infect humans. They've only been able to cross the species barrier under carefully controlled, highly artificial laboratory conditions.[26]

For deer it's another matter entirely. The prions that cause CWD are spread in feces, urine, and saliva and also through contaminated carcasses of deer that died from CWD or some other cause. Prions' multiyear persistence in soil is especially problematic. When animals are more concentrated, either in captivity or because they've been drawn to feed or bait, the conditions for transmission improve even further. Although infection rates in free-ranging populations are difficult to measure, those in captive populations have exceeded 90 percent. Modeling of CWD epidemics in free-ranging populations suggests they could cause local extinctions, and some states have taken the rather drastic step of preemptively eradicating deer from infected areas.[27]

By moving both live and dead animals, it seems likely that humans have begun to play a major role in accelerating the spread of CWD. A hunter returns from a successful outing three states away, butchers his elk, and disposes of the head, hide, and bones in a nearby county forest. A deer farmer buys new breeding stock and trucks the animals halfway across the country. The tall fences of a brand-new captive cervid operation enclose soil that was contaminated a decade ago by wild, free-ranging deer. A few years later, several of its deer and elk are sold to a hunting preserve three hundred miles away. All these scenarios could contribute to the spread of CWD. Although the origins of the disease remain unknown, it was first detected in Colorado in 1967. It's now known to be present in at least fifteen states and two Canadian provinces. Epidemiologists believe those numbers will continue to grow in the years ahead.

Hunters. Predators. Motor vehicles. Long, cold winters or long, hot summers. Diseases, parasites, and prions. Random mishaps. For all these reasons, and generally in about that order, even pampered suburban deer rarely live to be more than three or four years old. Once deer are deceased (or subdued and anesthetized), biologists can age them fairly precisely by examining the wear on their teeth. By the time deer are about ten years old, their teeth are worn to the gum line. If the resulting nutritional deficiencies don't lead to outright starvation, they leave the animal more vulnerable to cold, heat, diseases, parasites, and predators.

The rare deer that live longer than ten years can only be aged by using a microscope to count the annual layers in the cementum of the tooth root. In principle it's similar to counting growth rings on the cross section of a tree trunk. Using this technique, biologists determined that a doe from Orange County, New York, had lived to be twenty years old.[28] By then she would have outlived nearly all her great-great-grandchildren.

A SOCIAL ANIMAL

Although deer vocalizations include a wide range of grunts, bleats, snorts, and wheezes, many of their social interactions depend on their sense of smell and on special scent-producing musk glands. Deer have these glands in surprising places: tarsal glands on the inner surface of the rear "knee" joint, metatarsal glands on the outer surface of their rear "ankles," interdigital glands between their hooves, and preorbital glands at the front of the eyes. Deer also use urine as a scent, sometimes in combination with scent from their metatarsal and interdigital glands. They urinate on their ankles, rub them together, and mark their territory with every step they take.

Just before the peak of the mating season, which biologists and hunters term the "rut," deer often communicate at what's known as scrapes. At intervals along a trail, bucks paw at a spot under an overhanging branch. They chew on the end of the branch, rub their preorbital glands against it, and then urinate in the spot where they've been pawing the ground. If the mood strikes them, they may also defecate there. The next buck does the same, and so does the next. Some scrapes can grow to half the size of your living room, but most are just a couple feet across. Every October they can be found at regular intervals along some trails—perhaps even at the edge of your suburban lawn.

Although deer of both sexes pause to sniff these scrapes, they don't appear to play a major role in courtship. Deer may just view them the same way dogs do fire hydrants. Still, scrapes excite hunters at least as much as they do deer. Devious hunters armed with a garden rake and a bottle of scent often create mock scrapes, and deer do fall for them.

Hunters get even more excited about another signpost behavior called "rubs." Every fall, bucks attack the trunks of small trees they've chosen as sparring partners. By thrashing their antlers against the tree and rubbing off large patches of bark, they strengthen their neck muscles in preparation for any actual combat that could ensue later. Besides actually rubbing the spot with their antlers, bucks slide their preorbital glands against the exposed wood, lick and chew the tattered shreds of bark, and then check back every now and then to see who else is doing the same.

Although there's not a strict correlation, larger bucks generally choose larger trees. When hunters spot trunks ten inches in diameter that are missing a large patch of bark two or three feet off the ground, they know their preseason scouting may have paid off. When you're sipping your morning coffee and spot fresh rubs this size at the edge of your suburban lawn, you may be tempted to invite one of those hunters over to help defend your trees before they've been girdled completely.

Knowledgeable deer hunters are fascinated with scrapes, rubs, and any other deer behaviors that occur during the rut—and not just out of prurient curiosity. The rut occurs during the fall and roughly coincides with most states' hunting seasons. By better understanding deer courtship behaviors, hunters can greatly improve their odds of success. Sometimes it's as simple as taking unfair advantage of a distracted buck whose mind is on other things. Other strategies are more sophisticated. Every year this accounts for the sale of many calls, scents, and even an alluring doe decoy sold under the name of Miss November.

Once the rut is over, the woods become calmer. Bucks are less combative and more companionable, and spend much of the year hanging out together in what biologists call "bachelor groups." Does have social groups of their own, and fawns tag along. If deer have a society, it's a matrilineal one. Deer don't, however, have families in any human sense of the word.

Nor are deer true herd animals like bison, cattle, or antelope. If you ever see a hundred deer out in some unfortunate farmer's hay field, you're actually watching a sprinkling of lone deer among a dozen or more social groups. The only thing these acquaintances and strangers have in common is that they all happened to be hungry for alfalfa that evening. When deer biologists speak of "the deer herd," it's meant to be understood at a landscape level, as in "Pennsylvania's deer herd."

In the absence of population pressures or habitat changes, some deer never leave their ancestral homes. These homebodies rarely travel more than a mile or two in their entire lives, remaining within a well-defined territory whose size and shape vary with the terrain and the availability of food and cover. Typically it's an irregular oval rather than a perfect circle.[29]

Buck fawns are generally the ones that do the most dispersing. Once they reach a certain age, their mothers encourage them to head out on their own—often against their strenuous objections. Later they're often chased even farther from home by territorial bucks that don't want additional competition. Dispersal rates vary; a comprehensive 2011 meta-analysis of fourteen different studies found that from 5 to 50 percent of yearling does dispersed outside their original range, compared to 46 to 70 percent of yearling bucks.[30] Some wander far, perhaps in search of food, shelter, or safety from predators. Or maybe they're just curious, ready to boldly go where no deer has gone before. One way or another, deer can colonize new spaces and new suburbs with surprising speed.

Head Bones

Antlers are bony structures that grow from the head of a male deer. They're different from horns, which are made of the same substance as a deer's hooves or your fingernails. Another difference is that horned animals grow their horns and keep them. Instead, cervids grow a new set of antlers every year. In late winter, photoperiod changes trigger hormonal shifts, which in turn cause deer to shed their antlers. A few months later they start all over and begin growing a new set.

This is also true of cervids like elk, caribou, and moose that possess even larger, more extravagant antlers than deer. Older animals generally have larger antlers than young ones, and both nutrition and genetics play a role in determining how large any individual's antlers will grow.

Seemingly a tremendous waste of calcium, these antlers must provide some sort of evolutionary advantage. Although they do offer some measure of protection against predators, simpler spear points might have been just as effective for that purpose. Deer antlers seem best suited for competitive head-to-head sparring and wrestling that's more than playful but less than lethal. True, older bucks often carry scars from previous encounters. But if each fight were to the death, it would not bode well for the long-term survival of the species. Every now and then, of course, it does happen.

Similarly, on rare occasions the antlers of sparring bucks become hopelessly entangled, leaving them vulnerable to predators or to a long, slow death from thirst and starvation. (This happens most often to bucks with larger, more complex antlers, which may be one reason hunters find these incidents so fascinating.) If they're lucky, these deer will get their own YouTube video and be safely separated by their new friends—often with a well-placed bullet that shatters a key tine and unlocks the whole stalemate.[31] Even more rarely, three bucks have become entangled in this fashion. Later they're sometimes found dead in a tragic pinwheel of anger, antlers, and carrion.

Whole books have been written about the physiology and lore of deer antlers, and hard-core trophy hunters are especially fascinated by unusually large ones. However, freakishly large antlers are less important to deer than they are to deer hunters. And contrary to popular folk wisdom, the bucks with the biggest antlers are not necessarily the ones that get all the does. In fact, just the opposite may be true.

Evolutionary biologist and noted deer expert Valerius Geist has found that the most active participants in the rut are much less likely to grow trophy antlers the following year. They're gaunt and exhausted from fighting and chasing, and even months later they'll have less energy to spare for such nonessentials as outsize antlers. If their passions were too ardent, they may not even have the fat reserves needed to survive a long, cold winter. Geist learned from his research with mule deer that bucks with exceptionally large antlers are almost invariably unambitious "cowards, shirkers, and abstainers."[32]

Up to a point, bigger deer with bigger antlers are more likely to be dominant bucks that win every fight they start. But only to a point. True trophy-class antlers, according to Geist, make deer "biologically incompetent. Their unwieldy antler mass dooms them to failure in fighting, and they are readily defeated by normal males. Should two trophy stags meet and fight, they stand a high risk of locking antlers and dying."

Geist also points out another reason most bucks don't have antlers extending much wider than the tips of their ears: A rocking chair–size basket of forward- and upward-facing tines can be a huge liability when being pursued by a predator through thick woods—or when pursuing a flirtatious but coy doe through similar terrain. Evolutionarily, trophy-size antlers just might be one of Mother Nature's dead-end experiments.

If huge antlers did provide an evolutionary advantage, it stands to reason that more deer would have them. Geist notes that although it's relatively easy to breed captive deer with trophy antlers, they're quite rare in the wild. This, he suggests, is one more "hint that trophy-sized antlers may not be all that advantageous to their bearers."

Still, hunters prize these trophies precisely *because* they're so unusual. It's one reason an entire industry has been built on deer and their antlers. If you're a deer hunter, this assertion won't seem the least bit surprising. If you're not, it's time for a peek inside America's deer-industrial complex.

CHAPTER 2

Inside America's Deer-Industrial Complex

Our tools for the pursuit of wildlife improve faster than we do, and sportsmanship is a voluntary limitation in the use of these armaments. It is aimed to augment the role of skill and shrink the use of gadgets in the pursuit of wild things.

—Aldo Leopold

America's deer-industrial complex, like the pastime on which it's based, is largely invisible to the average citizen. The deer industry is huge, it's built on big antlers and small packages of venison, and most of its revenues come from new products that didn't even exist twenty years ago.

If we follow the money, we'll be following a lot of it right back out into the woods. All those billions—yes, billions—sloshing back and forth in just the right places can sometimes give the deer industry and the hunters who support it a surprising amount of influence over public policy. Maybe, some would argue, too much influence. And yet deer hunting, uniquely among all other types of North American hunting, now performs an essential and necessary role in restoring an ecological balance we've disrupted. However we may feel about deer hunting, its continuation is vital to the preservation of entire ecosystems and landscapes.

Even if you don't spend much time out in the woods, and even if your idea of a wilderness experience is taking a shortcut through Central Park, this is a story you should know. Because this land is your land, and these deer are your deer. Literally.

What's Good for Deer Is Good for America

The first thing you need to know about America's deer industry is that it's big. In 2011, 13.7 million Americans went hunting. Although only 6 percent of our adult population, hunters spent a combined total of thirty-four billion dollars on equipment, licenses, and other expenditures. A full 11.6 million of them (85 percent) were hunting big game—mostly deer. Despite our current recession, hunter participation has increased 9 percent since 2006, with a 6 percent increase in big game hunting. (These figures seem to signal a welcome change in what's until now been a decades-long decline.) During those same five years, total hunter expenditures increased a full 30 percent.[1]

The numbers suggest that deer hunters accounted for around 75 to 80 percent of that thirty-four billion dollars. To be conservative, let's peg deer hunting's share at just 50 percent. This would mean that if deer hunting—not all hunting, just deer hunting—were a single corporation, its seventeen billion dollars in annual revenues would place it 154th in the most recent Fortune 500 listing—just behind JCPenney but ahead of Colgate-Palmolive, Medtronic, and Southwest Airlines.[2]

It's quite possible, though, that these numbers from the US Fish & Wildlife Service are a bit on the low side. They're based largely on data compiled from state-level hunter surveys. Even though these self-reported numbers are offered anonymously, it's likely that many respondents underestimate how much they really spent on deer hunting last year. It's best not to look at those credit card statements too closely.

Remember too that these numbers don't fully capture real estate purchased as hunting land. In much of America, deer are now the number-one driver of the rural real estate market. Deer hunters also spend big on travel, tourism, and entertainment. Apart from deer hunters, tourists can be scarce in November. Deer season boosts the cash flow of many rural and small-town businesses right when they need it most.

It's simple, really. More deer and bigger bucks mean more happy hunters spending bigger bucks. So in a way, what's good for deer is good for America. Mostly.

WE'RE IN THE DEER BUSINESS

As for hunters' most visible, direct expenditures, consider this: Although most outdoor retailers sell a wide range of hunting, fishing, and camping gear, a huge percentage of their revenues are deer related. This industry isn't driven by moose, elk, or caribou. Nor is it driven by grouse, ducks, or pheasants. We're in the deer business.

Take Cabela's, for example. The largest of the big-three outdoor retailers, it's a publicly traded company (NYSE: CAB) with thriving catalog and Internet channels, plus thirty-one gigantic destination stores boasting a total of over 4.4 million square feet of retail space. In 2011, 40.2 percent of Cabela's $2.8 billion in revenues came from hunting equipment, 27.2 percent from clothing and footwear, 13.2 percent from fishing and marine, 9.8 percent from camping, and 9.1 percent from gifts and furnishings.[3]

What these figures don't tell you is that hunters, especially deer hunters, also account for most of Cabela's clothing and footwear sales. Similarly, its camping category is heavy on such deer gear as hunting knives, flashlights and headlamps, and even home meat-processing equipment.

The 1,288-page Cabela's catalog on my desk includes more than two hundred pages of hunting clothing, about 170 of which feature clothing meant for deer hunters. In contrast, the corresponding springtime catalog features fewer than twenty pages of clothing intended specifically for fishing.[4]

One retailer's clothing buyer told me that apart from Gore-Tex rainwear and the occasional pair of convertible pants with zip-off legs, it's much more difficult to sell specialized clothing to anglers. "Most guys," he told me, "just wear their oldest clothes. You catch a fish, you wipe the slime off on your pants, and you keep casting. Clothing just isn't part of the fishing scene like it is with hunting. Fish slime is."

Deer hunters also spend big in profitable subcategories like optics, which includes riflescopes, binoculars, spotting scopes, and laser rangefinders. Even at the riflescope counter, nonhunters would recognize familiar names like Bushnell, Nikon, Swarovski, and Zeiss.

Gander Mountain sees similar sales patterns on its website, in its catalogs, and at its chain of 116 stores. So does Bass Pro Shops, the third member of outdoor retailing's big three. Like Cabela's and Gander

Mountain, it sells through multiple channels—catalog, Internet, and sixty-five gigantic destination retail stores. John L. Morris, its founder and owner, had this to say in a 2011 *Outdoor Life* interview: "The whitetail deer is the backbone of the hunting industry in America, and not just in the fall, prior to hunting season. In the last decade we've seen deer hunters become year-round customers as they develop land and intensively manage their property."[5]

These three retailers are the largest. After them come smaller chains, many of which sell a broader range of sporting goods. And don't forget, big-box retailers like Walmart often do a surprising amount of business selling guns, ammunition, and accessories.

Many smaller retailers are quietly in the deer business, too, including, quite possibly, your neighborhood hardware store. Then there are the small specialty shops, such as gun shops, gunsmiths, and bowhunting shops. The other day I talked with Paul Korn, owner of A1 Archery in Hudson, Wisconsin. His shop is one of the largest archery retailers in the nation, and nearly all his business revolves around whitetail deer. "Take deer out of the equation," he said, "and we wouldn't have an industry. If there were a bear plague that killed every single bear in the woods, it wouldn't affect my bottom line. And sure, I'd feel bad if elk became extinct. But without deer, I'd be out of business."

The same is true for hundreds of manufacturers. Some are small entrepreneurial operations—low-tech start-ups, you might call them. Others have long ago outgrown their humble beginnings. One example is Mathews, the world's largest manufacturer of archery equipment. A company built on bowhunting, mostly for deer, it's no longer just a couple guys in a garage.

Some of the deer industry's biggest players are hidden in plain sight. But they're not camouflaged. They *are* camouflage. These companies don't actually manufacture camo clothing—or camo anything, for that matter. Instead, they license their unique, painstakingly created designs to other companies, just as Disney licenses its characters. And like Disney, they're also in the entertainment and real estate businesses.

Take Mossy Oak, for example. After developing photorealistic camo patterns designed to make hunters invisible in a variety of environments, the company began licensing them to manufacturers all over the world. Today you can find Mossy Oak patterns not only on hunting clothing, but also on binoculars, knives, flashlights, cell phone covers, GPS units, and Bibles. Mossy Oak has its own TV network and produces or sponsors about a dozen hunting shows. It also owns BioLogic, a company that sells seed for food plots designed to attract deer. Its real estate division is called Mossy Oak Properties.

Realtree, Mossy Oak's largest competitor, has followed a similar business model. According to its website, "more than 1,500 manufacturers produce over 10,000 products using its camouflage patterns. Thousands of retailers sell those products to millions of consumers." Like Mossy Oak, it produces or sponsors a number of hunting shows. Realtree is also a NASCAR sponsor; if you're a fan, watch for its antler-and-camo logo.[6]

When deer hunters aren't deer hunting, they're reading about it or watching it on TV—often on shows sponsored by Mossy Oak or Realtree. They can get their vicarious deer hunting fix on the Outdoor Channel (thirty-five million subscribers; NASDAQ: OUTD), the Sportsman Channel (twenty-five million subscribers), and Pursuit (twenty-four million subscribers). At all three networks, over half of all programming involves deer hunting.

The two largest North American magazines that cover hunting and fishing in general are *Field and Stream* (1.26 million subscribers) and *Outdoor Life* (755,000 subscribers). Today both are owned by the Bonnier Group, a Swedish media conglomerate that owns about 175 companies in seventeen countries.[7] The editorial content in both magazines is heavy on deer hunting, especially August through December. In a typical year, images of large bucks with large antlers will be found on the covers of at least three or four issues.

Hunters in the United States and Canada can also choose from several smaller outdoor magazines, plus dozens more aimed specifically at deer hunters. The top thirty have a combined circulation of over seven million. Each has its own editorial slant. Some, like *Deer and Deer Hunting* or *Quality Whitetails*, manage to slip in a fair amount of deer science. Although they don't follow an official peer-review process, quite often one does occur behind the scenes. Other publications take an entirely different approach. After all, big bucks with big antlers sell magazines—especially when they're right there on the cover.

Keith McCaffery, a retired deer biologist from Wisconsin, is one of the most outspoken critics of this phenomenon. "A couple years ago," he told me, "I went into our local bookstore and counted. There were nineteen different magazines dedicated to putting a giant buck on the wall. Every magazine had a picture of one on its cover, and you can bet most of those pictures were taken at deer farms." McCaffery is widely credited with coining the terms "horn porn" and "hornographic" to describe these publications.

That's what America's ten or twelve million deer hunters are watching and reading. As for what they're joining, a surprisingly small percentage of them belong to the country's two largest deer organizations, Whitetails Unlimited (WTU) and the Quality Deer Management Association (QDMA). Both, however, have far more influence and impact than their size would suggest.

With around fifty thousand members, up from just over two thousand members in 2000, the QDMA has a mission "to ensure the future of white-tailed deer, wildlife habitat, and our deer hunting heritage." When I talked with CEO Brian Murphy, he explained that the goal of QDM is to produce healthy deer herds that are in balance with their habitat and have balanced adult sex ratios and age structures. It's a philosophy that takes some explaining, and it's sometimes misunderstood as "quality antler management," or simply "letting young bucks walk." But there's more to QDM than planting food plots, shooting does, passing on young bucks, and waiting patiently for a mature buck with trophy antlers to stroll by your deer stand.[8]

Even if many hunters and landowners practicing QDM are motivated by their quest for mature bucks with trophy antlers, they quickly realize that bucks are more likely to grow large antlers when herds are balanced and habitats are healthy. For the most part, the goals of QDMA adherents are remarkably congruent with those of state wildlife agencies—and even with those of foresters, botanists, and ecologists. It seems telling, in fact, that Murphy is only one of several trained wildlife biologists on the QDMA staff.

With a less focused mission but around ninety thousand members, WTU is "a nonprofit organization interested in conservation, education, and the preservation of an American tradition." Patterned after similar organizations like Ducks Unlimited and Trout Unlimited, it's most known for its member magazine and its community-based fundraisers that feature plenty of refreshments and nonstop raffles and drawings. Everyone has a good time, and no one complains if he wins a new rifle by spending slightly more on raffle tickets than what he'd have paid for the rifle at the local hardware store. Although some of the proceeds support national programs like hunter safety initiatives, most funds stay in the local community. *Whitetails Unlimited* editor Jeff Davis told me about one chapter donating night-vision equipment that would give their local game warden a better chance of apprehending poachers.

You may have noticed that until now I haven't even mentioned two key essentials: guns and ammo. They're fascinating segments of the outdoor industry and deserve a whole book of their own. Few of us who aren't hunters or shooters realize the magnitude of their sales. In 2011 on Black Friday, the day after Thanksgiving and traditionally the biggest shopping day of the year, online background checks reached a new one-day record of 129,166. Since some would have been related to the purchase of multiple firearms, the actual number of guns sold was undoubtedly higher still. One industry insider estimated that on Black Friday Americans bought more guns than iPads. By the end of November, the number of online background checks for the month as a whole reached a new record of 1,534,414. That record lasted less than a month and was eclipsed a few days before the end of December.[9]

Although the gun and ammunition industries depend on deer hunters for much of their core business, they've recently been experiencing more growth in the military, tactical, and self-defense categories. The problem is that deer rifles last a long time, and most deer hunters don't burn up nearly enough ammunition.

You Need This

With average use a well-maintained deer rifle can last a century or two. Nearly as durable are those orange parkas that only get worn one week of the year. Fortunately for outdoor retailers, today's hunters spend the vast majority of their money on products that didn't even exist a generation ago. Although we somehow didn't realize we needed them, these items have suddenly become indispensible. We take them for granted and can barely remember a time when they didn't exist.

To get a sense of how sweeping these changes have been, let's go shopping. On my desk right now are two massive mail-order catalogs. One is a six-hundred-page Herter's catalog from 1967. The other is this year's 1,288-page catalog from Cabela's. They make for an interesting comparison.

The vintage Herter's catalog contains very few items that are missing from this year's Cabela's catalog. Among them, however, are around fifty pages' worth of firearms that could be ordered through the mail and delivered right to your door. A year later the federal Gun Control Act of 1968 would change all that; it was also one of the events that led to Herter's closing its doors in the early 1970s. But the front of this year's Cabela's catalog does include three or four pages of firearms after all—just enough to whet one's appetite and trigger plans for a visit to one of the company's thirty-one stores scattered around the United States and Canada.

(Strictly speaking, it's still possible for twenty-first-century Americans to buy a firearm through the mail or over the Internet. You'll just ask the seller to ship your purchase to a local dealer who has a federal firearms license [FFL]. For a small "transfer fee," your neighborhood gun shop or hardware store will be glad to run a background check and help you with the paperwork. You will, however, still have to come down and pick up the firearm in person.)

This year's Cabela's catalog also contains thousands of deer hunting essentials that hunters from 1968 never could have imagined. Some are low- and medium-tech innovations that could easily have been manufactured back then. We just didn't know we needed them. Others are high-tech devices that today's digital deer hunter just can't do without.

Even though your phone may have its own built-in GPS, a dedicated five-ounce handheld unit offers better reception, better resolution, better maps, and more features you definitely need. Go ahead. Download that high-resolution topo map that covers all of North America, including the Canadian Arctic. It's best to be prepared. True, the hardware and maps add up to over five hundred dollars. That's a hundred dollars an ounce, and it's more than you paid for your first deer rifle. But who can put a price on five ounces of never getting lost?

While sitting at a larger screen during long winter evenings, savvy hunters use other topo maps to do much of their preseason scouting. For aerial photos they visit state and county websites or use tools like Google Earth. Hunters hoping to turn maps and aerials into meat and antlers have made *Mapping Trophy Bucks* one of the best-selling books about deer hunting.

There's nothing like actually being there. But when you can't, your motion-sensing digital trailcams can surveil your hunting spot for you, twenty-four hours a day. Their batteries last for weeks, and their memory cards have room for thousands of images. A favorite of the well-equipped digital deer hunter, these cameras capture high-resolution color photos in the daytime and black-and-white infrared shots in total darkness. The invisible flash of their infrared light-emitting diodes (LEDs) doesn't alarm deer or alert any humans who happen to be nearby. This feature is especially important for hunters who place their cameras out on public land. That way no one will see the flash and steal their camera—or worse yet, steal their hunting spot.

These cameras start at around one hundred dollars and go on up to three or four hundred. Some models can even capture video and audio. If one is good, more is better. Guides and outfitters buy them by the case. Serious trophy hunters don't just use these cameras to discover whether deer are present. They use them to learn precisely which deer are where and what time of day or night they tend to pass by. On opening day these hunters will be waiting in ambush for one particular deer with large antlers. They've already seen it in dozens of photos, and they may even have given it a pet name.

As these trailcams are strapped to more and more trees and fence posts across rural America, their incriminating photos have been the downfall of numerous trespassers, poachers, marijuana growers, and ordinary burglars. Sometimes they've even meant trouble for the camera's owner. More than one carefree hunter has shot deer out of season, illegally baited, or violated some other game law, all in full view of his own trailcam. When wardens checked the memory cards, they found all the evidence they needed.

Think you can poach or trespass safely if you spot the camera and remove its memory card? Think again. The latest models use cellular technology to upload their images instantly and in real time. In at least one case, an out-of-state landowner sat at a computer five hundred miles away and e-mailed incriminating photos back to the county sheriff. The sheriff, in turn, immediately recognized the unshaven and less-than-photogenic trespasser. A high-resolution image, complete with time and date stamps, was enough to get a confession and a conviction.

These trailcams are not the only cameras out in the woods. Many deer hunters are now mounting miniaturized, ruggedized digital video cameras on their bows, crossbows, and rifles. They've seen enough hunting shows on cable TV, and they're ready to shoot their own. Although product descriptions invariably mention "sharing the hunt with your family and friends" or "analyzing and improving your shooting skills," most customers buy these cameras for one purpose: to get the kill shot. This is the climactic moment of most TV hunting shows, and there's nothing quite like capturing your own for "sharing with family and friends."

To improve their odds of making such a shot, today's deer hunters often use laser rangefinders that emit an invisible laser pulse, measure the time it takes to reach the target and return, and then calculate the range to the nearest yard or meter. The catalog on my desk includes five pages of rangefinders sold under eight different brands. The simplest go for under a hundred dollars and fit in a shirt pocket. For more features and greater range, hunters need only spend a few hundred dollars more. And for a couple thousand more, they can buy rangefinders built into premium binoculars from Zeiss, Swarovski, or Leica.

Better yet, you can buy a riflescope with a built-in laser rangefinder. For targets under 150 yards or so, just use the crosshairs. At longer ranges, activate the rangefinder and aim with the red dot that's floating at just the right distance below the crosshairs' intersection. Ahead of time, of course, you'll need to sight in the scope as usual and then calibrate its software to match the cartridge and bullet weight you're using. But don't worry. At the manufacturer's website, all these settings are just a click away.

Even hunters' clothing has gone high-tech. One company's slogan is "Turning clothing into gear." Today's hunters can choose from a huge selection of specialized fabrics and camo patterns. They can be ready for sun, rain, and below-zero blizzards, and they can blend in perfectly with sagebrush, tree bark, oak leaves, pine needles, or snow.

Despite their undeserved reputation among nonhunters as a rather slovenly bunch, experienced deer hunters tend to be very concerned about personal hygiene and odor. That's especially true for bowhunters, who engage their quarry at shorter ranges. Before they head for the woods, they shower with scent-free, scent-killing soap and shampoo. Some even use breath mints and underarm deodorant formulated especially for hunters.

They also wash their hunting clothing in special unscented detergent with no UV brighteners. After they're dressed they spray their camo outerwear with scent-killing and UV-blocking potions like UV-Killer, Scent Killer, Scent-A-Way, and Dead Down Wind.

In hopes of improving their odds even further, many bowhunters wear scent-blocking clothing like Scent-Lok and Scent Blocker. A layer of carbon absorbs odors and is, in theory, "reactivated" by the heat of a clothes dryer. The effectiveness and longevity of these barriers are difficult to measure, and one brand recently faced a class-action lawsuit from hunters who felt its advertising claims were, let's just say, overconfident.

Once they've done everything they can to conceal their scent, some hunters use another scent strategy that involves attractants—sometimes the scent of apples or acorns, but more often the scent of rutting bucks or does in estrus. Most scents come in tiny, one- or four-ounce bottles filled with a liquid or gel. Some are available as aerosols, solid wafers, or incense sticks. (No matter how tightly bottles are closed at the factory, and no matter how well these products are sealed, the scent aisle of a large outdoor retailer is always especially aromatic, even for humans. Apple and acorn scents smell delicious. The others do not.)

One company packages its attractant scents in a convenient stick identical to those used for deodorant. It offers three scents, the most popular of which seems to be a testosterone gel called Rutting Buck in a Stick. According to the instructions on the package, you can "Simply wipe on an exterior surface (not for clothing or body)."

Most of these products are totally natural. They're made from urine that's carefully collected from farm-raised deer, right on the proper schedule. Urine collection on this scale involves rows of indoor pens whose slotted floors are drained by highly specialized plumbing. Raising deer primarily for their hormone- and pheromone-laced urine, and only secondarily for meat, antlers, or release at high-fence hunting preserves, has quietly become a multimillion-dollar industry. But please don't do the math too carefully.

Outdoor writer Scott Bestul did just that in a 2006 *Field and Stream* article. Based on some rough, back-of-the-envelope calculations, he estimated that every year America's deer hunters buy enough deer scent to nearly fill a 660,000-gallon, Olympic-size swimming pool. But when he talked with a few deer farmers to learn where all that urine was coming from, the numbers just didn't add up—especially when so much of it is being sold as estrous urine, which can only be collected from a doe during its three-day estrous cycle.[10]

Bestul calculated that on all of America's licensed cervid farms put together, there aren't nearly enough captive deer to fill all those millions of one- and four-ounce bottles being sold to hunters. Someone, he realized, was definitely doing a little diluting out there. That may still be the case; the scent industry remains totally unregulated. Another, more serious concern is that it's theoretically possible for hunters using these products to spread CWD. Although several states and provinces recommend that hunters avoid using urine-based scents, so far only Nova Scotia, Ontario, and Alaska have banned them outright.[11]

To improve the odds that deer will be sniffing around your back forty in the first place, you can feed them, bait them, or plant food plots featuring some of their favorite menu items. All three practices are exploding in popularity, and all three require a substantial investment of time and money. They're permanently changing American hunting culture, and not necessarily for the better.

For outdoor retailers, however, they've meant an entire new product category. First, unless you plan to just pour corn out on the ground, you'll need a feeder. Some are simple gravity-fed hoppers. Others are controlled by photocells or programmable timers that can be overridden by a hunter's remote. They range in size from five-gallon canisters to elevated hoppers that hold over four hundred pounds.

For feeding or baiting, nothing beats plain old corn—unless maybe it's one of the high-octane attractants that come in powder, pellet, or syrup form. They have names like Deer Co-Cain, Buck Jam, Stump Likker, BoneDmonium, Acorn Rage, and Greens N-Raged. To attract deer to you property, or to build bigger and better antlers on the ones already there, you can also buy a special mineral block called a "trophy rock." Although it's unclear exactly where these irregularly shaped, reddish-brown lumps of salty-tasting rock are being mined, someone is making a lot of money selling them to deer hunters.

If you have time on your hands, and if you'd like to try a more subtle approach, you can plant small food plots with crops specifically chosen to please the palates of deer. Later you'll be ready to harvest the deer as they harvest their last mouthful. You'd never guess that these blends incorporate such ordinary crops as clover, alfalfa, canola, turnips, soybeans, rye, and oats. They're marketed under exciting brand names like Oatrageous, Monster Mix, Pure Attraction, Autumn Buffet, and Outfitter's Blend. Knowledgeable hunters often sound like Latinate botanists as they discuss the pros and cons of their favorite "brassica blends."

You'll need more than seed. Fortunately, an entire food plot industry has sprung up almost overnight. In addition to seed, hunters are buying fertilizers, sprays, and entire arsenals of miniature farm equipment that can be pulled behind all-terrain vehicles (ATVs). These implements include mowers, spreaders, sprayers, tillers, disks, drags, harrows, cultivators, rakes, plows, and scarifiers.

Dedicated deer hunters now have a whole new hobby: In their spare time they've become small-scale farmers who enjoy the farming as much as the hunting. They love seeing more deer on their property year-round, and they generally keep a few trailcams aimed at their food plots to see who's stopping by for a midnight snack.

When hunting season arrives, many of these hunters will be watching over their food plots from above. Although Grandpa may have been happy to walk out into the woods on opening morning and sit on a stump, today's hunters would rather be up in a tree. Treestands first caught on among a growing population of bowhunters. To make a good shot and a humane kill, they need to be within twenty or thirty yards of an unsuspecting deer. Treestands made that easier, and it wasn't long before gun hunters took to them too. As the popularity of treestands has soared skyward, wary deer have learned to look up.

Today far more hunters are injured by falls from treestands than by accidental gunshot wounds. Some falls happen when ascending or descending. Others . . . just happen. Many hunters fall when the action is slow and they begin to nod off. To stay safe, hunters can choose from dozens of harnesses and clip-in safety systems similar to those used by rock climbers.

Even the finest safety gear, however, works best when used with careful forethought. If you find yourself dangling upside down six feet below your treestand and six feet above the ground, there's no one within earshot, and you can't reach your knife or cell phone, you could be out of luck. And unless your harness is one of the more sophisticated designs that suspends you in an upright position and doesn't interfere with normal circulation, chances are good that you'll lose consciousness in another five to ten minutes.

Sadly this is not an imaginary scenario. It happens every autumn. I was once riding along with our local game warden when a call came over the radio from dispatch. A hunter was in precisely this predicament, except maybe a little higher off the ground. He'd been able to reach his phone and pull it out of his pocket without dropping it. Dialing 911 saved his life. A sheriff's deputy was only ten minutes away. (A moment later I checked my own phone. It turned out that we were bumping along a dirt logging road in an area with no coverage.)

For hunters with a fear of heights, there's a new concealment alternative. It, too, has become a whole new product line for outdoor retailers. Called a ground blind, it's a small, camo-colored tent with windows through which you can watch for deer and shoot them when they step within range.

In most states bowhunters enjoy special seasons that are much longer than firearm seasons. Depending on the state, these seasons may even begin a month or two sooner. Similarly, hunters with muzzleloaders have often been granted their very own "primitive weapon" season. In both cases hunters looking for an edge have benefited from a primitive weapons arms race. Suddenly what's old is new, and what's primitive is not.

True, a few purists still take to the woods with flintlocks. They're far outnumbered, however, by hunters carrying a scope-sighted weapon whose description may sound just slightly oxymoronic: the modern muzzleloader. To the untrained eye, these rifles look just like a modern centerfire rifle. The only giveaway is a ramrod in its holder under the barrel. Within 150 yards they're every bit as accurate and lethal as a modern breech-loading rifle.

Bowhunting has followed a similar demographic and technological trajectory. Twenty years ago bowhunters were rare. Today they account for a significant portion of the deer harvest. They also account for a significant portion of the sales at outdoor retailers. Their modern compound bows are thousand-dollar, high-tech instruments that bear little resemblance to the simple recurves used by bowhunters a generation ago. Today's bowhunters aim through fiber-optic sights and launch carbon-fiber arrows with better accuracy than many hunters can manage with rifles.

To learn more, I packed my bags for a quick road trip through bowhunting history. Before I made it home, I'd also get a glimpse into its future.

A STICK AND A STRING

My first stop was the Pope and Young (P&Y) Club's headquarters and museum in Chatfield, Minnesota. When the club was founded in 1961, it patterned itself after the Boone and Crockett (B&C) Club. Both promote ethical hunting, support conservation programs and habitat improvement, and maintain official trophy records for all twenty-eight native North American big game animals. (That "native" qualifier was added to exclude zebras, wildebeest, and antelope hunted behind high fences on Texas ranches.)

The difference is that P&Y is an archery-only organization. And rather than Daniel and Davey, it's named for bowhunting pioneers Saxton Pope and Art Young. Both organizations are best known for their records programs, and currently 46 percent of all new P&Y entries are for whitetail deer. Although submissions must meet certain minimum standards, the most recent edition of their record book for whitetails ran to 850 pages of fine print. Even a casual skim reveals much about the history of bowhunting for trophy deer.

But today I was more interested in the broader story of North American bowhunting's twentieth-century reboot. To its credit, the P&Y museum pays respectful tribute to earlier bowhunters. It acknowledges that Native peoples had been perfecting the technology over the past five hundred to two thousand years, ever since they began setting aside their atlatls in favor of a stick and a string. The change didn't happen overnight, and it happened earlier in some places than others. Later the same was true for the adoption of firearms. But by early in the twentieth century, very few Native Americans still hunted with bows. Almost no Euro-American newcomers did. Bows and arrows were toys, not tools.

That's where a new story begins, and today I'd learn about the bowhunting renaissance that came next. First on the agenda was a guided tour from P&Y president Glenn Hisey. Later I'd sit down for a visit with him and his son, Kevin. For the Hiseys and their handful of employees, it's a full-time job administering the club's records, membership, and conservation programs. They've also built the museum into the world's largest publicly displayed collection of bowhunting artifacts and memorabilia.

My tour began with a series of dioramas providing context for the exhibits and collections to follow. If you're a significant figure in the world of bowhunting, your photo is on the wall at the P&Y museum. If you're one of the legends, you get your own waxwork figure carefully posed in a diorama simulating your own native habitat.

The very first diorama depicted a scene from Deer Creek, a wilderness area in the mountains of northern California. The guy in the loincloth squatting beside an electric campfire was Ishi. He's described on the brass plaque and in the museum's brochure as "the last truly primitive Indian in North America." It was Ishi who would give all-day bowmaking and archery lessons to a young surgical instructor named Saxton Pope.

We moved on to the next diorama, and the next. In 1918: Pope with a bow and a bear. In 1922: his friend Arthur Young packing out moose antlers in Alaska. In 1925: Pope and Young on safari in Africa. Next a photo of Howard Hill as Errol Flynn's archery double in *The Adventures of Robin Hood*. Fred Bear in his trademark Borsalino hat . . . and more. Down the hallway, around the corner, and a century was gone.

Around another corner and we arrived at the collections. The museum houses mounted specimens of all twenty-eight North American big game animals whose scores are kept in the P&Y record books, including deer, elk, moose, sheep, goats, and bears. Hundreds of bows, hundreds of arrows, and thousands of stone and steel points of every design imaginable are also on display.

The longbows and recurves were simple but elegant. Many of them, even the very newest, were quite beautiful. I saw timeless designs executed in modern composites that still revealed the beauty of natural wood; laminated layers of contrasting colors; and warm, glowing wood that begged to be touched. It couldn't get any better.

But then we literally and figuratively turned a corner in the history of archery. The next wall was labeled "The Evolution of the Compound Bow." In the 1970s these bows began sprouting pulleys, cams, and cables that provided an extra mechanical advantage. They stored more energy and propelled the arrow at higher velocity, and yet they were much easier to aim while at full draw.

For thousands of years bows had offered progressively more resistance as the string was pulled rearward. Once drawn, they were difficult to hold steady for more than a second or two. Bowhunters shot almost the instant they reached full draw, and they shot instinctively, with no sights. Bowhunting success depended on serious muscle and continuous practice.

Modern compound bows have changed all that. Their resistance peaks as the string is pulled partway back and then falls to a mere 20 percent of that peak. When bowhunters draw a seventy-pound compound bow, it takes only fourteen pounds of force to hold it at full draw. This makes it relatively easy to linger at full draw while waiting for just the right moment to release an arrow.

That's fortunate, since modern bowhunters invariably need more time for each shot. They aim through a tiny peep sight wound into the string, carefully aligning it with a glowing fiber-optic sight mounted on the bow. They no longer pull the string and release it with their fingers. Instead they use a mechanical release aid that straps onto their wrist. After nocking an arrow, they open the jaws of the release aid and clamp it onto the string. When they've drawn, aimed, and are finally ready to release their arrow, they pull a trigger just like the one on a rifle. Given a quality compound bow and a little coaching, a beginner who's already proficient with a rifle can achieve impressive accuracy in a single session.

Today's compound bows are incredibly accurate and lethal. With enough practice, so were the longbows and recurves that preceded them. But in the early and mid-twentieth century, it was an uphill battle convincing fish and game departments. Back then bowhunters were in the same position as today's atlatl advocates. Bowhunting was illegal in most states, and officials didn't believe the bow was an effective weapon for taking big game—despite the obvious fact that a hundred generations of nonvegetarian Native Americans had been using them to bring home the venison.

In 1930 an experimental archery deer season was held in northern Wisconsin. Although dozens of bowhunters took to the woods, only one was successful. The spike buck Roy Case arrowed that fall is one of the least impressive trophies I've ever seen enshrined behind glass in a museum. But it was a start. Case, Aldo Leopold, and other Wisconsin archers maintained their lobbying efforts, and the first statewide bow season was held in 1934. Other states soon followed suit.

Glenn Hisey explained that this debate about the effectiveness of archery equipment was one of the primary reasons for the club's founding. Once bows were used to harvest a long list of trophies that included larger animals like elk, moose, bison, black bear, and even grizzly and polar bears, their effectiveness against a 75- to 150-pound whitetail deer would no longer be in dispute.

Later I learned more about the sport's continued tension between seeking a challenge and seeking an extra advantage. "In the beginning," Glenn explained, "it was all about making hunting harder. Bowhunters wanted an extra challenge. Some still do.

"But others," he said, "just want more hunting opportunities. In most states the bow season for deer is earlier and longer than the firearm season.

You might have a gun season that lasts a week or two and a bow season that lasts three or four months. New bowhunters who start for that reason want the most effective hunting tool they can get."

His son, Kevin, speculated that these tensions between tradition and technology would only continue. "We like to think bowhunting is more about the pursuit than the harvest," he said. "But it's now an important tool for managing deer populations in the suburbs. We're making the case that bowhunting is lethal, humane, and effective. Even though a bow doesn't have the same range as a rifle, it's getting harder all the time to claim that we're doing it solely for the extra challenge."

Still, with their rules for record-book entries, both B&C and P&Y have done much to shape hunters' thinking about ethics and fair chase. "In the '60s," Glenn told me, "a lot of those rules became ingrained in society and even became law. At the time it was legal to use poison-tipped arrows, but our rules said no. Same with shooting caribou from a boat while they were swimming."

Fair chase, or not fair chase? I asked about a few deer-hunting specifics.

Baiting? "I'm personally not a fan," said Kevin, "but we can't prohibit it in our records program if we allow it for some other animal. And other than hunting with hounds, baiting is pretty much the only way it's possible to get a black bear."

Crossbows? "For us," Kevin said, "it's not a matter of fair chase. But bowhunting is a subset of hunting in general. We have standard definitions of what constitutes a bow, an arrow, and a broadhead. They're hand-held and hand-drawn, with no locking devices. Just as we don't accept shotgun harvest in our record book, we don't accept crossbow kills."

"But we do support their use by someone with a severe disability," Glenn added, "someone who can't hunt otherwise. And we have nothing against able-bodied hunters using them—in the firearms season, not in the bow season."

(By popular demand more states are allowing crossbows to be used during the regular archery season. Crossbows have an even shorter learning curve than compound bows, and beginners love them. Their critics, however, see them as being more like rifles than bows. And although there's little evidence of this, they're said to be quite popular among poachers.)

Trailcams? Kevin and Glenn exchanged glances before answering. "That's a tricky one," said Kevin. "They're already hugely popular. Can we ban them altogether? I don't know. But now there's more electronics in there, and some new capabilities. In theory, with models available right now, you could sit in your treestand with a laptop, or even your phone. You could watch a live feed from multiple cameras. You could know when a trophy buck is coming down the trail, which direction he'll be coming from, and when to start drawing your bow. Not fair chase."

And the future? What's next? "Here's one that's more low-tech," said Kevin. "It's an issue we're wrestling with right now: dogs trained to trail wounded deer—not to hunt with, but to help recover deer. It's illegal in eighteen states, and some people want to change that. At first glance it's a great idea. Still, tracking dogs have their pros and cons."

Glenn agreed: "We want to expend every possible effort to recover a wounded animal. But at what point have we gone too far? What if it becomes a crutch? What if someone takes a shot that's less certain, knowing he'll have a dog there if something goes wrong?"

Kevin described another technological advance that could be just around the corner, one that would make tracking dogs obsolete in a hurry. "What if we had a tiny, nearly weightless transmitter built right into the arrow? What if you could use that transmitter and a directional receiver to find a wounded deer? Great idea, but how would that influence the choices hunters make about when to shoot and when not to shoot?"

"And what about lighted nocks?" Kevin asked. "Was that even going too far?" (A word of explanation: At the tail of every arrow, the bowstring fits into a slotted "nock" made of translucent plastic. Standard versions can be replaced with one whose tiny LED switches on at the instant an arrow is released. They're sold under brand names like Firenok, Lazer Eye, Lumenok, Nockturnal, and Tracer Nock. They go for seven or eight dollars apiece, and their batteries last about as many hours.)

In the low-light conditions when deer are most likely to be on the move, these lighted nocks make it easier to see an arrow's flight. If an arrow misses its mark or, as is usually the case, passes completely through an animal, it will at least be easier to find and recover. But if the shot isn't what bowhunters call a complete pass-through, and if the arrow's nock and fletching are still protruding from a fallen deer, then a lighted nock could make that deer much easier to find and recover—especially if the shot is made at dusk. In darkness these lighted nocks are visible for up to one hundred yards.

"Sure," said Kevin, "maybe they'll tempt someone to take a shot he shouldn't, or to stretch the daylight just a little. But they've probably helped a lot more hunters recover deer they otherwise wouldn't have found. So lighted nocks can be a good thing. But an arrow with a radio transmitter in it? Somehow that's not the same."

KAIZEN IN THE ART OF ARCHERY

After I thanked the Hiseys and said goodbye, I walked out into the parking lot, blinked in the sunlight, and set out for Sparta.

That's Sparta, Wisconsin, not Sparta, Greece. I was on my way to Mathews, the world's largest archery company. Although dozens of small companies make archery equipment, three or four major players dominate the industry. Of those, Mathews is by far the largest.

The P&Y display showing the evolution of the compound bow had ended with the latest model from Mathews. Already, however, the museum's exhibit was out of date. A new 2012 model had been unveiled two days earlier, just in time for the company's upcoming twentieth anniversary. Tomorrow I'd learn more about how the company's history and growth over those twenty years has paralleled that of the sport itself.

My tour guide was Bob Ohm, Mathews public relations director. He's been with the company for most of its twenty-year history and was one of the very first employees hired by founder Matt McPherson. Today the company has just under four hundred employees, around one hundred thousand square feet of manufacturing space, and over eleven hundred dealers in the United States plus another hundred or so abroad. Including all four of its product lines, it sells about 150,000 bows a year.

Bob explained how bows made by Mathews and its competitors have changed over the past twenty years. "First, they're quieter," he told me, "with a lot less vibration. They shoot harder, with higher arrow velocities. But the silence and smoothness are a big deal too. Plus, they're more efficient and easier to draw. They're lighter, and they're also a lot shorter than they used to be.

"Bows fifteen years ago were forty, even forty-five inches long," he said, "and now they're as short as twenty-eight inches. A thirty-four-inch bow is considered long. Because of the more acute string angle, you can't even shoot these bows with fingers, only with a release aid. As bows shrank, their limbs became more parallel. Now they've gone beyond parallel. Risers are longer, limbs are shorter, and we've packed a lot more power in a smaller, lighter package.

"I remember our first thirty-two-inch bow," he said. "It was called the MQ 32. Back in '98 I was at a trade show when a guy rolled up in a wheelchair. He saw that bow and his eyes lit up. He picked it up and held it full draw. He let it down, and then he drew it again. He had tears streaming down his face. He finally had a bow he could draw from his chair."

Bob's not the touchy-feely type. That day he was wearing a neatly pressed black Harley-Davidson shirt, and he seemed like a no-nonsense kind of guy. But I could see his own eyes were moistening at the memory.

"So what about efficiency?" I asked him. "How has that changed?"

"That's changed too," he told me. "We used to have a special Safari model that weighed over seven pounds. In a hundred-pound draw weight, which very few bowhunters could even pull back, it was our only bow that met minimum kinetic energy standards for hunting Africa's big five. Today you can get the same kinetic energy from a seventy-pound bow that weighs 3.5 pounds."

I asked Bob about the company's core values noted so prominently in its catalog and on its website: Innovation, Integrity, and Impact. The innovation part was obvious, but what about the other two? He told me integrity was about putting people first and business second. The idea was that if you took good care of your people, they'd take good care of your business. From what I saw that day, it appears to be working.

From the customer's perspective, Bob said, integrity was all about quality, truth in advertising, and knowing that both Mathews and its dealers would be straightforward, forthright, and honest. "If it says on the box that your bow will shoot 232 fps," he said, "you can bet it will shoot at least that, and probably a few feet per second more."

For Mathews impact means giving back. The company supports dozens of missions and philanthropic organizations in developing countries. Some bring food or clothing to needy children and families, and one drills wells so that more villages will have a source of clean drinking water. Closer to home, every year Mathews donates thousands of bows to fund-raisers for wildlife and habitat organizations. It's giving back; it's good PR too.

Mathews has also provided millions of dollars worth of support to the National Archery in the Schools Program (NASP), which gives students in grades four through twelve an introduction to archery during their physical education classes. Over the past decade, more than nine million students from eighty-eight hundred schools in forty-seven states and five countries have participated in NASP. Virtually all of them used the same brightly colored, easy-to-draw bow. Built by Mathews, it's called the Genesis.

Mathews recently launched Centershot, a similar program for church youth groups. Today Centershot and NASP reach over a million participants a year. Potentially they add up to a lot of future customers.

Innovation, the first of Mathews's core values, applies to both products and processes. As we began our tour, Bob told me about materials requirements planning (MRP), lean manufacturing, rapid continuous improvement (RCI), and a kaizen continuous-improvement process fueled by suggestions from front-line employees. Having worked on a few corporate writing projects in a manufacturing environment, I knew just enough to realize I was seeing a world-class operation. And from the charts, graphs, and statistical analyses I saw posted on the walls and at individual workstations, I could tell that around here quality was more than just a slogan.

Although assembly operations still require a great deal of careful craftsmanship, most of the actually machining is done by rows of million-dollar robotic computer numerical control (CNC) machines. But everything, right down to the cams, pulleys, and strings, is made right here. It was an impressive tour.

Bob did ask me to leave my camera out in the lobby. But as far as I know, the only department I wasn't allowed to see that day was the string room. Today even a bowstring is a marvel of top-secret technology. Before a bow is ever drawn, these small-diameter strings are already under tremendous tension. If one were to break, the consequences would be catastrophic. A bowstring can't twist or stretch even a millimeter; if it did, the bow would be out of tune and its sights would be out of alignment. And yet a bowstring must be lightweight, totally flexible, waterproof, abrasion resistant, and durable enough to last for thousands of shots before needing replacement.

Since even you or I could hop on the Internet and order a roll of high-tech fibers like Spectra, Vectran, or Dyneema, the secret is in what we'd do with them next. That's the tricky part. So the door to the string room remained closed.

In fact, because Mathews had been building and assembling the very first shipments of its top-secret new bow, the entire factory had been off-limits to visitors for nearly two months. It happens every year at Mathews, and this year's tour "blackout" had only been lifted two days earlier, when the new bow was unveiled to the press and the public. The first day, sight unseen, dealers placed initial orders for just under ten thousand of them.

MEAT HUNTERS AND HEADHUNTERS

During the past two decades, the values and priorities of today's deer hunters have changed just as dramatically as their gear. Not long ago a large buck might have been described as "a ten-pointer that weighed 230 pounds field-dressed." Instead, today's trophy hunters speak knowledgeably of Boone & Crockett or Pope & Young scores.

Both use the same formula, which takes into account the number of points, the length and thickness of the tines, and the width of the antlers' "inside spread." A 120-inch buck is now considered average, no matter how many points it has. A 150-inch buck is still brag worthy; one over 180 inches merits a magazine cover; and one over 200 inches can light up the blogosphere, be featured in a major magazine article, and even garner its hunter a couple of small endorsement contracts.

Truly exceptional antlers can also be worth big money. If a lucky hunter sells them to a collector, the check might be enough to pay for a new treestand, a new rifle, and a new pickup in which to haul them. Since Milo Hansen harvested the current world record whitetail, he and his antlers have earned over six hundred thousand dollars in appearance fees.[12] For Realtors who specialize in prime hunting land, harvesting a record-book buck has in many cases increased the value of a single parcel by one hundred thousand dollars, two hundred thousand, or even more.[13]

In turn, dreams of antlers like these fuel much of the spending at outdoor retailers. Want further proof that theirs is a business built on antlers? Many deer hunters have now become obsessed with the new springtime sport of shed hunting. For a month or so every spring, they spend their weekends searching the forest floor for antlers that bucks have already shed. Shed hunters become especially excited when they find a large antler—despite the fact that it's no longer attached to a deer. And that's "antler," singular. Finding a matched pair is an even greater challenge, since after shedding the first antler, a buck might travel a mile or more before losing the second. Hoping to gain an extra edge, some hunters are now training shed-hunting dogs. In places where large-antlered bucks are known to be roaming private land, wardens are now receiving complaints of "shed poaching."

It's true that many hunters are still more interested in venison. But it could also be argued that there's a direct connection between big antlers, big dollars feeding the deer-industrial complex, hunters' eagerness to see more deer and bigger bucks every time they step out the door, and wildlife management decisions that are good for deer but not necessarily for other wildlife or for the forest ecosystem as a whole. To better understand these connections, we need only follow the money back out into the woods.

PLEASE TAX ME

Here in North America, hunting and fishing licenses provide much of the funding for wildlife conservation and habitat improvement. They also help fund a wide range of other conservation initiatives and environmental protections. That's especially true in states and provinces where the same agency charged with wildlife conservation also enforces environmental regulations related to things like feedlot runoff, point-source water pollution from a paper mill, or emissions from your local, coal-fired power plant.

These agencies go by a variety of names, but typically it's the Department of Natural Resources or, in Canada, the Ministry of Natural

Resources. Since a portion of license fees are typically used to support the agency as a whole, this means that hunters and anglers do more than the rest of us to foot the bill for clean air and clean water—not to mention things like state or provincial parks, habitat preservation, and of course wildlife management.

Every since President Franklin D. Roosevelt signed the Migratory Bird Hunting Stamp Act in 1934, many American hunters have also been chipping in a little extra federal money on top of their state licenses. Currently the annual fee is fifteen dollars. Although the stamp is also required to hunt migratory birds like doves and woodcock, most hunters know it as simply "the duck stamp." The stamps are issued by the U.S. Postal Service, which holds an annual competition to select the following year's artwork. If you're a wildlife artist, the duck stamp is a very good thing to have on your résumé.

Ducks themselves should be glad for the duck stamp. So should the many rare and endangered species that depend on wetland habitats. Since 1934 the program has brought in over 750 million dollars that's been used to purchase or lease more than 5.3 million acres of wetland habitat that houses roughly a third of the nation's threatened or endangered species. If you're a nonhunter who cares about wildlife, especially if you're a birder, you might want to consider buying one of these stamps. Many do. It's hunters, however, who purchase around 87 percent of them.[14] Hunters also make further contributions to habitat preservation through their memberships and donations to organizations like Ducks Unlimited, the Ruffed Grouse Society, and Whitetails Unlimited.

In 1937 American hunters lobbied Congress to be allowed to pay a special 11 percent tax on arms and ammunition. The Pittman-Robertson Wildlife Restoration Act became law, and during the past seventy-five years, it's generated more than $7.2 billion for the purchase, restoration, and protection of wildlife habitat.[15] When bowhunting began to grow in popularity, the archery industry asked that its products be included. It essentially told Congress, "Please tax us too." In 1975 the industry got its wish.

These funds aren't restricted to "game" species and can be used to create habitat for the benefit of any wild bird or mammal. According to the US Fish and Wildlife Service, over 70 percent of users at the refuges and wildlife management areas established with these funds are nonhunters such as hikers, anglers, campers, birders, photographers, and picnickers. In some areas nonhunting usage is as high as 95 percent.

Hunters who question the fairness of all this will be delighted to learn that some states have begun asking nonhunters to chip in too. The latest was Virginia, which now charges four dollars for a day pass and twenty-three dollars for an annual pass that gives visitors without a hunting or fishing license full and equal access to state-owned wildlife management areas. Still, when a columnist and blogger from *Field and Stream* asked readers to comment, not everyone was thrilled. Wrote one commenter, "As long as we as hunters provide the majority of the funding, we also hold the power when it comes to access, land use, etc. I would much rather pay somewhat higher fees than potentially lose access . . . or get locked into a perpetual battle to keep that access."[16]

Nonhunters, on the other hand, wonder if current funding methods give hunters a little too much influence over public policy and wildlife management decisions that affect the rest of us. If hunters provide most of the funding, they reason, and if hunters are seen as customers, then decisions will be made that benefit hunters at the expense of other users—even at the expense of the environment.

Nonhunters might also point to the US Fish and Wildlife Service telling us that in 2011 America's 13.7 million hunters spent thirty-four billion dollars on their pastime. The same survey, it turns out, found that 71.8 million wildlife watchers spent fifty-five billion dollars.[17] Although each of them may have spent less, together they spent significantly more. And even though myriad other outdoor pursuits might claim sizable numbers of their own, it seems unlikely that new Pittman-Robertson–type surcharges will be levied anytime soon on binoculars, sleeping bags, kayaks, or mountain bikes. For now, hunters are paying more than their share. This may help explain something called the North American Model of Wildlife Conservation.

THESE DEER ARE YOUR DEER

Really. They are. The wild deer of North America belong to you. They also belong to me and to everyone else. This radical idea is a key tenet of the

North American Model of Wildlife Conservation.[18] According to wildlife biologists' professional organization The Wildlife Society (TWS),
"The Model" is based on seven key principles:

- The public trust doctrine. This one's most important. Wildlife
  belongs to the people, and the states or provinces hold it in
  trust for the benefit of all. When deer walk onto your land, they
  don't become your property. They still belong to everyone. In the
  United States this principle dates back to an 1841 Supreme Court
  decision, which in turn referenced the Magna Carta.

- Elimination of markets for game. In North America it's illegal
  to sell wild game. If you select venison from the menu at a fancy
  restaurant anywhere in the United States or Canada, it will be
  from a deer that was raised on a farm.

- Allocation of wildlife by law. These deer may be your deer, but your
  state or province can tell you when and how you'll be able to acquire
  one. In my state, for example, this year's deer hunting regulations
  run to fifty-six pages. Separate regulation pamphlets for small game,
  waterfowl, and trapping are roughly the same length.

- Kill only for legitimate purpose. As TWS notes, most people
  would consider food, fur, self-defense, and property defense to be
  legitimate purposes. If someone's mainly interested in antlers but
  eats venison from the deer to which they were attached, then that's
  still considered legitimate.

- Wildlife as an international resource. Since migratory birds
  cross international borders as they're flying north and south, we
  Americans had better be talking with Canada and Mexico. All
  three countries are among the 175 signatories to the Convention
  on International Trade in Endangered Species of Wild Fauna and
  Flora (CITES). This has little to do with deer, but it's a key part of
  The Model.

- Science-based wildlife policy. Wildlife management decisions
  should be based on sound science rather than folk wisdom or
  political considerations. As we'll learn later, that's not always true
  when it comes to deer management.

- Democracy of hunting. The United States and Canada have
  worked to preserve hunting opportunities for everyone, even those

who aren't wealthy and don't possess their own private hunting land. It's one of our most egalitarian and democratic traditions. It's also one of our most endangered.

In North America these ideas shape the policies we use to manage and conserve *all* wildlife, not just the "game" species that most interest hunters. If you're a nonhunter learning this for the first time, you may find it disturbingly "hunter-centric." And even hunters, once they begin thinking critically about The Model, will have questions: Who, for example, gets to decide what's a legitimate purpose, and where do we draw the line? Which scientists get to influence policy? Just because this is our history, should it be our future? And what about other countries with very different models of wildlife conservation that are working just fine for them? What can we learn from those examples?

Still, most of us would agree that The Model is at least a reasonable set of principles on which to base our management of whitetail deer. At this very moment America's deer-hunting culture is changing rapidly in ways that are undermining almost every one of The Model's seven principles. Practices like feeding, baiting, and food plots, for example, are leading to the de facto privatization of what's in theory a public resource. Worse yet, what happens when farmers and ranchers encircle their property with high fences that keep wild deer from leaving to wander in front of someone else's rifle? There goes the public trust doctrine. And that's only the beginning.

— —

To sum all this up, the deer business is big business, and the outdoor industry is built largely on deer and their antlers. What's good for deer is good for the industry, and what's good for the industry usually turns out to be good for deer—at least in the short term. This often has unintended consequences for deer, their habitat, and the entire landscape. (Not to mention your suburban landscaping.)

In North America all these things are interwoven and inextricably entangled: conservation and its funding, public policy surrounding how we manage deer populations and hence entire ecosystems, and an influential outdoor industry based largely on the pursuit of a single species. That's not true anywhere else in the world.

So remember, this land is your land. So are its deer. For now, states and provinces are holding them in public trust for you. Should you decide to try and take possession of one next time deer season rolls around, you'd better be ready. And if you'd like to find a deer with record-book trophy antlers, I know just the place.

CHAPTER 3

The Deer of Buffalo County

Land is going for how much per acre? So, let's see . . . Times three hundred acres, that's over eighteen hundred thousand—almost two million! If I hadn't let the farm go back to the bank in '97, I'd be a millionaire!

—OVERHEARD IN A BUFFALO COUNTY TAVERN

Venison is delicious. This I know for certain.

Antlers, however, are different. Their magic is lost on me. And yet for many hunters, antlers weave a spell of enchantment. For them venison is almost a by-product. They're more interested in what goes to their taxidermist than what goes on their table.

Most nonhunters feel OK about hunters who eat what they shoot. If they feel a little uncomfortable with the whole idea of trophy hunting, well, so do many hunters. Serious trophy hunting is definitely outside the mainstream of American hunting culture. Hunters of a certain age like to remind their younger counterparts, "You can't eat horns." Still, the fascination persists. In fact, evidence suggests that hunters have been fascinated by magic antlers for millennia.

Take, for example, the sixteen-thousand-year-old Paleolithic cave paintings of Lascaux. They include hundreds of horses, bulls, and bison—plus seven felines, a bird, a bear, a rhinoceros, one dead human who seems to have just had an unpleasant encounter with a bison, and more than ninety stags with implausibly gigantic antlers.

It's quite possible, however, that the antlers on those Paleolithic deer *weren't* exaggerated. After all, consider the canvas on which they were painted. The caves of Lascaux were formed when percolating groundwater dissolved passageways through a type of limestone that's very similar to the rock found under Buffalo County, Wisconsin. Today the Lascaux region of southwestern France is no longer a prime destination for trophy deer hunters. Instead, the best place on the entire planet to find magic antlers is one small county in southwestern Wisconsin.

Buffalo County covers 684 square miles. It has only one stoplight. And yet somehow it has yielded more record-book bucks than any other county in America. Only two or three entire states can match it. It's unmatched by any province in Canada—or even by all of Canada's provinces combined.[1]

Buffalo County's annual crop of record-book antlers has made it the world's most deer-driven real estate market. Although sales have cooled during the current recession, during one five-year period land values increased nearly fivefold.[2] And rather unfairly for landowners just across the county line, the prices stop there—even though the bucks don't. For some local residents it has been a winning lottery ticket.

Farmers who aren't ready to sell can lease out the hunting rights to their land—often for an amount that matches their annual profits from the entire farm. Many of these leases are to outfitters and guides; they in turn hope to sell a guided, five-day hunting experience to enough clients so there's a profit left over at the end of the year. Some years there is; some years there isn't.

Trophy hunters make the pilgrimage to Buffalo County from all over America; a few even arrive from other countries. They all have one thing in common. Whether they're investing a million or two in a piece of prime hunting land or merely dropping four or five thousand for a week-long guided hunt, none of them are impoverished subsistence hunters hoping to put a winter's supply of venison in the freezer.

Still, whatever you might think of trophy hunting, it's important to note one important fact: If venison is a Buffalo County by-product, it's one that rarely goes to waste. Even most trophy hunters value their venison and look forward to filling the freezer every year. It's true that some out-of-state hunters visiting Buffalo County are only interested in antlers. If they're successful, they have their buck's head and antlers sent to a local taxidermist; later the finished mount will be carefully packaged and shipped to their home or office.

The meat from these deer is donated to local food banks. At the risk of stating the obvious, large deer with large antlers tend to also contain a lot of venison. Although perhaps less tender than meat from a younger, smaller deer, it still makes great hamburger. If our obsessive trophy hunter hadn't worked so hard to kill his oversize deer, there would easily be a hundred fewer pounds of ground venison at the food bank.

Figure ten meals each for ten different families, and trophy hunting doesn't seem so bad. If a hunter enjoys his vacation, shoots a deer, and heads for the airport empty-handed, then it's at least ground venison for the local food bank, some extra business for guides and outfitters, some lease money for a struggling dairy farmer, another project for the local taxidermist, and more money spent on gas and groceries. Think of it as economic stimulus money.

Trophy deer have definitely stimulated the economy of Buffalo County. While these deer and their magical antlers may not have stimulated everyone's economy equally, there's no arguing with the fact that they've changed Buffalo County forever. I was curious to learn more—especially about the more surreal aspects of the county's deer-driven real estate market.

What do these wealthy hunters do with their new land once they buy it? I knew they didn't just wait until opening morning of hunting season and then tiptoe out into their newly purchased woods. But once they own the land, just exactly what do they do to shape it in their own image?

And what about the guides and outfitters who lease so much land in Buffalo County? What sort of hunting experience justifies the prices they need to charge their clients? And why are so many of those hunters repeat clients who return year after year?

I was curious to meet some of these people, and I had lots of questions for them. To begin with, I wanted to learn more about just *why* all this is happening—especially why it's happening here.

The first question I wanted to answer was this: Just what makes Buffalo County, well, Buffalo County?

Magic Dirt, Magic Antlers

In Buffalo County taverns you'll hear many theories. Some hunters believe it's because the steep terrain and wooded bluffs make it easier for big bucks to evade hunters. That lets them live longer and grow even bigger.

Others are certain it's because the steep terrain makes deer bigger and stronger from climbing up and down those hillsides every day. Still, that doesn't quite explain the antlers. Wouldn't the deer be more tired, with less energy left over for antler production?

I also heard a lot about something called "Quality Deer Management," or QDM. Some said QDM was the answer to my question. When landowners manage their land correctly and let the small bucks walk, they're rewarded with larger ones next year. It's as simple as that.

But it's not. The QDM story itself isn't so simple. I'd learn more later. Plus, I knew that QDM is only part of the story. After all, QDM advocates are applying the same concepts all over North America without achieving the same results. The potential just isn't there.

Hunters in Buffalo County have been shooting large deer with freakish antlers for at least the past century and a half. Old-timers remember seeing giant deer in these hills long before anyone had ever heard of QDM. The potential was already there.

I had a hunch the answer might be something deeper—like maybe even deep underground. Maybe it was the soil itself. Maybe it takes magic dirt to make magic antlers. To confirm my suspicions, I decided to find a soil scientist.

I ended up talking with Todd Mau. He's with the US Department of Agriculture's (USDA's) National Resources Conservation Service (NRCS), and he knew the secret. Having spent his entire life in southwestern Wisconsin, he also knew about the dramatic changes magic dirt and magic antlers have brought to Buffalo County over the past twenty years.

After we exchanged a few e-mails, Todd agreed to tell me everything I wanted to know. He even promised to take me out in the field so that I could learn about the soil science firsthand. In the end the science would turn out to be relatively simple. It was the rest of the story that got complicated.

In fact, if Todd had only explained the chemistry and geology that have made the deer of Buffalo County possible, our visit would have been over in about two minutes. He saved that part for the end, as almost an anticlimactic afterthought. The magic in Buffalo County's dirt is a simple quirk of fate and geology. The story he most wanted to tell me, and the story I most want to tell you, is what that magic dirt and the resulting magic antlers have meant for the people of Buffalo County.

Todd's office is in the county courthouse. Alma, the county seat, is a long, skinny town wedged in between the Mississippi River and the five-hundred-foot bluff that overlooks it. With the train tracks running alongside the river, and with Lock and Dam Number 4 located about halfway through town, there isn't much room left for Alma.

The courthouse is partway up the hillside, on the street farthest up the hill. From his office Todd has one of the best views in town. On a clear day he can see all up and down the river, way over into the backwaters, and maybe twenty miles over into Minnesota.

Todd told me that right now we were looking at the one reason most tourists came to this area—at least before that whole deer thing got started. Anglers came for the river's walleye, pike, catfish, and panfish. Waterfowlers came for the ducks and geese in the backwaters. Birders came to watch the eagles or the annual migrations of tundra swans.

By itself, however, tourism isn't always enough. "Here in Alma," Todd told me, "we no longer have a grocery store. We don't have a single hardware store. You can't buy a hammer in Alma. Sure we have plenty of shops for the tourists. But that's only good for four or five months out of the year."

I asked Todd about jobs. "Well, apart from those souvenir shops and a couple of restaurants and taverns, there isn't much. What you see down there along the main street is pretty much it. There are a few government jobs in this building. And then there's teaching. But even that isn't so secure anymore."

As in much of rural America, Buffalo County's population is shrinking rapidly. In recent years its deer-driven real estate market has only accelerated that trend. Today over 50 percent of the land in Buffalo County is owned by nonresidents—most of whom bought it as hunting land.

"It's great that they pay taxes," said Todd, "and they do contribute to our local economy in other ways. But for the community's long-term survival, we need property owners who live here and raise their families here. Right now our schools are hurting; their student populations are dropping fast. Our three kids went to school in Alma, and they got a great education. But in ten more years . . . I just don't know."

Since the state and federal funding received by school districts is based in part on student enrollment, these trends have serious budgetary implications. To make matters worse, state assistance is also based on local income levels, which in turn—theoretically, at least—are reflected in local land valuations.

In Buffalo County these standard formulas don't work so well. Recent land sales to out-of-state hunters have skewed their results with some large numbers. On paper these school districts are suddenly much wealthier and hence eligible for much less assistance. They've been, quite literally, defunded by deer.

Deer have also meant some changes for Todd and his job. As a district conservationist, he consults with farmers and private landowners on issues like managing barnyard runoff, preventing soil erosion, and planning crop rotations in a way that maximizes short-term yields while still preserving the soil for a sustainable future.

Until 1985 Todd's agency only worked with farmers who voluntarily asked for its advice. Since then farmers who want to participate in any USDA subsidy programs—and most of them do—have been required to work with the NRCS to formulate and implement an approved conservation plan.

Todd told me that whole "mandatory" part was an adjustment for him and the farmers both. He says most farmers are great to work with though. They're friendly, they welcome him onto their place, and they're glad to talk. They know he's there to help them out.

His job is more challenging when he's working with absentee landowners and newly arrived "deer farmers." To start with, he needs to explain what the subsidies and management plans are all about.

"Suppose we've got an absentee landowner who's rarely here outside of hunting season," said Todd. "He rents to a farmer, maybe even the one who sold him the land. When he hears about subsidies, he thinks he should get them, too—or maybe raise the farmer's rent. But it doesn't always work that way. And he may not be excited about having to work with us on a management plan.

"We need to help him understand the long-term benefits of a good management plan and a good renting arrangement. If it means renting the land for more per acre, he may want to cash in on corn, year after year. The farmer's only renting, so he's OK with the deal. But in the long term, it's in that new landowner's best interest to not deplete the soil."

Todd also encounters new landowners with different values and expectations. "Take one guy I talked with a couple months ago," says Todd. "He asked me what he should do to improve deer habitat. I start to tell him about winter cover, bushes that would produce berries, that sort of thing. I tell him it would be great for turkeys, songbirds, and all the wildlife, not just deer. The guy stops me and says, 'Wait a minute. That's nice, but I don't give a shit about the birds. I only care about deer.' What do you tell someone like that?

"Or there was the guy who called and asked, 'What kind of trees should I plant along the road so people won't be able to see my deer?' It was 'my' deer. I had to kind of bite my tongue on that one."

Todd then told me about out-of-state landowners who give special instructions to the farmers who rent from them. One farmer was asked to not drive his tractor out into the field and disturb the deer during prime morning and evening hunting hours. Another was told he couldn't harvest his corn until after deer season—even though it might mean losing the entire harvest. While en route to a rented field a couple miles away, a third farmer was stopped while driving his tractor on a public road. An angry hunter, someone he'd never met, told him to turn back so that he wouldn't disturb the deer.

Todd's heard lots of stories. After doing this sort of work for more than twenty years, he knows just about every farmer in Buffalo County. He's met their families. He knows their children's names, and he knows their dogs' names. He drives and walks their farms with them, and he's become good friends with many of them.

For some of these Buffalo County farm families, the past decade's deer-driven real estate market has been the answer to their prayers. Imagine a husband and wife, struggling dairy farmers who face rising feed prices and falling milk prices. One day, at the end of their long gravel driveway, there's a letter in the mailbox. It might be from a local Realtor or from a stranger in Minneapolis or Chicago. They open the letter, read it together, and their lives are changed.

Other stories are less happy. Thanks to deer, some Buffalo County families are estranged and no longer speaking. Let's say a farm couple is approaching a certain age when they receive an offer to lease hunting rights. They tell sons and daughters—some still at home; others returning every Christmas, every Easter, and every November for deer season—that they won't be able to hunt on the family farm anymore. A commodities trader from Chicago has leased exclusive hunting rights for an annual payment that exceeds last year's profits from the entire farm. And, yes, that "exclusive" part includes the landowners and their family. The children don't take it well.

Or after receiving an unsolicited offer to purchase, other parents reconsider their plan to deed the farm to an eldest son. They'd told him it would only be another year or so, but . . . they're not so young any more. They don't have much saved up, it's still a couple more years until they're eligible for Medicare, and two million dollars is a lot of money. The son doesn't take it well.

And then there was the story about those two brothers . . . No. Maybe that's one to save. And even in the two brief stories I've already told, I've changed certain details.

From Todd, and from others, I heard stories about many families like these. When I asked him about putting me in touch with a couple of them, he politely demurred. And after a moment's reflection, I realized he was right. Some secrets should be kept, and some stories are better left untold.

I can, however, tell you the secret behind those bizarrely huge Buffalo County antlers. Todd finally told me, but only after I reminded him why I'd come.

His explanation was bedrock simple. For the deer and the people of Buffalo County, however, its implications and consequences are not.

Before I left his office that day, Todd revealed the secret. He showed me the secret, and he even let me hold some of it in my hand. He didn't swear me to a Buffalo County code of silence, and now I can finally tell you the secret behind the magic dirt that makes those magic antlers possible. It's dolomitic limestone with just the right ratio of calcium to magnesium. Just like at Lascaux. That's it. That's the secret.

Without really understanding what I was looking at, I'd already seen it everywhere—in outcroppings on the highest bluffs, in streambeds at the bottom of coulees, and in cliffs where roadways are carved into steep hillsides. It's everywhere—under the ground and sometimes lying in plain sight right on top of the ground.

Most of all, it's *in* the ground. It's in the soil, and it's in everything that grows here. It's in everything deer eat: the acorns, the browse, the food plots planted by hunters, and every bite of the corn, soybeans, and alfalfa planted by farmers.

Rich soils anywhere are great for raising crops; the magic dirt in Buffalo County is great for raising trophy deer. Antlers contain lots of calcium. But unless dietary calcium is accompanied by the right amount of magnesium, deer can't utilize it effectively. It turns out this optimum ratio falls within a relatively narrow range.

You may not live in Buffalo County, and you may not live in any of America's other hidden hot spots with the same kind of magic dirt. But if you still want to grow deer with trophy antlers, you might try feeding them special mineral supplements—or even scattering special trophy rocks in your woods.

Unlike the square, fifty-pound mineral blocks meant for cattle, these sixteen-pound chunks are tastefully formed into irregular shapes. Mottled brown in color, they look like any other rocks that just happen to be lying out in the woods.

Depending on where you live, this might be a good thing when your local game warden stops by. In some states, including Wisconsin, the use of these minerals is highly regulated. Deer love them. When these "rocks" are gone, deer will lick away the dirt underneath to get any remaining residue. These mineral supplements are considered bait and can only be used in limited quantities and at certain times of the year.

Deer, however, need minerals year-round. And in Buffalo County they get them every day.

Elsewhere hunters annually buy many tons of these trophy rocks. Legal in most states for year-round use, they're not necessarily a bad thing. We all need vitamins and minerals. Presumably the deer slurping away at these trophy rocks gain other health benefits besides larger antlers. The deer in Buffalo County, however, do just fine without them.

Now I knew the secret, and I'd heard a few stories about what that secret has meant for Buffalo County. It was time to leave the office and head out into the field. By now I knew I wouldn't have to worry about perplexing chemistry lessons or an evening in the lab performing soil analyses. Instead we went for a drive.

We headed upward and eastward, away from the Mississippi. It was a steep climb; the narrow roadway was cut into the side of a deep coulee penetrating the river bluff. One side dropped off steeply, and I was glad for the guardrail. On the uphill side we drove past a sheer face of dolomitic limestone.

After a mile or so, we found a spot where it was wide enough to pull over and park. Just for fun, I took a few photos of Todd pointing to the limestone cliffs. Next I got a shot of him down in the roadside gravel on one knee, pointing to the barely visible corner of a protruding boulder. Like a limestone iceberg, most of it was still submerged beneath the surface.

Then we spotted some boulders that had recently fallen from the cliff. Most were too heavy to lift, but Todd found one that was smaller—about as big as his head. He hefted it in one hand, pointed to it, and gave me a knowing, conspiratorial look.

I still have the photo. It's the secret Buffalo County Trophy Rock.

MARKET FORCES

"Wanted: Woman with truck. Please send picture of truck."

This "redneck ad in the personals" joke, along with its many variations, has worn a bit thin. It does, however, resemble many Buffalo County real estate listings. Only this time it's "For sale: Land with trophy deer. Please see picture of deer."

Typically the listing's main photo shows an embarrassed and startled-looking trophy buck that's just been surprised by an electronic flash at around 2:00 a.m. It's the deer version of those unflattering celebrity photos on the cover of grocery-store tabloids. These deer haven't been ambushed by human paparazzi. Instead they've been caught by motion-sensing trailcams.

Those are the lucky deer; the ones in other real estate photos are already dead and being posed with their hunters. The implied message is that this deer is taken. But if you buy these 320 acres, there are plenty more where that one came from.

There are no guarantees of course. Because these trophy deer aren't fenced in, they may have already left for your new neighbor's woods by the time you get out your checkbook. Still, they're a big part of what you're buying. That's why the listing's other, smaller photos show even more trophy deer and a couple aerial photos to show why the terrain would make deer want to stick around.

Property descriptions rarely mention curb appeal or granite counter-tops. Instead they include key phrases like "waterholes and food plots," "a hot spot where rutting bucks check for does in bedding areas," and "good access and good ambush spots, no matter which direction the wind is blowing." If a perfectly sound farmhouse and barn are included, they're rarely mentioned until the last paragraph. They may not even merit a photo.

When Buffalo County Realtors meet with someone who's buying or selling hunting land, the dress code is strictly "business camo." Most are themselves avid deer hunters. In this market a few sets of record-book antlers on one's office wall can go a long way toward establishing credibility with new clients.

One of these Realtors is Gordy Weiss. I met with him in the fall of 2009, when we were still nosing our way into a recession. Since then the local market has cooled considerably. But if the rush has slowed, it could be about supply as much as demand. Buffalo County landowners are now holding tight to what they believe is an excellent long-term investment, one that pays yearly deer dividends. This is no deer bubble.

"Yes," Gordy told me back then, "it's true that prices have fallen back by 15 or 20 percent. But we're still seeing some sales. Some people out there still have money, and they see Buffalo County hunting land as a safe long-term investment."

Gordy explained that most of these buyers are from Minnesota and Wisconsin—mainly Minneapolis, Green Bay, Milwaukee, and Madison. A few are from Chicago, but not so many. About 90 to 95 percent are bowhunters; some don't even hunt during the gun season. At least 75 percent of these transactions are strictly cash. For most of these buyers, financing is not an issue.

Rather unfairly for sellers in adjacent counties, the Buffalo County mystique stops precisely at the county line. Gordy's office is in downtown Durand, just a couple blocks from the Chippewa River. "Over on the other side," he explained, "that's Pepin County. Last year, right over in the river bottom, a guy shot a buck that came close to being a new state archery record."

Gordy then pointed to one of the deer up on the wall; its antlers were especially massive. "I also got *that* one over in Pepin County," he said. "Doesn't matter. Anything over the county line goes for seven hundred to a thousand dollars less per acre."

Tom Fedie is a Realtor over on the other side of the county. There he sees even more of a differential. "If it's over in Trempealeau County," he said, "it goes for about a thousand to fifteen hundred dollars less per acre. Obviously the deer don't know where the county line is. But for buyers it's just not the same as being in Buffalo County."

These buyers are doing their homework. Every week the county mails out five or six plat books to addresses all over the country. During hunting season that figure doubles or triples. County Clerk Roxann Halverson remembers sending one to an address in Pennsylvania. "He called first to get our address. Had a strong German accent. Rudi was his name. Very nice man, but very hard to understand. At first we thought someone down the hall was playing a joke on us. But a couple days later, there was his check in the mail."

Some farmers, even though their property isn't for sale, have occasionally noticed small planes circling overhead. Later, when an unsolicited offer arrives in the mail, they're relieved to learn the flights were nothing more than buyers out scouting.

These buyers are most interested in large, contiguous blocks of wooded ridgelines and steep bluffs—the untillable land that until recently was worth far less than the fertile farmland in the valleys below. In fact, if they can buy a wooded ridgeline without having to waste money on all the flat farmland in an adjacent valley, so much the better.

The edge of the woods is rarely a straight line. The uphill limit of what's tillable generally corresponds to a meandering contour line beyond which tractors tip and hillsides erode. That's probably why so many Buffalo County property descriptions include terms like "apparent boundaries" and "287 acres more or less."

In other cases these new landowners rent their tillable farmland to the previous owner or to one of the neighbors down the road. Or they may simply take it out of production. After all, they're not really all that interested in corn or soybeans. The one crop they most want to grow and harvest is whitetail deer with trophy antlers.

—◆—

To really understand the market, the buyers, and the sellers, I sat down to talk with Stu Hagen, a Realtor and hunter who's been at the center of Buffalo County's transformation from the very beginning. According to some, he's one of the two or three people most responsible for that transformation.

Stu is Buffalo County's number-one Realtor specializing in prime hunting land. He owns a couple thousand acres of his own; in partnerships with a few friends, he owns a couple thousand more. All of that land is carefully managed for bigger and better deer; Stu was one of Wisconsin's early advocates of QDM. He's also an avid bowhunter who's taken several trophy bucks. His name pops up in Boone & Crockett and Pope & Young record books as often as it does in Buffalo County real estate listings.

We met at Stu's log home, just outside a small town that's roughly in the center of Buffalo County. On both sides of the valley, steep, oak-covered hillsides rise above the farmland below. Although Stu's home overlooks the valley, it's perched atop a smaller foothill. The ridgeline behind it, like so many in Buffalo County, is reserved for the deer.

Later he'd take me up the trail for a tour. But first he began with a little history—complete with helpful visual aids. From where we sat sipping Diet Cokes in Stu's living room, I could see a panoramic view of the entire valley. On this morning in early September, the fields and the woods overlooking them were still green and lush. Up on the wall I could see several head-and-shoulder mounts sporting massive, record-book antlers.

Stu gestured toward them. "Around here," he explained, "we've always had large deer with large antlers. Then about fifteen years ago, QDM came to Buffalo County. There's more to it than this, but basically QDM is about balance. Rather than just shooting bucks, we're harvesting does and letting the young bucks go. Initially it was a matter of waiting until they were three years old. Now we're letting them get to be at least four years old. That's the difference."

Stu explained how QDM quickly reached a critical mass in Buffalo County. Once a couple neighbors start practicing QDM, a few more people buy land around them—and then a few more. Soon there's a huge block of land where nearly all landowners are practicing QDM. So far, Buffalo County has at least four areas like this.

I wondered where this left the hunter who just wants to get out and shoot a deer for venison—or, for that matter, a first-time hunter who'd be happy with just any deer. In this neighborhood would peer pressure and doctrinal purity still leave room for those kind of hunting experiences?

In theory, yes. Rather than just harvesting trophy bucks, QDM adherents also harvest enough does to keep the population in line with what the habitat will support. This also helps maintain a relatively normal balance between does and bucks. QDM, in principle, is more than just "quality antler management." Letting small bucks walk until they turn into big bucks is only one small part of the QDM equation. By itself that's not QDM.

Indeed, I'm told that several landowners in Buffalo County are now practicing a very different sort of regimen. They're shooting no does, no younger bucks, and only a small number of trophy bucks. They're careful to shoot, trail, and remove these trophy deer with a minimum of disturbance; they also venture into their best hunting spots as infrequently as possible. Apart from antlers on the wall, their number-one priority is ensuring that "their" trophy deer never feel unsafe enough to begin spending time on a neighbor's land. To keep a low profile, some of these hunters are swearing their taxidermists to secrecy and no longer having their trophy antlers officially measured for the record books.

Those hunters are the exception, and Buffalo County is still producing more than its share of record-book antlers. Stu told me that a 150-inch buck used to be considered pretty impressive, even in Buffalo County. But now, unless they're at least in the 180s, no one even talks about them. Hunters are even bringing in more bucks with antlers over 200 inches. It's these magazine-cover deer that are driving up prices. As a result, very few pieces of Buffalo County land are now being bought for farming. "Farmers don't like hearing this," Stu told me, "but it's only accelerating. That's just the way it is."

For Stu and other local Realtors, the trend has been good for business. But for local hunters who don't own land, it's been less of a godsend. There isn't a lot of public land around here, and suddenly Buffalo County private land is a lot more private than it used to be.

A generation ago, locals could easily get permission to hunt on a farm down the road. Even if they lived in town, they'd know someone. If they didn't, they could go for a drive in the country a month or two before hunting season. When they saw a promising patch of woods and stopped at the closest farmhouse, their odds of getting permission were generally pretty good. Although no payment was expected, a package of venison and a bottle of something to go with it was always a welcome thank-you gift.

Today that doesn't quite cut it. One hunter explained it quite simply: "If you don't own it, lease it, or hunt with an outfitter who leases it, then you're not hunting on private land in Buffalo County. Period."

Gone, too, are the neighborhood deer drives that followed a ridgeline for miles. "We'd get together in a big group," Stu told me, "and all do a drive together. No one cared whose land we were on, and no one cared where we happened to be standing when we got a deer. But not anymore. Now people hunt on their own land. Usually they're hunting by themselves, sitting in a treestand."

Not surprisingly, some local hunters resent the new absentee land-owners. They resent the outsiders, they resent the outfitters, and most of all they resent the Realtors. Stu says that's unfair. He tells me the outfitters aren't to blame, and neither are the Realtors. Stu insists that he's not driving up prices; buyers are. The price of the land is whatever the market will bear. He's following a market that's already there. His commissions might be bigger, but he works a lot harder to get them.

Stu does indeed work hard on his clients' behalf. But if it's his job to sell their listings, well, part of that job is to sell Buffalo County in general. Today the best way to do that is to sell the deer of Buffalo County, and Stu is doing his part.

To further support his deer-related marketing efforts, he's also started a separate consulting business called Midwest Whitetail Management Services. Its slogan is "More Bucks for Your Bucks." If you're selling, Stu's company can help make your land more marketable to hunters. If you're buying, they'll help you find hunting land and improve it. If you already have hunting land, they'll help you enhance it with food plots, waterholes, and access roads. After that, if you want help deciding where to hang your treestands and trailcams, they'll give you expert advice. If you like, they'll even do it for you.

The basics are simple enough; deer need food, water, shelter, and places to hide. But Stu tells me there's a real art to knowing where and how to make these improvements, and then knowing how to integrate them with your treestand placement so the whole system works together—for the deer year-round, and for you when it's time to hunt. In other words, you might want to hire a trained professional.

By using some of these same techniques, Stu has been quietly buying and transforming farmland in out-of-the-way pockets all over the Midwest—even in other parts of the country. A few short years after making these improvements, he sells what's now "prime hunting land" for a substantial profit—sometimes, in fact, doubling his money.

As with Stu's other deer-related business ventures, his treestands, trailcams, and trophy shots are all tools of the trade. He told me one story about purchasing a farm in a sparsely populated corner of a certain midwestern state. He'd seen its potential, made lots of improvements, and eventually captured trailcam images of a Boone and Crockett buck that would be one for the record books: a "Booner," as they say.

"We really wanted to sell this property," said Stu. "We had lots of stands out, and three of us were hunting hard. But no luck."

I interrupted to make sure I understood correctly.

Stu grinned sheepishly. "Well . . . no. I wouldn't exactly say we had to kill that particular buck before we'd be able to sell the place. But we knew it wouldn't hurt—especially if we could do it during bow season. And in the end, it did make a difference. Once that photo was on the listing, it wasn't long before we had a buyer."

Stu's a friendly, likable guy. We spent the morning together, and I could tell he'd have been happy to talk deer all day. He clearly loves what he does. And who wouldn't? We chatted a bit more, and then it was time for a tour. First we headed for the machine shed behind Stu's house. (There's also an office and a bunkhouse in the back half of the shed; Stu needs the extra room when he invites friends and relatives over to hunt.) Stu's shed held the usual tractors, discs, and seeders. I also saw equipment that you wouldn't find in most farmers' machine sheds.

Right inside the door we squeezed past a pallet-load of treestands that had just been delivered. After they're assembled these twenty-foot steel ladder stands will be strapped to strategically located trees. At the top of the ladder, there's a platform just big enough to sit on. A typical bowhunter might own three or four of them. By placing them at multiple ambush sites, he'll always have at least one that's downwind of the direction from which deer are expected to approach. Stu orders them by the pallet-load. He has forty-seven on just one farm. "We have some large properties," he explained, "and you need different stands for different wind conditions and different times of day. Still, I do have my favorites."

To keep tabs on the deer, Stu deploys hundreds of motion-sensing trailcams. I only saw a dozen or so stacked over in the corner. Most of his trailcams were already out in the woods, strapped to trees in various corners of Buffalo County and points beyond.

Stu gestured toward two pruning saws that they were bungeed onto the roll cage of his Polaris Ranger, a two-person ATV with a cargo bed in the back. "We use these saws for clearing shooting lanes in front of the treestands. But we won't need them this trip. You want to grab the other one?"

Stu reached for a telescoping pole with a toothy foot-long blade on one end. I unstrapped the other saw, a shorter fiberglass pole with a tiny chainsaw on the end. We carefully leaned them both against the wall and then hopped in the ATV.

Once we'd backed out of the machine shed, we headed toward the ridgeline. As we bounced along the trail, we passed small fields of soybeans, corn, canola, and sunflowers. Rather than small farm fields that would be soon be harvested by and for humans, these were actually oversize food plots meant to attract and hold deer. Like everything else I was about to see, they were here for the deer.

I was puzzled by what appeared to be alternating rows of short and tall soybeans. "Two different types," explained Stu. "The short one's a normal variety, for the pod and the beans. Good protein for later in the season. The tall variety is less pod, more leafy vegetation. The deer love it. Down here they've only nibbled a few of the tips so far. Up closer to the woods, they really take it down."

As we came over a small rise, I noticed a trailcam on a fence post up ahead. Stu gestured toward it and grinned. "Smile for the camera." I did, waving for extra measure.

As the trail started uphill, we passed another food plot with rows of alternating soybean varieties. It was perhaps a two-acre strip, right along the edge of the woods. Here, just as Stu had predicted, deer had browsed the green, leafy variety to a uniform height of only six or eight inches.

As we entered the woods and climbed toward the ridgeline, I saw more deer sign—tracks, scrapes where bucks had pawed at the dirt, and even a few rubs where they'd been polishing their antlers and testing their neck muscles against small saplings. After reaching the top of the hill, we bounced along a narrow, meandering trail that followed the ridgeline for the better part of a mile.

At one point we stopped at a small waterhole just off the trail. A bulldozer had been used to scrape a depression about twenty feet across; after recent rains it was nearly full. Around its edges we saw an unbroken carpet of fresh deer tracks. Overlooking the waterhole, and well within bow range, was a strategically placed ladder stand.

"We've taken quite a few nice deer from this spot," Stu told me. "We have lots of oaks along this ridge that are dropping acorns, and there's plenty of cover along the hillside. These waterholes really bring them in."

I stepped out of the ATV to get a couple photos. I was just about to walk all around the rim of the pond. I especially wanted a wide-angle shot from near the edge of the water, one that included both the waterhole and the treestand overlooking it.

Fortunately I caught myself just in time. It was less than a week until bow season, and I knew Stu wouldn't appreciate my leaving a human scent trail all around the perimeter of his favorite ambush site. When I told him why I'd stopped after only three steps, he laughed and told me not to worry about it. I could tell, however, that he appreciated my caution. He hadn't even stepped out of the ATV. He could wait until next week.

During my travels, and through my own experiences as a new deer hunter with a lot to learn, I've found that the most successful hunters aren't just lucky. They earn their deer. While money can indeed buy more land, more treestands, and more trailcams, it can't guarantee success. Hunting still requires skill, patience, and luck.

Suppose you can't spare a million or two for a Buffalo County backyard like Stu's. But after some scrimping and saving, you're at least able to fork over five thousand dollars for a weeklong guided hunt somewhere down the road from Stu's place. The rest is still up to you. It's good to know that your outfitter has already positioned a treestand in just the right spot. Now you'll need to sit motionless in that stand from dawn until dusk. (Actually, you'll want to get in position an hour before dawn. And don't come down until it's hard dark. You're especially likely to see deer right at dusk.)

If you move a muscle at the wrong moment, you're busted. Deer's eyes are good at detecting motion, and deer have far better peripheral vision than we do. And when bowhunters in treestands become more common, deer learn to look up.

You could arrow a trophy deer on the first day. But chances are good that you'll wait for days on end. A deer with massive antlers wanders by at dusk, right when the light is fading and almost gone. Your opportunity will last for three seconds. You're stiff from sitting motionless in the freezing rain for the last twelve hours. Your arms shake as you draw your bow. To make this moment possible, it took five thousand dollars, round-trip airfare, and a week's vacation. Don't miss.

At three or four points along the ridgeline, and then again on the way back down, Stu reminded me to smile for the trailcams. Trespassers beware. The woods are watching.

Each time, we turned to wave at the trailcam as it snapped our photo. When Stu or one of his employees swaps out the memory cards and reviews the captured images, we'll be in there, right among the usual shots of deer, turkeys, raccoons, and coyotes.

After we parked the ATV, I persuaded Stu to take a short walk so that he could smile for *my* camera. I took several shots: Stu in front of soybeans. Stu in front of sunflowers. Stu in front of corn.

Stu's a cheerful, positive guy. Still, to make sure of a smile, I made a couple lame jokes—including the obvious one about him being an excellent farmer who's out standing in his field. But the truth is, Stu really *is* a deer farmer who's outstanding in his field.

A CASH CROP

Before I left, Stu encouraged me to get in touch with Ted Marum, who was at the time his lead consultant at Midwest Whitetail Management Services. Ted was out at a client's site that day, but Stu said he was someone I should definitely meet. Ted's lived all his life in Buffalo County. He's a former guide and outfitter, and every fall he still spends time harvesting whitetails. The rest of the year, he works full-time growing them.

A couple months later, Ted and I finally connected. We'd have met sooner, but he was out of the office on a couple of weeklong hunting trips. They weren't exactly vacations though. Ted had been on filmed hunts for Mossy Oak; he's a member of their pro staff. These action-packed, half-hour hunting shows—shorter still if you don't count the commercials—are generally edited down after a week or two of sitting in the woods. Ted had just returned from a long, rainy week in Iowa.

Mossy Oak, you'll recall, isn't just in the camo business. It has its own TV network and produces or sponsors about a dozen hunting shows. It even has a real estate division called Mossy Oak Properties. The company's slogan is well understood in Buffalo County: "It's not a passion. It's an obsession."

Ted has a firm handshake and a quick grin. Like Stu, he obviously loves his work. He was eager to show me around. We loaded a Polaris Ranger on his trailer, climbed into his truck, and headed up the gravel road for a spot two or three miles away.

It was now mid-November. It had frozen hard the night before; by late morning the temperature was still in the low forties. The leaves were down, and the underbrush had fallen back. Crops were either ready to harvest or already out of the fields.

The same, I suppose, was true of the deer. They are, after all, Buffalo County's most important cash crop. Bow season was well under way, and gun season would begin in a few days. Plenty of deer were still out there. Over the next hour or so, we saw several, all of which saw us first.

When we arrived, it only took Ted a moment to back the Ranger off its trailer. Our first stop was a two-acre patch of sunflowers, now dead and brown. The plants were still shoulder high, providing both food and cover. Ted pointed to the sunflowers in the center of the patch that still had their seed-filled heads; deer had already eaten the ones near the edge.

Our next stop was a rub tree that a buck had used to polish its antlers and strengthen its neck muscles—perhaps getting ready for combat. These markings also serve as a territorial signpost; although the correlation isn't perfect, bigger bucks generally prefer bigger trees. Every fall I see these rubs in my own neighborhood. Most are on small saplings. This tree was eight or ten inches in diameter. Two to three feet above the ground, nearly all of its bark was torn free and hanging in ragged shreds that fluttered in the breeze.

As we continued down the trail, we saw more rubs, scrapes, and other deer sign. Ted also pointed out more of the enhancements he'd made to the property. Here he pointed to "hinge-cut" trees felled to make extra cover for bedding deer. There, another waterhole . . . and another. Above each pond was an elevated treestand. Although these ponds were frozen over with a thin skin of ice, there was still open water at the edges. Fresh tracks showed where deer had come to drink during the past hour or two.

Emerging from the woods we passed food plots planted with corn, clover, or canola. Still green, the clover and canola were browsed nearly to the ground. Some food plots were only slightly larger than my living room; they generally had treestands overlooking them. These were, quite literally, the killing fields.

Other food plots covered three or four acres. In the middle of one, I saw three cedar fence posts whose surface had been battered and torn by deer antlers. There were fence posts but no fence. The posts weren't even in a straight line.

"That's kind of a large open area," explained Ted. "This time of year the testosterone is flowing. If you want more than one or two bucks out there at the same time, the fence posts are a nice outlet for their aggressions. They do a little rubbing, they go back to eating, and everyone's happy."

These same primitive instincts seem to motivate some hunters. During my tour Ted told me about the changes he's seen over the years. Camaraderie, he told me, has all too often given way to competitiveness; deer disputes have ended more than a few friendships. In Buffalo County big antlers and big egos can be a bad combination. The worst," he said, "is coming up next week when gun season starts. Get ready for nine days of hate.

"Well, maybe it's not that bad," he laughed. "But you know, as handy as those motion-sensing trailcams are, they're one of the worst things to ever happen to the sport. I'm serious," he said. "They really are. Once people get pictures of a giant buck, they assume ownership of that deer. In their mind, it's now *their* deer. They don't tell anyone about it, not even their neighbor. The neighbor shoots it, and the guy's all mad. 'You killed my deer. That's the one I was hunting.' Yeah, well, the other guy was too.

"People need to remember it's just a deer," said Ted. "It's a wild animal. It doesn't live and die on the same farm. People get so jammed up. If they didn't have a camera, they wouldn't know it was there. They'd be happy for their neighbor when he gets it."

Ted's definitely someone who does take pleasure in other hunters' success. For nearly ten years he ran an outfitting business here in Buffalo County. The first couple years he just saved up vacation from his day job and did a little guiding on the side. But after he went full time, it was really full time.

"People don't realize all that goes on the rest of the year," he explained. "And then in the fall, there are plenty of eighteen-hour days. I didn't see much of my family for about two and half months. And obviously I didn't get to hunt myself."

Ted talked it over with his wife, and they decided it was time to think about getting out of the outfitting business. That January he heard from Scott Kirkpatrick, a former client from Vermont. Scott had always dreamed of being a guide and wondered if there might room for one more outfitter in Buffalo County.

Ted told him there were plenty of clients to go around, but said that for the right price his own outfitting business might be for sale. Scott flew out for a week to get a closer look, they talked numbers, and by June the deal was done.

Meanwhile, Stu's consulting business was really starting to take off. He and Ted talked, and that was that. Four years later Ted still misses the out-fitting business. Mostly. "A lot of people think outfitters have a dream job," he told me, "that they're just living the dream, relaxing out in the woods. But it's not like that at all. You don't believe me, you just talk to Scott."

LIVING THE DREAM

It was midmorning when I met Scott Kirkpatrick, the new owner of Buffalo County Outfitters. He'd already had a long day.

"During hunting season," he told me, "I usually set my alarm for 3:20 a.m. We need to get our hunters fed, pack them a lunch, and get them out into the woods before the sun's up. After that, every day is different. I may get a break midday, or I may not. And most days I'm lucky if I get to bed before 11:00 p.m."

That morning, things were getting complicated fast. Scott would have to leave soon to recover a deer one of his hunters had shot. Since the deer had made it a short distance onto the neighbor's property before expiring, Scott had to first secure permission. The neighbor wasn't at home and couldn't be reached at his first work number. After several calls and much texting, everything was arranged.

Another hunter was having a bad morning. He was sitting in a tree-stand overlooking a doe decoy meant to lure amorous bucks, but a dog from a neighboring farm spotted the decoy first. Puzzled and agitated, the dog continued to circle and bark at a Styrofoam deer that for some reason refused to be intimidated.

The hunter had called Scott on his cell phone, and he wasn't happy. He was paying a lot of money for this hunt, and at the moment he wasn't exactly getting his money's worth. Scott promised to get in touch with the dog's owners immediately. They'd come and get their dog, and everything would be OK. Scott reassured his hunter that deer were used to farm dogs and would be filtering back out into that field within the hour.

The landowner at that particular location lived in another state. From the client's description, Scott recognized the dog as one belonging to a couple down the road; it took three or four calls to track them down. The apologetic owner said she'd go get her dog right away.

Meanwhile a bored hunter on another farm texted Scott with an urgent message: GOOD COOKIES. PLZ BRING MILK. Scott texted back: HA. HA. HA.

Once all that was out of the way, Scott could take a few minutes to explain how the business works. He gestured around the room where we sat. "One of our little expenses was this new lodge."

The building had just been completed that summer; it still smelled like new carpet. Although its wood paneling and abundant taxidermy gave it an authentic backwoods feel, it definitely deserved at least two or three more stars than the small-town motel where I'd find myself staying that night.

Scott explained that hunters' expectations have changed. Just five or ten years ago, a bunkhouse with indoor plumbing was considered the height of luxury. Hunters were here for the deer, and that was all that mattered. Not anymore.

The lodge, of course, is just one expense; there are also guides, cooks, and housekeeping. Then there are treestands, trailcams, and ATVs. Scott also burns a lot of gas and puts a lot of miles on his truck. And despite all the signed waivers, liability insurance is a significant expense for any business that sends its clients out in the dark and into elevated treestands every morning.

Finally there's land. Scott currently owns or leases more than three thousand acres in ten different locations. He hosts dozens of hunters every year, and it takes a lot of land to produce the deer he needs. For Scott it's not enough to just put hunters out on stands. He wants to put them on a stand where they'll actually have an opportunity at a nice buck.

Scott uses the word *opportunity* a lot. "There are big deer here," he says, "and I'll probably get you an opportunity. You'll probably see one, and you might get a shot. But you won't see a two-hundred-inch buck standing behind every tree."

"This is fair chase," he emphasizes. "There are no high fences, and there are no guarantees. I'd say our success ratio is about 30 percent—same with all the other outfitters. If I have a dozen guys in camp and three or four of them get a deer by the end of the week, then we're doing great.

"And really," he asks, "would you want a guaranteed 100 percent success ratio? That's not hunting."

Scott takes genuine pleasure in his clients' success. "Where I grew up," he told me, "the tradition and camaraderie were a big part of the hunt. It was great to get a deer, but it was just as fun to see someone else get one. Myself, I'd just as soon help someone else get their big buck."

That's fortunate, because these days Scott doesn't have much time to hunt himself. He hasn't shot a single buck during the four years he's lived in Buffalo County.

I couldn't quite put my finger on it. But there was definitely something very strange about the four deer at the far end of Tom Indrebo's dining room. The massive head-and-shoulder mounts were all on pedestals and occupied a place of honor, centered across the full span of the lodge window. The tableaux transcended mere taxidermy; it was more like a shrine.

All four deer had huge antlers with almost too many tines to count. While I'm no connoisseur, these mounts seemed flawless. Still, there was something jarring, something not quite right. I could tell Tom was enjoying my confusion.

Finally I realized what was wrong: They were four deer, but they were one deer.

By now I'd learned to discern small differences in the shape and configuration of deer antlers. If you look closely, they *don't* all look the same. Except for these four. True, from left to right the antlers became progressively larger. Other than that, they appeared to have all come from the same deer.

Were they identical quadruped quadruplets? Was it divine deer reincarnation? No.

"It's Moses," explained Tom. "The first time a hunter saw him, he said that deer had to be as old as Moses. The name stuck."

Moses lived to be older still, somehow eluding hunters for three more years. Every spring Tom managed to find Moses's shed antlers. One year they were only a few yards apart; the next, they were half a mile apart. Finally Moses's luck ran out; the antlers on the fourth deer were obtained in the usual fashion.

The other three mounts were Moses's shed antlers paired with skin from the head and shoulders of another large but anonymous deer. Because taxidermists begin each mount with a Styrofoam form, it was possible to find some sheds, swap some skins, and create a marvel of time-lapse taxidermy.

These aren't Tom's only mementos of Moses; he also has over two thousand stills from his trailcams, plus enough video footage for a half-hour DVD. Besides starring in his own DVD, Moses was the subject of an entire chapter in Tom's book *Growing and Hunting Quality Bucks*. Moses just might be the most photographed wild deer ever.

Tom made Moses famous. According to some, he's also the person most responsible for making all the deer of Buffalo County famous.

For months everyone I talked with in Buffalo County had been telling me there was one more person I should be sure to meet. Tom Indrebo, they said, was the one guy who put Buffalo County on the map. The deer were already here; it took Tom to make them famous. Once I talked with Tom, I realized all those people were probably right.

To reach Bluff Country Outfitters, I'd turned off the main road and followed Tom's gravel driveway for nearly a mile before reaching the old farmstead. The renovated farmhouse is the "main lodge"; Tom and his wife, Laurie, live upstairs. Nearby are cabins, a bunkhouse, and a converted barn that features workspace, storage, and a lounge with a game room and a well-stocked bar.

During my tour I noticed that, not surprisingly, the decor relied rather heavily on taxidermy. That theme began in the lodge and continued to the cabins, the bunkhouse, and the lounge. Moses and his various incarnations weren't the only deer on display. Tom explained that all these deer heads with their massive antlers aren't just decoration; they're important visual aids.

The moment hunters arrive, he starts educating them. They're in Buffalo County now; the bucks he wants them to pass on here would be monsters back home. Most hunters have never been around deer like these and have no idea what one looks like. But here they're on display everywhere you go. And with a little luck, Tom's clients will see a few of them out in the woods.

The first place many hunters saw deer like these was in one of Tom's videos. The first, filmed in 1990 and 1991, was *Monarch Valley*; sequels included *Legend Lane* and *Monster Alley*. Call me old-fashioned, but I found Tom's videos refreshingly different from today's typical cable-TV hunting shows. There are no fences, no feeders, no kill shots, and no high-fiving over a dead deer. All these deer are wild deer behaving naturally in their natural habitat.

Even without listening to Tom's homespun narration, it's easy to tell that he's more amateur naturalist than professional hunter. Indeed, it's been years since he's hunted with a rifle or bow; today he hunts exclusively with a camera.

Thirty years ago Tom and a couple friends started climbing into treestands with their 35mm cameras. They used deer calls to grunt in rutting bucks, and there was some friendly competition to who see could get the closest shots of the largest bucks. Although he wouldn't say, I suspect it was Tom.

A few years later his brother-in-law bought an early video camera. By today's standards it was huge. Tom managed to hoist it up into a treestand a few times, and before long he had a camera of his own. He was getting hours of footage, and some of it wasn't bad. It didn't hurt that he was filming deer with the sort of antlers rarely seen outside Buffalo County.

After assembling some of the best segments, Tom placed a small ad in the back of a hunting magazine. The phone starting ringing, and soon he had orders for over six hundred copies at twenty-five dollars a pop. He used the first checks to buy several cases of blank VHS tapes—plus five VCRs that he cabled together for making copies.

One of those orders came from *Deer and Deer Hunting* magazine. A couple issues later, Buffalo County wasn't a secret anymore.

Another tape went to the Quality Deer Management Association, which asked Tom if he'd create a more polished version they could use to promote QDM and the QDMA. (Back then its members numbered in the hundreds; today it has over fifty thousand.) If he could do that, they'd be happy to sell the tape for him. Tom agreed, and he spent the next two months in the edit suite at a local public television station. The result was *Monarch Valley*.

Today the project would be much easier; Tom has his own digital editing suite at Bluff Country Outfitters. He also maintains a few terabytes of digital stills from his custom-built trailcams. Ordinary trailcams are fine for surveillance; they'll tell you where deer have been. But Tom wasn't satisfied with their image quality. When he couldn't find trailcams with the lens and specs he wanted, he built his own.

Tom opened up one of his trailcams to show me. On the outside is the same weatherproof plastic casing that might house a standard trailcam. On the inside are a motion sensor and a couple switches, all neatly wired to a high-end, point-and-shoot digital camera.

Tom works hard, and he loves gadgets. He especially loves computers and cameras. Other outfitters may save digital photos from their trailcams. Tom studies them and thinks about what they mean. He files them carefully away and then returns to study them again. And again.

Every photo in his collection is cross-referenced by location, date, and sometimes by the names of individual deer. Although all these deer are wild, some with distinctive antlers get nicknames after they show up on a few trailcam photos. Moses was one. Others included Garth, Boonie, The General, and Elvis.

When trailcam photos show these bucks wading through the snow in January, Tom knows they've made it through one more hunting season.

When their luck inevitably runs out, Tom includes one or two final photos of the deer with its hunter. He then, to use his words, "closes the file."

For years Tom worked hard to spread the word about Buffalo County and Bluff Country Outfitters. Now most of his hunters are repeat customers. He has a website, but otherwise he doesn't advertise much. With the website and word of mouth, he stays pretty well booked up.

Over the years Tom has hosted dozens of celebrities and professional athletes. "They're just like anyone else," says Tom. "Just regular people. And when they're here, they don't talk much about football, baseball, or whatever it is they do. They're on vacation, and they're here to hunt—just like everyone else."

Although clearly not one to drop names, Tom couldn't help mentioning that Hank Williams Jr. would be here in a couple days. He'd booked a weeklong hunt during Wisconsin's gun season. "Hank called last year," said Tom, "but I had to tell him we were already booked up. Talked with him on the phone the other day. Seemed like a heck of a nice guy."

Later I learned that Hank didn't have any luck that week. He did however have an enjoyable hunt. As they say, that's why it's called "hunting," not "shooting." Being a country boy, Hank will survive. He'll probably be back.

THE COUNTY LINE

After I left Bluff Country Outfitters, I rolled down Tom's mile-long gravel driveway, turned left, and headed northward. As I drove through the fading afternoon light, I saw several deer. Once I braked hard to avoid a doe that stumbled out onto the pavement in front of me.

The hills of Buffalo County were luminous in the autumn sunset. The road wound through flat farmland, oak-covered hillsides, and the occasional outcropping of dolomitic limestone—limestone that possesses just the right ratio of calcium to magnesium. Like at Lascaux, only different. Very different.

Although Buffalo County has little to do with mainstream American hunting culture, what I'd seen here told me a lot about hunters' complex relationship with deer. It also gave me a glimpse into one possible future—and not one I especially relished.

In the morning I'd be leaving Buffalo County for the last time. During my visits here I'd talked with dozens of people. I'd met ordinary people in small-town taverns and cafes. I'd met Realtors, outfitters, guides, farmers, and hunters. I'd even met a soil scientist who revealed the secret of Buffalo County's magic dirt and magic antlers.

Some of the people I met have been blessed by deer; others have been cursed. Still others have simply become obsessed with deer—most of all, with their magical antlers. As for myself, I'll probably always be more interested in meat than magic. Still, after the time I spent in Buffalo County, I have a new understanding of trophy hunters, guides, and outfitters. I found myself liking nearly everyone I met; they were all genuine, decent people whom I really enjoyed being around.

Once or twice I was warned to not expect that. Somehow those warnings never quite fit the people I met. Maybe there's a little envy here and there in Buffalo County, and maybe some of those people should get to know one another a little better.

True, those magic antlers have been a tremendous windfall for certain local landowners. But most of the people I met in Buffalo County—Stu Hagen, Ted Marum, Scott Kirkpatrick, Tom Indrebo, and lots of others—have worked long and hard for their luck.

By now I knew my way around Buffalo County pretty well. I didn't need a map. I recognized the turn for Stu's place, Ted's office out behind the machine shed full of treestands, and the oak-covered ridgeline where so many other treestands are so carefully placed.

A few miles later I passed the turn for Scott Kirkpatrick's new lodge. I hope he's booked enough hunters to make his payments and cover all his leases for another year. If he doesn't, it won't be because he hasn't provided his clients a good hunt. Just the other day I'd visited his website and seen fresh photos of smiling hunters with their trophy deer. And like all the other outfitters in Buffalo County, Scott works long and hard to ensure his clients' success—or at least their opportunities.

CHAPTER 4

Feeders, Baiters, and Plotters

A peculiar virtue in wildlife ethics is that the hunter has no gallery to applaud or disapprove of his conduct. Whatever his acts, they are dictated by his own conscience, rather than by a mob of onlookers. It is difficult to exaggerate the importance of this fact.

—ALDO LEOPOLD

On a frigid January afternoon, the sun is setting early over a snowy back-yard just outside Boston. A half dozen deer emerge single file from a wooded ravine to take their places at a trough filled with corn. At the window a father lifts his toddler so she can see their dinner guests. She squeals with delight.

As the scorching August sun sets over an arid ranch in the Texas hill country, a timer on an elevated four-hundred-gallon mechanical feeder releases a precisely metered trickle of corn to a semicircle of waiting deer. They've learned what time of day this machine will feed them breakfast, lunch, and dinner. Fifty yards away and twelve feet in the air, an enclosed stand overlooks the feeder. It's empty tonight, but it won't be at breakfast time on opening morning of deer season.

As dusk approaches, a cold November rain falls on the woods of northern Michigan. It's late afternoon, just three days before opening morning. Until then, it's the last time this aging pickup will bounce slowly along the muddy logging road and stop in this unmarked spot. Its driver gets out, climbs up into the bed of his truck, and empties a sack of corn into two white plastic five-gallon pails. He sets the pails down on the tailgate, climbs to the ground, grabs the handle of a pail in each hand, and heads into the woods. He's glad to be wearing his camo rain jacket. It's starting to rain harder. Fortunately he isn't going far. He'll be back in a minute or two, and the cab of his truck will be warm on the way home.

It's Saturday, a warm, sunny spring morning on a hobby farm in central Ohio. Golf can wait. Today this software engineer has one more field to disk and plant. At almost an acre, it's his largest. He's already planted a half dozen smaller food plots, all of them tailored to the specific tastes and nutritional needs of deer. All summer long he and his family will enjoy watching the deer attracted by these plantings. Come fall he'll have a pretty decent hunting spot too.

All these scenes have one thing in common: Someone is spending time and money to manipulate the diets and behavior of deer. As different as their purposes might seem, in the end they all want the same thing. Millions of Americans have become feeders, baiters, and plotters because they want to see more deer. It's a simple enough desire, and a very natural one. Its consequences, however, are not.

It's true that feeding, baiting, and growing food plots are three very different things. Still, sometimes the lines between them can blur. At sunrise on opening day, year-round supplemental feeding can instantly become baiting when a hunter slips off the safety of his rifle. And while planting food plots may feel very different from dumping buckets of corn out in the woods, critics argue it's only a baiting technique that happens to take a little more work and planning. One thing is certain: Each of these practices has unintended consequences, and each raises troubling questions about who we are and how we relate to the natural world.

FEED MILLS WITHOUT FARMS

Here in far northern Wisconsin, we have feed mills but few farms. I live in one of those "sand counties" that inspired the title of Aldo Leopold's *A Sand County Almanac*. In point of fact, however, Leopold lived in a county whose soil is much richer. His old homestead, now a shrine for environmentalists, is a four-hour drive south from here.

Here in the north, our soil is poor, our winters are long, and our wolves are hungry. It's not a great place to farm. When the whole topic of agriculture comes up, people often wave in a vaguely southerly direction and use a phrase I've never heard elsewhere: "Down in Farm Country."

Mysteriously a surprising number of local feed mills still do a booming business—especially in the fall and winter. Every day they sell many tons of grain, mostly corn. You'll also find sacks of these precious golden kernels at every gas station and every hardware, grocery, sporting goods, or liquor store for miles around. At each of these businesses, all that corn accounts for a significant portion of revenues. As it's being hauled in from somewhere far to the south, it also means job security for dozens of truckers.

The corn isn't being fed to cattle cowering in a barn to escape the blizzards raging outside. It's being fed to deer. Some of those deer had better be careful though. They're not being fed, they're being baited—lured into range. If hunters aren't watching over those bait piles yet, they will be soon. It's only a matter of time.

All the other deer can relax. They're being fed by humans who wish them no ill. The owners of feed mills can relax too. Their revenues for October and November will be eclipsed by those for December, January, and February. Once deer season and baiting season are over, feeding season begins in earnest.

A little over a decade ago, all this very nearly came to an end, at least here in Wisconsin. When CWD was discovered in the state's deer herd, biologists were concerned it might spread more quickly among deer concentrated by feeding and baiting. The state declared an emergency ban on both feeding and baiting, but the ban was rescinded less than two years later.

After talking with biologists, epidemiologists, and deer managers, I've learned a lot about why feeding and baiting can be bad for deer, bad for deer hunting, and bad for a lot of other reasons. There is, however, another side to the story. To learn what Wisconsin's bait debate looked like from the office of a feed mill, I talked with Patty Rantala.

She'd never boast about it, but she's the person responsible for almost single-handedly getting the ban rescinded. She and her husbanded owned the feed mill in Iron River, a small town in northern Wisconsin. During just the first winter that the ban was in effect, they lost over eighty-five thousand dollars in revenue. Her husband started driving a truck to help make ends meet (they still didn't), and Patty started driving to hearings down in Madison.

From Iron River, Wisconsin's state capital is nearly in the far corner of the state. On good days it's a five-hour drive each way. On days when the roads are covered with snow or ice, the round-trip can easily take sixteen hours. Patty made thirteen trips altogether. On some trips she was joined by her husband and son. She made most trips by herself. Often she'd drive down, testify before the state legislature, and then drive back, all in a single day.

In the beginning other feed-mill owners joined her on the trips to Madison. So did a few customers. Eventually that tapered off. At most of the hearings, Patty was the only one testifying from this corner of the state. She was relentless, but not entirely alone. "An anonymous person put together a modest website for us," she told me, "and I started doing a little e-mailing. Sometimes customers would donate fifty dollars, one hundred dollars, or whatever they could, just to help me with gas. Sometimes it was just ten bucks. But it all helped."

Patty never gave up. This pocket of north woods Wisconsin was settled by Finnish immigrants who would have described her as having *sisu,* a term that doesn't fully translate. It means incredible stubbornness, but with a slightly more positive connotation. More like determination. Perseverance. Tenacity. Refusing to give up, even in the face of overwhelming odds. Kind of like Patty.

There was a lot at stake. "Before we got into this business," says Patty, "we had no idea how big feeding and baiting were. My husband was sitting in the sauna with a friend of his, and the guy said, 'You know, someone ought to buy that feed mill. I heard the co-op is trying to get rid of it.' That's how it all started. And we quickly learned that deer would account for at least a third of our revenue. During some months it would be almost 100 percent."

The first few winters were especially long and hard. Bad for deer, good for business. Deep snow forced the deer to yard up even more than usual. They weren't able to reach enough browse, and by late winter a lot of them were starving. Patty figures that locally, at least, all the feed her customers hauled out into the woods did a lot to save the herd.

When CWD appeared in 2001, Patty and a lot of others were skeptical—especially when the biologists started talking about a ban on feeding and baiting. "It was just an excuse," says Patty. "It was all politics. There was one guy on the Natural Resources Board who wanted to ban feeding and baiting. I'm convinced that it was his personal political agenda. There was no science. It was nothing but politics."

Whether that's true or not, the ban definitely hurt the Rantalas' business. It went into effect in the spring of 2002 and lasted almost a year and a half. During that period Patty figures she and her husband lost over one hundred thousand dollars in revenue. They came perilously close to bankruptcy, and they still teetered on the edge for a long time after that.

Patty walked me through the math. I'll leave out most of the numbers, but I was surprised at how openly she shared them. I suppose they'd once been at the heart of her testimony during all those legislative hearings.

A pie chart showing the mill's revenues would have been divided into three roughly equal slices. The first was livestock feed, birdseed, and pet food. The second was the greenhouse and gardening operation. The third was feeding and baiting.

All three were seasonal, but they tended to overlap nicely. Still, without any one of those pieces, the business would sink fast. It wasn't just a matter of total revenue for the entire year, but of cash flow during any given month. "Most of our livestock customers were hobby farmers," explains Patty. "They'd buy in the spring and butcher in the fall. So they weren't feeding over the winter. And obviously the greenhouse isn't doing much in the winter. From about October through March, feeding and baiting were what kept us afloat."

Bow season begins in September and lasts until January. Gun deer season is in November. That meant the mill's baiting revenues would peak in October and November. After that, recreational feeding kicked in. For the rest of the winter and on into spring, it would account for around 90 percent of the mill's revenue.

All across America's north woods, and in exurbs and suburbs everywhere, thousands of other small feed mills operate on a very similar business model. Here in Wisconsin it almost ended. But not quite.

The final day of testimony began at 8:00 a.m. and continued until 6:30 p.m. Thousands of constituents who couldn't be there in person called their representatives, and they set a new one-day record for incoming calls at the capital switchboard. The bill that would have extended the ban was defeated by a wide margin. In its place there would now be a two-gallon maximum "compromise." During the years to come, the two-gallon limit would be largely ignored.

When it was time for Governor Jim Doyle to sign the bill into law, Patty didn't need to make a fourteenth trip to Madison. Instead the governor came to her. He held the signing ceremony just down the road in Ashland, the closest town of any size. As Governor Doyle reached for his pen, Patty stood at his shoulder. At his other shoulder stood her representative to the state legislature.

Thanks to deer, business was good. In 2009 Patty and her husband lost the mill in a fire. Although there wasn't enough insurance money to rebuild the mill, they were at least able to rebuild the greenhouse. They now have a thriving garden center that's open about six months of the year. *Sisu.*

But don't worry. If you need to buy deer corn in Iron River, you still have several options. For starters there's the grocery store and all the gas stations. They'll have a few twenty- and fifty-pound sacks. For larger quantities you might want to check out the tack shop over at the edge of town. Although there aren't many horses around here, and even though horses are more commonly fed hay and oats, every winter this tack shop somehow manages to sell a surprising amount of corn.

Today both baiting and feeding are more popular here in Wisconsin than ever before. Baiting is currently legal in twenty-five states, partially restricted in twelve, and totally unrestricted in thirteen. On a local level, hundreds of counties and municipalities with serious deer problems have banned both baiting and recreational feeding. Clearly both practices would attract even more deer. That is, after all, the whole idea.

Most state-level restrictions have been on the books for decades. Although Minnesota banned baiting in 1991, I'm told illegal baiting is now quite common in certain parts of the state. Due to concerns over CWD, Vermont banned both feeding and baiting in 2005. Virginia banned baiting in 2006, and then later banned feeding in four counties where CWD is a concern.

Several other states have attempted bans and failed. Apparently state legislators who want to be reelected have decided it would be safer not to oppose baiting. That's even more true of recreational feeding. It's usually only banned locally, typically in municipalities where overabundant deer have become a serious nuisance.

But feeding deer is a harmless enough pastime. Isn't it?

A HARMLESS PASTIME?

In a word, no. If you're a nature lover who enjoys feeding the deer, you may want to reconsider the whole idea. But don't just take it from me.

Nearly every state and province in Deerland produces pamphlets explaining to its citizens why it's a bad idea to feed deer. From New Hampshire there's *More Harm Than Good*. From Vermont, *Thinking About Feeding Deer This Winter? Think Again*. From Mississippi, *Deer Feeding Concerns: A Biological Perspective*. From Pennsylvania, *Please Don't Feed the Deer*.[1]

Every November these same agencies issue press releases reminding people once again to not feed the deer. From Wyoming's Game and Fish Department, "Feeding Deer—Bad Idea." From Utah's Division of Wildlife Resources, "Don't Feed the Deer." From Ontario's Ministry of Natural Resources, "Don't Feed Deer This Winter."

Somehow we're still not getting the message. Every winter, especially in the North, we insist on feeding deer. The reason is clear: Whether we're hunters or watchers, the main reason we feed deer is to see more deer more often.

More selflessly, many kind-hearted souls genuinely believe that deer wouldn't survive the winter without our help. Even though we know better, it's easy to anthropomorphize—to perceive animals as being a lot like us. If we were sleeping naked in the snow all winter, and if we had to paw through two feet of snow for just a few mouthfuls of frozen spinach, wouldn't we want someone to feed us a little corn? If they didn't, would we even survive?

Deer of course are not people. They do fine sleeping in the snow for months at a time, mainly because they have a warm coat that doubles as a toasty sleeping bag. They take it with them wherever they go. A deer's primary metabolic strategy for surviving long, cold winters is to store up as much fat as possible and then burn as little of it as possible while waiting for spring. Its metabolism slows dramatically, and it spends most of the night—and, for that matter, most of the day—bedded down in a spot where it's sheltered from the wind, preferably under the thermal cover of conifers. (Deer that invade suburbia have also learned to hunker down near warm dryer vents.)[2] Even on the coldest winter nights, temperatures are a few degrees warmer in these hidden microclimates.

When lured away from cover, a deer may burn more calories traveling to and from a backyard feeder than it's able to take in while it's there. During these nightly excursions, it's also more vulnerable to cold, predators, and automobiles. There's no need to ask a game warden, forester, or botanist for subtle clues about where wildlife lovers in your area are feeding deer. Just ask a state trooper, tow truck driver, or auto body technician.

So far, deer in North America have survived around four million cold winters. Some individual deer haven't survived some winters, but the species as a whole has survived them all. Deer have evolved to do just fine most winters on the browse that's still available. When they don't, supplemental feeding only delays the inevitable. Deer reach numbers that exceed the land's long-term carrying capacity and then, in the words of that *Please Don't Feed the Deer* pamphlet from the Pennsylvania Game Commission, "eat themselves out of house and home."

When homeowners feed deer in the hopes of diverting them from trees, shrubbery, and vegetable gardens, the strategy invariably backfires. Feeding lures in more deer and concentrates them in a small area. They eat all the corn they're offered, but they also browse heavily on any natural food that's nearby.

At the risk of anthropomorphizing a little myself, it's as though deer know they're eating junk food. Corn is like Doritos for deer. They love its concentrated carbohydrates and fat, and they can't stop eating it. But after they've polished off a few bags, they find themselves feeling full but still vaguely dissatisfied. They'll be craving a little salad, and that new arbor vitae you planted last summer will do just fine.

In fact, for deer accustomed to a normal diet of woody browse, corn can literally be toxic, causing debilitating illnesses that leave them vulnerable to hypothermia or predators. Quite often the results are fatal. Biologists use the broad umbrella term "corn toxicity" to describe three noninfectious diseases that can affect deer—acidosis, enterotoxemia, and aflatoxin.

To really understand why winter feeding does deer more harm than good, it helps to know a little more about deer digestion. Like us, deer have bacteria in their stomachs and intestinal tract that help digest their food. Unlike us, they have four stomachs, with a different mix of microflora in each. These organisms are particularly adept at breaking down the cellulose and lignin in woody browse. Normally, however, they're not the right mix of bacteria to break down corn or commercial pelletized food.

When deer switch from their normal diet to one that's low in fiber and high in carbohydrates, it takes three or four weeks for their digestive system to adjust. Eventually it may. The mix of microflora in their stomachs will change, and they'll do just fine on their new diet.

Until then they continue filling their stomachs with food they can't digest. In the rumen, the deer's first and largest stomach, microbial populations change rapidly within just a few hours. Streptococcus bacteria become more numerous, producing enough lactic acid to kill other microflora that aid with digestion—and also the ones that normally keep lactic acid levels in check by metabolizing it.

In a vicious cycle the situation can worsen rapidly. The rumen stops working, and the deer suffers from severe diarrhea and dehydration. By this point it will be lying down, staggering, or standing quietly.

In severe cases of corn-induced acidosis, digestive acids literally eat away at the walls of the deer's stomachs. A necropsy reveals black or maroon-colored lesions, most of which are in the abomasum, the deer's second of its four stomachs. Performing necropsies on deer that have died from acidosis can be a messy business, as their stomachs are usually packed with large quantities of undigested corn.

Most deer that are fed corn or commercial feed don't die. They just experience a two- to three-week transitional period of weakness and diarrhea. Although they're eating plenty, it passes through largely undigested. Well-meaning wildlife lovers hope to provide deer with an extra energy boost to see them through the winter. Instead they give deer extra weeks of severe stress under an energy deficit.

But if you're one of those people, and if you're reading this by the fire during a long winter's eve, then please don't stop feeding the deer tomorrow morning. Until deer rebuild a normal, balanced population of microflora in their digestive tract, they need to go through the same sort of transition again. Feeding deer in the winter and then suddenly stopping could push them over the metabolic edge. If you've already started feeding the deer, please do stop—but gradually.

A second type of corn toxicity is called enterotoxemia. It's less common but more often fatal. Like acidosis, it occurs when ruminants ingest unusually large amounts of high-carbohydrate feed. In many cases it occurs in combination with acidosis.

Although corn is usually the culprit, enterotoxemia can also occur when animals consume large amounts of apples, sugar beets, or pelletized feed. It's caused by *Clostridium perfringens*. These bacteria live in a ruminant's lower digestive tract and thrive on high levels of starch and carbohydrate, which normally would have already been metabolized earlier as food passed through the deer's stomachs.

At normal levels *Clostridium perfringens* is harmless. At higher levels it releases potent toxins that usually cause death within twenty-four hours. "Visible symptoms," according to the Michigan Department of Natural Resources, "can include circling, rapid eye movement, convulsions, tremors, and pushing of the head against fixed objects. Diarrhea, frothing at the mouth, grinding of the teeth, and generalized weakness may also be seen."[3]

More often, however, these visible symptoms remain invisible. Instinctively, weak, sickened deer tend to bed down in thick cover. When that happens, well-meaning nature lovers remain oblivious to the sickness and death they've caused.

A third type of noninfectious disease occurs when spoiled or moldy feeds contain aflatoxins produced by fungi. It's not the mold itself that's the problem, but rather its toxic by-products. According to a 2006 technical review from The Wildlife Society, these aflatoxins are "immu-nosuppresive, hepatotoxic, and carcinogenic, and can cause disease or death in wildlife, domestic animals, and humans."[4]

These aflatoxins are deadly in concentrations so small they're measured in parts per billion (ppb). The US Food and Drug Administration (FDA) regulates maximum allowable concentrations in food destined for both humans and livestock. For humans it's 20 ppb—except for milk, which is 0.5 ppb. For corn being fed to immature meat animals and dairy cattle, it's 20 ppb, the same as for humans. For corn being fed to mature beef, swine, and poultry, it's 100 ppb. Corn being used to "finish" swine just before slaughter can contain up to 200 ppb, and corn being used to finish beef can contain up to 300 ppb.[5] Presumably these higher levels are considered an acceptable risk for animals that will soon be on their way to slaughter anyway.

Deer corn, however, isn't regulated like livestock feed. It may, in fact, be where some corn ends up after it flunks the aflatoxin test. Biologists in one study purchased bagged, shelled corn being sold as wildlife feed. They found that 20 percent of samples contained over 100 ppb of aflatoxin; 8 percent contained over 300 ppb.[6] In another study biologists tested corn samples from bait piles across the southeastern United States. At some sites they found aflatoxin levels over 750 ppb—nearly 40 times the maxi-mum concentration allowed for dairy cattle, and 7.5 times what's allowed for most other livestock.[7]

Although acidosis, enterotoxemia, and aflatoxin are more than just minor deer indigestion, they're at least noninfectious diseases that can't be transmitted from one deer to another. Feeding and baiting are also fac-tors, however, in the spread of infectious diseases like bovine tuberculosis (TB) and CWD.

Bovine TB can infect birds, cattle, deer, humans, and a number of other mammals. It's transmitted through respiration or by ingesting bac-teria in feces, saliva, or other bodily secretions. At temperatures below freezing, TB bacteria can live on the surface of corn or other feed for up to four months. The prions that cause CWD are even more persistent; they can remain infectious in the soil for years—possibly even decades.

Many of those who enjoy feeding deer or hunting over bait would argue that these practices don't necessarily increase the spread of disease.

They're quick to point out that a deer's normal social behavior includes a great deal of licking, grooming, and sniffing. While that may be true, feeding and baiting create a whole new set of conditions that are perfect for disease transmission.

To really understand this story, I've waded through several papers filled with dense scientific language. If you still don't believe that feeding deer is a bad idea, you can do the same. With minimal effort you'll find yourself digesting technical phrases like "persistence outside mammalian hosts," "ingestion of bacteria in bodily secretions," or "increased number of prions in gut-associated lymph tissues." The science is solid.

Here is a simpler, less technical explanation: Too many hungry deer with poor table manners crowd into the same small space all winter long. They fight. They spill corn. More corn drips from their jaws as they chew. Other deer eat the corn where it falls. Deer urinate and defecate everywhere. As a result of eating feed to which they're unaccustomed, every single animal will at some point during the winter have a compromised immune system and debilitating, often bloody, diarrhea that's filled with undigested corn. The wind is cold, the deer are hungry, and no kernel is left uneaten.

Speaking of crowding and poor table manners, here's one more reason not to feed deer. In the face of unnatural crowding and competition, fed deer exhibit behavior that's unusually aggressive and competitive. Apparently they don't quite grasp that there's plenty for everyone. Even among normally collegial groups of does, for example, you're far more likely to see deer rearing up on their hind legs and lashing out viciously with their front hooves. Biologists call this behavior "flailing."

Larger males eat first, then dominant does. Although these older does do fine, subordinate does going into their second or third year tend to get less food and hence experience a higher rate of neonatal mortality the following spring. Last year's fawns, whether bucks or does, are the last to eat. After expending extra energy traveling to the feeder with their social group, they get little or none of that high-energy food. For them especially, the trip has been a net loss.

Even without the extra stress, these are precisely the deer least likely to make it through a long winter. When spring arrives late after an unusually harsh winter, fawns from the previous year are the first deer to die. Some winter the majority of them die. They've spent their short lives growing instead of building fat reserves that could carry them through the winter. Being smaller, they can't push through deep snow as easily or reach as high toward a browse line. When there's a limited food source, adult deer may push them away. All these factors are exacerbated by recreational feeding.

So maybe feeding deer isn't such a harmless pastime after all. The extra conflict and competition is a significant stressor, and not all deer get their fair share. The ones that do may experience some form of corn toxicity—acidosis, enterotoxemia, or aflatoxin. All the deer will leave their bedding area and expend precious energy traveling to and from the feeding site. Along the way they'll be exposed to cold, predators, and automobiles. To once again borrow that phrase from the New Hampshire Fish and Game Department, feeding deer truly does do "more harm than good."

Finally, that unnatural crowding, competition, and aggression bring to mind one last reason not to feed deer. If you love watching wildlife and fancy yourself something of an amateur naturalist, then you should know that feeding deer is not the best possible way to learn about their behavior and social structure. Although you may observe fascinating behaviors at your backyard feeder, very few of them are normal, natural deer behaviors.

Fed deer become domesticated and habituated to human presence. Although not quite tame, they're no longer wild. When they're fed like cattle, they act like cattle. They don't interact with us normally, and most of all they don't interact with one another normally. Watching deer at a backyard feeder is a lot like that *Planet of the Apes* scene where laughing apes toss loaves of bread into a cage filled with starving humans. Although it's hugely entertaining for the apes, it provides few insights into the secret lives of humans.

Still, it sure is fun to see more deer. Especially if you're out hunting.

THE GREAT BAIT DEBATE—AND A MYSTERIOUS THING CALLED "FAIR CHASE"

To bait or not to bait?

That's the question more and more deer hunters have begun asking themselves. A generation ago they took pride in their woodsmanship and their hard-earned knowledge of deer and their habits. They could track and stalk, and they could choose the perfect ambush spot where unsuspecting deer were sure to pass by as they waited undetected.

Today however, many hunters prefer to bait and wait. After all, who needs all those other skills when you have a rifle and a five-gallon pail of corn?

Although apples, sugar beets, carrots, sweet potatoes, and even pumpkins have all been used as bait, corn is most hunters' bait of choice. It's relatively inexpensive, it lasts, it's convenient, and deer love it. Worried about all that neon yellow being spotted by an observant game warden? One company in Alabama now markets its own brand of carefully dyed "Camo Corn." Separate batches are dyed in muted greens and browns, then mixed back together. No longer yellow, this corn is almost invisible when spread on the forest floor. Its scent, apparently, allows deer to still find it easily.

For those spreading bait on public land, it's the perfect solution to the problem of other hunters spotting their bait site and crowding in on "their" spot. With a nudge and wink, the makers of Camo Corn advise their customers to be aware of and follow all local hunting regulations. In states where feeding or baiting is illegal, it's not against the law to possess this product, only to use it.

Times have changed. But is this progress? What does it say about the future of hunting? More broadly, what does it say about our changing relationship with the natural world—and even about our national character? Are deer hunters becoming lazier and less enterprising? Do they have shorter attention spans? Is all this, to use a term popular with hunters, "fair chase"? And does it even matter? Are these questions about ethics, or merely aesthetics? And by the way . . . Is that even legal?

Before asking more of these awkward questions, I should pause for a moment to acknowledge that many of my friends and neighbors hunt deer over bait. Some are far more experienced and skilled as hunters than I am. They are upstanding citizens and pillars of our community.

I should also point out that hunting deer over bait is not universally a subject of debate. Nor, in some regions, is it a recent phenomenon. All across the South, hunters have a long tradition of baiting. For many it's a natural extension of their daily, year-round supplemental feeding. Since every refill of their elevated, four-hundred-gallon mechanical feeders would require several fifty-pound sacks, many prefer to buy feed in bulk, by the ton.

When farmers and ranchers are willing to spend a little on feed, their marginal or degraded land can support far more deer. Those deer are also likely to be healthier. They'll be larger, and they may even grow larger antlers. Plus, they're more likely to stick around rather than wander off to some neighbor's back pasture. Come hunting season, those same feeders make a great ambush site. It's not only legal and socially acceptable, it's a social norm. It's how deer are hunted.

In most of the United States and Canada, however, social norms are far less clear. Deer hunters often argue among themselves about whether baiting fits the definition of fair chase. This is a term I've already mentioned once or twice, and it's roughly what it sounds like. But if you're not a hunter, it's a rather slippery concept that deserves some explaining.

Both Boone and Crockett (B&C) and Pope and Young (P&Y) have defined the term very similarly. In their rules for record-book eligibility, they also provide more detail about what is and isn't allowed. But here's P&Y's basic definition of fair chase: "Simply defined, fair chase is the ethical, sportsmanlike, and lawful pursuit of free-ranging wild game animals in a manner which does not give the hunter an improper or unfair advantage over the animal."[8] And yet if we examine this definition more closely, it's not so simple after all. What exactly is ethical and sportsmanlike? What's free-ranging, and what's an improper or unfair advantage?

Our standards of what's "ethical and sportsmanlike" have changed over time, and they vary from one region to another. They even vary from one species to another in ways that can seem arbitrary and illogical. Why is it legal to hunt bears over bait, but not deer or ducks? Why is it OK to use hounds when hunting bears, but not when hunting elk? Why do hunters only shoot turkeys when they're on the ground, but pheasants or doves only on the wing? Why is it considered sporting to shoot a squirrel from a tree limb, but not a partridge—or, for that matter, OK to shoot sitting squirrels, but not sitting ducks? And who got to make all these unwritten rules anyway?

The next part of that definition is slightly easier to explain: "free-ranging." This phrase addresses the phenomenon of high-fence hunting, which is called that because it depends on fences higher than the usual sort that keep in cows but not deer. These fences keep in the deer too. Paying to shoot a tame, farm-raised buck with record-book antlers while it's standing in the middle of a half-acre pen is not fair chase. Paying to shoot its wilder counterpart on a densely wooded, ten-thousand-acre ranch might be. But somewhere in between is a line most hunters wouldn't cross.

Spread all across the United States are thousands of these high-fence hunting operations, nearly all of which specialize in whitetail deer with trophy-class antlers—antlers, however, that don't meet the definition of fair chase that would make them eligible for actual inclusion in the B&C or P&Y record books. Nor do regular hunting seasons and game laws apply at these establishments. Legally, and in every other way, these are farmed deer.

Even most deer hunters have no idea how numerous and widespread these operations are. Their ads in the back of hunting magazines are small and discreet, and they rarely advertise locally. Most locals, after all, can't afford the thousands of dollars that this "hunt" is going to cost. Although you'll find a few of these businesses online if you search for "high-fence hunts," you'll have much better luck if you search for code words like "hunting preserve" and "high success rates."

Despite the cryptic descriptions you'll find on these websites, a careful reader can infer much. Price lists alone are revealing; when you reserve a hunt, you'll be placing an order. At some hunting preserves it's even possible to view photos and order a specific animal that you'd like to "hunt." Does are typically one price and bucks another, much higher price that varies with the size of their antlers. Although you'll essentially be paying by the B&C inch, the correlation between these two numbers is not linear. Even on a deer farm, it's much more difficult to grow deer with unusually large antlers. One preserve's website states "For over 200", please call for pricing."

So that explains the "free-ranging" part of fair chase. But what about an "improper or unfair advantage"? And isn't a rifle already rather an unfair advantage? This is where it gets tricky. For hunters it's difficult to define "fairness" rationally and objectively. To be honest, it's more of a subjective feeling. For me personally, the best way I can describe it is that hunting feels just right when it's neither too hard nor too easy.

As much as hunters enjoy a beautiful day in the woods, and as much as they claim it doesn't really matter whether they get a deer, they tend to make these statements with less conviction after they've experienced a certain number of deerless days in a row. Still, if deer invariably showed up on cue precisely three minutes after hunters loaded their rifles and stepped into the woods, then that wouldn't feel quite right either. Not too hard, not too easy. Just right.

Which brings us back to baiting, and the story one hunter told me about the only time he tried it. He already had a deer in the freezer but was hoping for one more. His teenage daughter wanted to try for one during Wisconsin's late muzzleloader season, which immediately follows the regular gun deer season. But after being harassed by hunters for the past couple weeks, every deer in the woods was on high alert. Most had become nocturnal and weren't moving at all during the day. Since far fewer hunters were out during muzzleloader season, no one else was likely to be kicking up deer and moving them toward another hunter's stand.

By now there was snow on the ground. It seemed likely that deer would respond especially well to bait. The hunter and his daughter poured out a couple gallons of corn. The next morning it was gone. They did it again, and the next morning they were waiting in their stand. Just at dawn a group of does approached the corn pile. His daughter took aim, pulled the trigger, and their hunt was over before the sun was fully risen. A few minutes later, as they were field-dressing her deer, she told him she didn't care to hunt over bait again. "Dad," she said, "it felt like cheating."

Other hunters, however, sit in the woods for days on end without seeing a single deer. When chances of success seem impossibly remote, the whole business begins to feel absurd. Quite understandably they decide that maybe next year it will be time to give baiting a try after all.

"Besides," many hunters argue, "everyone else is doing it!" They bait defensively, knowing they don't stand a chance if they're the only one not doing it. This can often lead to an escalating arms race, with adjacent landowners dumping out progressively more and larger bait piles. When hunting stands and corn piles are both visible from the other side of the property line, it doesn't always make for good neighborly relations.

If anyone's hunting nearby on public land, they feel forced to join in the baiting too. And once they do, that piece of public land begins to feel more private—at least to them. Baiters become possessive. When other hunters presume to hunt nearby, tensions escalate. Words and blows have been exchanged, and in a few cases shots have been fired.

One story here in northern Wisconsin ended more peacefully, but just barely. Immediately after the incident, a warden filed this report:

A young hunter finds a promising hunting spot on public land within the Chequamegon National Forest. Along comes an older hunter who orders the youngster to leave the area because he's too close to the older hunter's bait pile. The older hunter has paid someone else to bait the site before he arrived. The older hunter tells the younger hunter to compensate him for the money spent to bait the site if he doesn't leave. The younger hunter contacts his own hunting party. . . . They tell the older hunter his actions are wrong. In the older hunter's presence, they contact the local conservation warden via cell phone. The older hunter decides to leave before the warden arrives.[9]

Although baiting can be an extremely effective way to kill unpressured deer, it can also backfire. Both feeding and baiting change deer behavior and movement patterns, but not always in the way hunters hope. When these hunters make frequent trips out in the woods to replenish their bait piles, deer can't help but notice certain patterns. Hunters often speak of "patterning" deer as they learn their daily routines and travel routes. What they may not realize is that deer are simultaneously patterning them.

Baiting, just like any other form of hunting pressure, makes deer more wary and causes them to alter their daily routines. They quickly realize dangerous humans are bringing them corn during the daytime but never at night. Once they discern a pattern, they're less likely to sample hunters' bait during legal daylight hunting hours. With so many concentrated calories available, they have even less need to move from their beds during the day. In just a few minutes, they can eat their fill, go back into hiding before the sun comes up, and spend the entire day safely ruminating on the situation.

One South Carolina study found that baiting does indeed reduce hunter success rates. In parts of the state where baiting is legal, hunters expended more effort to harvest fewer deer. Where baiting is prohibited, the study found, "total deer harvest rates were 33 percent greater, female harvest rates were 41 percent greater . . . [and] hunter effort per deer was 6 percent less."[10]

Other hunting techniques are arguably more effective. They're like baiting, but not exactly. Although similar in principle, they somehow feel more like fair chase. One strategy, for example, is to use scent-based lures that smell like a rutting buck. These lures attract territorial bucks that hope to confront an unseen rival, a stranger they don't remember seeing or smelling around these parts. Other perfumes, generally made from the urine of an estrous doe, lure in hopeful bucks that are sure to be disappointed. Their hearts, already pierced by Cupid's arrow, will soon be pierced by a hunter's.

If these magic deer love potions come in a tiny brown bottle, just exactly what sort of instructions are on those bottles? How do hunters use these scents, and what's the right dosage? How much deer lust is enough, and how much is too much?

It depends on whom you ask. Some hunters apply only a few drops on the end of a tree branch above a scrape, one of those olfactory message boards described earlier. One scent company sells a "dripper" accessory that can be hung from any convenient tree branch. Picture a tiny, two-ounce IV drip that's dripping an all-day scent of deerly love.

Most hunters choose an in-between approach that depends on absorbent felt wicks about three inches tall. Although each brand is a different shape, one end of the wick generally has some sort of hook by which it can be hung over a tree branch. Departing hunters almost always retrieve their wicks, especially when they're out on public land. They're not litter-bugs. And besides, they don't want to give away their hunting spots. But if you ever find one of these mysterious felt question marks hanging from a tree, that's the explanation.

Finally, there are dozens of high-octane attractants that fall some-where in between scent lures and bait. They're neither, and they're both. Legally, however, they're classified as bait. They're meant to be ingested, not just sniffed. Although they're not calorie free, their nutritive value is questionable. They're highly concentrated, and they're highly addictive for both deer and hunters. If corn is Doritos for deer, these products are more like meth or cocaine.

Some are syrupy gels that can be poured onto the ground—or better yet on a tree stump, where they'll soak into the wood. When deer find the gel, they lick the stump clean and immediately begin gnawing at its edges. Other formulations are powdered, and at least one is actually a white powder. This brand, not surprisingly, is called Deer Co-Cain. Although instructions on the bag suggest cutting it with water, most hunters just pour out a line on the ground. The next day it will be gone, and deer will be back looking for another fix.

THE FOOD PLOT THICKENS

Other hunters prefer an approach that feels more natural. They attract deer to their property by planting food plots with crops specifically cho-sen to please the palates of deer. These small plantings range from desk-size to living room–size plots, on up to an acre or two. Although critics view the practice as being no different from baiting, it definitely feels different from pouring a bucket of corn out on the ground.

If you own a small woodlot halfway between one neighbor's corn field and another neighbor's soybean field, the whole concept may seem superfluous. But even then, planting a few small clearings in food plots might entice deer to pause a bit longer as they're passing through. With luck, they may pause long enough for you to get a better, less hurried shot in your own private killing field.

Still, as the popularity of food plots has exploded during the past decade, that whole "private" part of the concept has begun to concern many hunters and wildlife managers. Reviewing a popular how-to guide, Wisconsin DNR biologist Keith McCaffery writes:

> *The growing fascination with food plots seems driven by the desire to sequester deer onto a privatized parcel. The author openly advises (p. 239), 'Place the major food and bedding areas in the center of the property, away from neighbors, public roads, and areas where other hunters may have access to the deer herd.' The book adds to others that are recipes for privatized wildlife management. . . . This book, with its blend of deer and self-interest, is likely to add many hunters to a slippery slope leading away from the North American Wildlife Model and inevitably toward the European system.*[11]

Indeed, there's no denying that the primary purpose of food plots is to attract and hold deer, thus privatizing what's in theory a public resource. No one is coy about stating these objectives in their catalogs and brochures, on their websites, and right there on every sack of seed.

(While heavily promoting food plots, the highly influential QDMA has to its credit come out publicly against the captive deer breeding industry and the shooting of genetically engineered bucks in small enclosures. They also advocate strongly that state wildlife agencies rather than departments of agriculture should have jurisdiction over these activities, and that deer should be classified as wildlife rather than livestock.)

As I began learning about food plots, I also had many other questions. I noticed that some outdoor retailers have a new sign hanging from the ceiling in this corner of the store. It's for a brand-new product category called "Wildlife Management." But how did all us amateurs get to be "wildlife managers"? And what do the professional wildlife managers think of all this?

Doesn't this whole practice, in the words of Wellsville, New York, outdoor writer Oak Duke, "take the wild out of hunting?"[12] When do amateur efforts at wildlife management become something more like agriculture and animal husbandry? Now that Roundup-Ready canola is a favorite among food plotters who don't want to contend with unsightly weeds, have we perhaps already crossed that line? And when do private feedings become an attempt to hold and privatize the deer themselves—deer that are in theory a public resource? Finally, what do all these trends mean for the future of deer and deer hunting?

These were the questions swirling through my mind as I began learning about food plots. I arrived skeptical, and I wanted to stay that way. I wanted to remain objective. Truly I did.

~ ~

The first food plot evangelist I talked with was Tim Bauer. He's with a medium-size seed company that earns only a small sliver of its total revenues from food plots. But he was right here in northern Wisconsin, only ninety minutes away. Plus, the name of his company is Deer Creek Seed. With a name like that, how could I resist?

That morning I learned a lot about the seed business. Tim knows seeds. He's an avid deer hunter himself, and in his spare time he does a little product testing on his own food plots. He had a pretty good sunburn that day, and he sheepishly admitted it may have been from working on his food plots over the weekend.

When we were done visiting in his office, Tim gave me a quick tour. I got to see bulk bins, bagging and packaging operations, and a warehouse stacked high with bags and boxes of custom seed blends with names like Autumn Buffet, Logger's Trail, and Brassica Blend. Each featured the Deer Creek logo plus slogans like "Attract & keep 'em on your land," and "Plant yourself in position for a great hunt."

Tim is a great guy, and I really enjoyed talking with him. His exuberance and enthusiasm were genuine and infectious. If my wife and I owned more than our two small acres, by now I'd probably be out working on my food plots every spring.

And that's one thing I'll have to say for food plots. Thanks to guys like Tim, dedicated deer hunters now have a whole new hobby. I've talked with dozens of hunters who find tremendous satisfaction in planting and tending their food plots; they seem to enjoy it as much as they do the hunt itself.

One enthusiast was Paul Korn, the archery shop owner you met briefly during our tour of America's deer-industrial complex. Paul does sell archery equipment at A1 Archery. But every year he also sells a lot of seed for food plots. And despite his surname, he only occasionally hunts over bait. "About the only time I'd do it," he said, "is late in the season when I'm hoping to get one more doe for the freezer. But food plots, that's different. I've got about a dozen on my own land. My favorite magazine used to be *Bowhunter*. Now it's definitely *Gamekeepers: Farming for Wildlife*."

Two days later I talked with Austin Delano of Biologic. Owned by camo conglomerate Mossy Oak and based in West Point, Mississippi, Biologic is one of the largest food plot companies around. It's also the publisher of Paul Korn's new favorite magazine.

"Education," Austin told me, "is definitely one area where our industry has grown. Not just when and how to plant. Sure, we put a lot of emphasis on doing soil tests, improving your soil, and getting your dirt right before you plant. But also on planting what's best for your location and best for deer nutrition. And knowing how to build the land. Taking a patch of dirt and making it better than it was when you got your hands on it. That's what gets people excited about food plots. There's a lot of satisfaction in it, especially for guys who didn't grow up farming."

Some customers, he said, aren't even hunters. "Our dealers sell a lot of seed to little old ladies who just want to watch deer out in the backyard. And I know of a couple guys, photographers who sell to hunting magazines. Without food plots they wouldn't get their shots.

"But our typical customer," he said, "is a deer hunter who's already been planting for a few years—maybe with someone else's seed. By now he's progressed beyond just wanting to attract deer. He wants to plant crops that are beneficial to the deer. Every year he's less interested in the killing part and more interested in growing a healthy herd."

And that whole privatization thing? "Deer," Austin noted, "are gonna do what deer are gonna do. They have a mind of their own, and it tells them what's good for them. If you have pregnant does, and bucks trying to grow antlers, and give them a nutritional resource, they'll take advantage of it."

Who could argue with that, I wondered? If farmers, even hobby farmers, begin taking better care of soil that's been abused for a century or two, if they become better stewards of the land, and if they're doing it for the deer, then maybe that's not so bad.

—————

I also talked with Steve Scott at the Whitetail Institute of North America. Although no one in the food plot industry is eager to share precise sales figures, it seems likely that Biologic and Whitetail Institute are the two largest companies in the business. They're definitely among the top three or four. Year after year, both have seen incredible growth. "We feel so blessed," Steve said. "Even in a bad economy, business has been tremendous."

The Whitetail Institute is located in Pintlala, Alabama. Like Biologic, it has its own promotional and educational magazine. Called *Whitetail News,* it's supplemented by an e-newsletter called *Breaking Ground.* And like Biologic, the Whitetail Institute places a great deal of emphasis on education.

"I wish I had a quarter," said Steve, "for every time I've said 'soil test.' Some people don't even read the instructions on the bag, and they get lucky. But I tell 'em, 'You're fixing to become a farmer, and the biggest gambler in the world is a farmer. You may as well get the odds in your favor.'"

But despite its academic-sounding name, Whitetail Institute was built on more than just soil testing and educational outreach. Steve Scott is Whitetail Institute's vice president of marketing, and he's good at his job. It runs in the family; the company was founded by his father, Ray Scott, who's still active in this and a number of other outdoor ventures.

Way back in 1967, Ray Scott single-handedly launched the big-money sport of tournament bass fishing. Over the next few years, he formed the Bass Angler's Sportsman Society (BASS), began publishing *Bassmasters* magazine, and set in motion a nonstop series of tournaments that now feature million-dollar payouts, glittering candy-flake bass boats capable of speeds over seventy miles per hour, NASCAR-like angler uniforms plastered with sponsors' logos, and crowds of up to twenty-five thousand spectators waiting at the docks to watch the nightly weigh-in ritual. Eventually, seeking new challenges, Ray began his new career in deer.

"It's been a steady, slow, consistent grind," his son Steve told me, "and we've been there right from the beginning. A few years back the industry started to grow like a snowball. Some people thought it would be a fad, but now it's just something people do. It's definitely here to stay.

"It's not a fad or a shell game," Steve said. "It really works. Now it does take an investment of time, money, and effort. You're gonna sweat, and you're gonna bang your knuckles and get dirt under your fingernails. But once you see those bucks out there, you'll forget the effort you put into it."

Like Biologic's Austin Delano, Steve also talked a lot about being a good steward of the land and doing what's right for deer. "If you have too many deer, they're going to damage native browse. We always preach population control. We're not farming deer, and you can't have five hundred of them running around where there's browse for fifty. Food plots aren't the magic bean. But they're a critical piece of the puzzle when it comes to deer management.

"A few of our customers," he said, "intentionally plant some of their plots late so they'll be ready after hunting season is over. When all the farmers' crops have already been picked for miles around, stressed deer can really use that extra boost.

"Hunters," he said, " are some of the most conservation-minded people out there—especially food plotters. Yes, we do it with ulterior motives. But it's good for the deer. And those anti-hunting folks who are out banging pans and garbage can lids to scare deer away from hunters? Best thing they could do is put down that stuff and go buy some seed."

With obvious delight, Steve told me about one customer who actually *was* against hunting. His property was adjacent to that of an avid hunter, and one year he planted several large food plots in hopes of luring the neighborhood's deer to safety. Worked like a charm. (By now, of course, the neighbor has probably planted food plots of his own.)

When I asked Steve what he'd tell someone with concerns about the whole "privatization of deer" issue, his answer was simple: "I'd tell that person you probably need to go get some seed and plant on your own side of the fence."

Steve did acknowledge that food plots have not always brought out the best in his customers: "Yes, they've played a role when people get ant-ler mania. It's like anything else. People get obsessed, and they take things too far. Pretty soon it's not fun anymore. There's jealousy, and they lose friends—even their marriages and families.

"But you know," he said, "for every one of those stories, we hear a hundred good ones. We hear from people all the time about how being on the land and working on their food plots has truly improved their lives. Maybe they had some bad habits they were struggling to break. All kinds of things. They tell us how we've helped their family life—even their spiritual life. Now I can't go connect that to the power company. But I know it's for real."

CHAPTER 5

Venison: The Other Red Meat

Now therefore take, I pray thee, thy weapons, thy quiver and thy bow, and go out to the field, and take me some venison. And make me savoury meat, such as I love, and bring it to me, that I may eat; that my soul may bless thee before I die.

—Genesis 27:3

Venison: the other red meat. It's what's for dinner. Newly popular among locavore foodies, it's been a favorite on American dinner tables since before either America or tables were invented.

The continent's first deer hunters were more numerous and more effective than most of us realize. Even ten thousand years ago, they used atlatls to accurately launch eight-foot, stone-tipped darts that hit a target thirty yards away with the same impact as an arrow from a modern compound bow.[1] Later, bows and arrows would help them bring home even more venison.

Since they were more interested in food than fair chase, America's earliest hunters didn't mind having an unfair advantage. Like many modern hunters, they used deer calls and bait. They also used snares and pitfall traps. They conducted massive drives, and with the help of fire and fences they herded deer toward enclosures, cliffs, water, and snowbanks. When snow was soft and deep, they donned snowshoes, chased down deer, and killed them with knives, hatchets, and clubs.[2] Not owning chest freezers out in the garage, they hunted year-round.

For them, nearly everything that moved was food. One archaeological site in West Virginia held identifiable bones from twenty-four mammal species, thirty bird species, ten reptile species, one amphibian, and thirteen fish species.[3] Bison and elk were hugely important in the West, and in the East bison, moose, elk, and black bear were all important locally. Wild turkey, bear, elk, waterfowl, raccoon, and various other creatures provided occasional variety. Archaeological evidence at middens all over the eastern United States and Canada, however, confirms that these early hunters obtained most of their daily protein from venison.

Newcomers Venture into the Woods

History tells us the new arrivals at Plymouth Rock were not especially skilled as farmers or hunters. Fortunately their neighbors were glad to share.

The most reliable written account of that first Thanksgiving in 1621 is from Edward Winslow. In it he makes no mention of turkey—only venison.[4] Contemporaries writing about wild game usually named waterfowl and turkey specifically, probably because each bird was larger and provided more meat. Winslow, however, only mentions some sort of generic "fowle" that was most likely heath hen. This two-pound bird, a relative of the prairie chicken, was once quite common along the entire Eastern Seaboard. Because they were easy to hunt and tasted like chicken, they are now extinct.

The only other written account of that day is from William Bradford, who does indeed mention turkeys. Bradford, however, was writing about his recollections twenty years after the fact. He appears to have made a number of other adjustments to the day's menu, and he also put a far more positive spin on the type and amount of food that Pilgrims enjoyed during the months before and after.[5]

Winslow, meanwhile, notes that the Indians "went out and killed five Deere which they brought to the Plantacion, and bestowed on our Governour, and upon the Captain, and others." So at that first Thanksgiving in 1621, it seems likely that turkey wasn't even on the menu. One thing is certain, however: The main course was venison.

At the time bumbling colonists were impressed by Native Americans' hunting and stalking skills. One in Virginia describes the Roanokes' stalking thusly: "these savages being secretly hidden among high reeds where oftentimes they find the deer asleep and so kill them." John Smith reported in the early 1600s, "When they have shot a deare by land, they follow him like bloodhounds by the blood and straine, and oftentimes so take them."[6]

Before long these newcomers were venturing into the woods and learning some woodsmanship themselves. Back in the Old World, hunting was a privilege reserved for royalty and nobility. Here, anyone could hunt. The colonists could pursue, shoot, and eat whatever they wanted, and what they most wanted was deer. It was an unheard-of freedom, one of the things that made America different right from the beginning.

Given these freedoms and colonists' entrepreneurial spirit, it was inevitable that some would try their hand at market hunting, primarily for deer. The best skins were sent to England until colonies enacted legislation to keep this valuable commodity at home. In 1677 the Court of Connecticut made illegal the "transport out of this Colony the skinns of bucks and does, which are so serveable and vsefull for cloathing."[7]

In the beginning deer seemed infinitely abundant. Soon, however, colonists found it necessary to enact the first game laws in the New World, beginning in 1646 when the town of Portsmouth, Rhode Island, ordered "that there shall be noe shootinge of deere from the first of May till the first of November; and if any shall shoote a deer within that time he shall forfeit five pounds." By 1700 similar harvest seasons had been set in New Jersey, Connecticut, Massachusetts, and Virginia. That didn't happen until 1911 in Tennessee, 1915 in Arkansas, 1916 in Oklahoma—and 1921 in Ontario.[8]

As a young nation grew, American immigrants quite literally hunted their way westward. Even in the East market hunting continued to grow in importance. Every year from 1698 through 1715, an estimated 13,755 deer hides were exported from Virginia, 50,250 from what's now North Carolina, and 75,000 from South Carolina. Between 1739 and 1765 annual hide exports grew to an estimated 151,000 from Charleston, South Carolina, alone. In just one year, 1771, 125 tons of hides were shipped from Pensacola, Florida, and Mobile, Alabama.[9]

In the 1750s and early 1760s, Daniel Boone supported his growing family as a market hunter. Much of the westward exploring he did was strictly a by-product of his hunting. To be precise, he was after hides rather than meat. What venison he couldn't eat for breakfast, lunch, and dinner, he left for coyotes.

Boone received 17 to 18 pence for each hide. It wasn't until much later that prices would reach one dollar. Buckskins first sold for over a buck a deer in 1815, when they went for $1.50 in Michigan.[10] And, yes, that's the origin of our slang term for the American dollar. Unfortunately for hunters, but fortunately for deer, the price of buckskins has not kept pace with inflation.

Throughout the nineteenth century market hunters sold deer for their meat, hides, antlers, hooves, hair that could be used for stuffing, and even their fat. In 1806, 120 kegs of deer tallow weighing 4,536 kilograms were shipped eastward from Green Bay, Wisconsin, for the purpose of making candles.[11]

More elegantly, the menu for Lincoln's second inaugural dinner in 1865 featured "Roasted Whitetail Venison with Herb Crust." At least some of the candlelight at that night's dinner was very likely from flames fed by deer tallow. Meanwhile, frontier families living in dirt-floored log cabins relied on venison, rabbit, and squirrel for most of their meat; chickens were kept for eggs and cows for milk.

In 1870 a Philadelphia man visiting Saint Paul, Minnesota, wrote home: "You can eat grouse three times a day if you please, and the finest flavored of trout and venison are a drug on the market."[12] During that same year, Saint Paul shipped 3,859 deer hides.

Just a few years earlier, in 1867, the first refrigerator cars had begun running between Chicago and New York City. One historian has argued convincingly that market hunting didn't just benefit from this development, but actually did much to bring it about. While these new refrigerator cars would eventually be hauling a lot more beef than venison, it's noteworthy that in December 1872, one small Minnesota town shipped out over six tons of dressed deer carcasses by rail.[13]

When market hunters began sending entire boxcars full of deer carcasses to big-city restaurants back East, it couldn't last. For a time it looked as though deer would be totally extirpated from the continent. They weren't. Efforts to preserve them and other game animals helped jump-start America's nascent conservation movement. As a result, today we often struggle with a very different problem. Rather than too few deer, in much of America we now have far too many.

In the end, all this history leads us to one inescapable conclusion: America wasn't just built on cod or corn. It was also built on venison.

WHY DEER MEAT STILL MATTERS

But is all that ancient history? In twenty-first-century America, has eating the flesh of wild animals, including deer, become a bizarre anachronism? At best, is it a harmless novelty from the fringes of the forest, a primal feast enjoyed by the very outermost fringes of our society? And what about the rest of us who live in the city, don't hunt, have never tasted venison, and never want to?

I'd argue that deer meat still matters, and not just because Americans eat a lot of it. True, annual harvest figures from state wildlife agencies add up to a total of over six million deer.[14] If each deer yields fifty pounds of boneless lean meat, that's three hundred million pounds of venison. Although hunters would say it's priceless, let's price it anyway, at a conservative ten dollars a pound. (At current prices this is a bargain for beefsteak. And depending on the cut, farm-raised venison is currently going for nine to forty-eight dollars per pound, not including shipping and handling.[15]) Even at only ten dollars a pound, our three hundred million pounds of venison adds up to three billion dollars.

But as large as those numbers may seem, they're less impressive when compared with beef production, which the USDA estimates at an annual 26.3 billion pounds and a retail value of seventy-nine billion dollars.[16] I should point out that the beef number is "commercial carcass" weight, which includes a large percentage of bones and fat. Deer, on the other hand, are usually butchered with a technique that yields lean, boneless cuts. Still, even if the comparison isn't entirely fair, there's a big difference between three hundred million pounds of venison and twenty-six billion pounds of beef. And if those three hundred million pounds of venison were evenly distributed among all Americans, we'd each get less than a pound a year.

All that venison, however, is not evenly distributed. For many Americans it's a regular staple that stretches their modest incomes a lot farther at the grocery store. For them and their families, hunting, gathering, and gardening are more than mere hobbies. These hunters were locavores before it was fashionable—indeed, before the word was even invented.

It's easy to make jokes about hunters who spend more freely on their sport, the kind who dine on venison whose true cost could be calculated at hundreds of dollars per pound. Those hunters are out there, and you've met some of them during the last few chapters. But don't make these jokes about my neighbors, or about others like them who live in small towns and rural areas all across America.

These hunters are different. They don't travel halfway across the country to hunt. Instead they hunt their own land, a neighbor's land, or the state forest just down the road. They don't own a safe filled with rifles in different calibers to suit the day's terrain and mood. They have one, which they refer to as simply "my deer rifle." They may have purchased it a decade or two back, or they may have even inherited it from a father or grandfather. Either way, it's a rifle that paid for itself many, many deer ago.

Hunting, whatever its recreational value, can be hard work. It takes patience and persistence. It takes time, and time is money. But for those with more time than money, the math works differently. And if you're a construction worker who's just been laid off for the winter, you'll have plenty of time this November.

Admittedly, hunters like these are outliers. They're far from typical. The same is true of other hunters you've been reading about during the past few chapters. Many of them are outliers too. All those amazing new gadgets available at your favorite outdoor retailer? I'll let you in on a little secret: Some hunters don't buy all of them. And whatever goes on in Buffalo County has very little to do with mainstream North American deer-hunting culture. It's something foreign even to most deer hunters. For them hunting is about venison as much as antlers.

Elsewhere, most hunters don't rely on truckloads of bait. Nor do most of them have the luxury of planting randomly distributed two-acre food plots all over the back half of their 320-acre hobby farm. The typical American deer hunter is someone of fairly modest means who just hopes to get out every fall for a hike in the woods, a little fresh air, time with friends, time alone to sit and think, and, with luck, maybe even a little venison.

For hungry hunters the phrase "overabundant deer" can seem a puzzling oxymoron. The same is true for vegan wildlife watchers. Both would like to see more deer. But when present in excessive numbers, deer can dramatically alter entire ecosystems—often at the expense of nearly all other wildlife. They ravage our farm fields, wander out onto our highways, and leave our suburban lawns crawling with Lyme disease–laden deer ticks. It definitely is possible to have too many deer, and quite often hunting is a big part of the solution. But as fewer Americans hunt, how long will the rest of us continue to tolerate the practice?

Although only 6 percent of Americans went hunting last year, a 2011 survey found that 74 percent approved of hunting and 94 percent felt it's "OK for other people to hunt if they do so legally and in accordance with hunting laws and regulations." Only 4 percent of respondents wanted to strip citizens of the right to hunt. Respondents' approval, however, appeared to be contingent on hunters' motivations. While only 28 percent approved of "hunting for a trophy," 81 percent approved of "hunting as wildlife management," and 85 percent approved of "hunting for meat."[17]

So for the American landscape, for Americans' suburban landscaping, and for the vast majority of us who have no interest in ever picking up a rifle and toting it out into the deer woods, these "hunting for meat" numbers are the biggest reason venison still matters in twenty-first-century America.

Only Five Hundred More Deer until Christmas

Once upon a time, every village had its butcher, baker, and candlestick maker. Today the candlestick makers are long gone, and so are most of the butchers and bakers. Modern economies of scale and supply-chain efficiencies mean that relatively inexpensive bread from the bread factory reaches your grocer's shelf literally overnight. Factory-farmed meat from giant processing plants flies from the kill floor to your shopping cart in two to four days.

Behind those swinging doors just beyond the counter in your grocer's meat department, very few beef and pork carcasses are being broken down into individual cuts for your dinner table. Most of those cuts are prepackaged, or at best repackaged. And with the exception of a few trimmings here and there, nearly all hamburger arrives either prepackaged or in eighty-pound plastic sleeves. Today most grocery-store meat departments could just as accurately be called unpacking and repacking departments.

Happily, thousands of independent butcher shops have managed to survive by giving their customers service and meats that are a cut above the ordinary. Brooklyn alone has nearly four hundred of these neighborhood meat boutiques, many of which now have their own websites and blogs. Very few, however, offer venison processing. For that you may need to venture a bit farther out into the heartland.

In small towns all across America, local butcher shops depend on deer hunters for much of their business. Every fall they take a break from beef, push aside the pork, and clear their decks for a flood of venison. Although the beginning of venison season mirrors that of each state's deer season, its ending does not. Long after deer season has ended, many of these butchers are still putting in twelve- and eighteen-hour days disassembling deer. With luck they'll be caught up by Christmas.

They do, however, have a lot to be thankful for at Thanksgiving. Deer season, in fact, is often the one thing that lets them end their year in the black. If retailers at the mall have Black Friday, these small-town butcher shops celebrate one of their own partway through deer season. In states that schedule their deer seasons for late November, butchers may even celebrate it on the same exact day.

━ ⌣ ━

To learn more, I'm visiting with Rob and Laura Hursh, owners of Hursh Meat Processing. Tonight, two days before the opening of Wisconsin's deer season, it's eerily quiet in their shop. It will be for one more day.

Tomorrow the November woods will be just as silent. For a single day, except at officially designated ranges, it will be illegal to discharge a firearm outdoors in Wisconsin. In theory this makes it easier for game wardens to track down any hunters who decide to improve their odds with a one-day head start.

The law's only other exception is for waterfowlers. But here in the North, the marshes are frozen and the ducks are long gone. Tonight's lows will be in the single digits.

Inside the shop, though, it's comfortably warm. A dozen or so hams in the smoker perfume the air with charred maple and sizzling pork fat. I haven't eaten yet, and my mouth is watering. I make a mental note to buy a couple pounds of bratwurst before I leave. Dinner. For now I'm taking actual notes as fast as I can while Rob and Laura tell me their story.

They live right across the parking lot from their shop. It's a family business, and over the coming weeks the whole extended Hursh family will be working seven days a week, sometimes for twenty hours a day. There's Rob's brother, Clyde; Clyde's wife, Carol; various nieces and nephews; and another six or eight seasonal employees from all over this part of the county.

We're a couple miles outside the village of Poplar, which is four miles down the road from Maple. And, yes, there are lots of poplar and maple trees around here—also plenty of oak, alder, tamarack, spruce, and pine. Nine days from now, a lot of the deer out in those woods will be stacked up right here at Hursh Meat Processing.

Of the thousand to fourteen hundred deer processed here every year, around seven hundred arrive during the nine-day gun deer season. (Wisconsin also has a much longer bowhunting season that began in September.) Depending on the weather, nearly all of them could arrive on the last day or two of the season. "If it warms up," explains Rob, "hunters will bring their deer in right away so they don't spoil. But if it stays below freezing, most of our deer will arrive on that final Sunday afternoon."

The crew will be ready. Everyone knows the drill. To speed the unloading process, they'll stack deer on the dozen or so hay wagons parked outside the shop. If the weather is unseasonably warm, Plan B is to cart them straight into the shop's walk-in freezers. Similarly, if a warm front arrives later in the week, the crew will drop everything and move every single carcass from the wagons to the freezers.

Most years, though, temperatures this time of year stay safely below freezing. Deer can remain on the wagons until they're brought in to be thawed, skinned, and processed. That makes the job more fun and less stressful for everyone.

"We like efficiency," says Laura. "But we take time to listen and visit with our customers too. Everyone's excited about getting a deer, and everyone has a story. We're hunters ourselves, and for us that's part of what makes all this fun."

If loyal customers are dropping deer off in the evening and want to crack open a beer while they visit, it's OK. If they're done working with sharp knives, and if they've already cleaned up, the Hurshes and their crew just might not turn one down themselves. But only in moderation. They'll be up early to begin another long day.

Over the next four to six weeks, they'll be putting in a lot of long days. One year they ended the season with a backlog of over nine hundred deer. Wisconsin's Department of Natural Resources estimates that this year's deer population is down slightly, so Rob and Laura figure that by the end of the season they'll only be behind by about five hundred deer. If all goes well, they and their employees will be caught up by Christmas—or at least by New Year's Eve.

They'll spend January and February making sausage and jerky for the hunters who requested it. Then it's back to pork and beef for most of the spring and summer. The Hurshes also do custom livestock processing and run a mobile slaughtering operation.

When bear season rolls around in early September, daytime temperatures could reach the eighties. Bears, typically 100 to 150 of them every year, will need to be skinned and processed fast. They'll also need to be skinned carefully and patiently—most bear skins are bound for the taxidermist. On the other hand, that's all the more reason for speed. In warm weather any delays mean the hairs will "slip." That's taxidermy talk for when the animal's hairs loosen and fall from their follicles. Since no customer wants hairless, balding bearskin rugs, Hursh employees keep working around the clock. On one or two occasions, they've skinned bears for forty-eight hours straight.

In mid-September, long before bear season is over, deer season will begin for bowhunters. A few hundred deer will trickle in, and along with them a hundred or so moose. After that it will be time once again for the main event.

The woods were dark as I drove home from my Thursday-night visit. Twice I braked hard for deer stumbling out onto the pavement. By the time my wife and I sat down to enjoy the bratwurst I'd brought home for dinner, it was almost eight o'clock. For one smug moment I felt as though I'd just put in a very long day. Then I remembered the week ahead at Hursh Meat Processing.

━ ⁓

Three days later I was back. As I drove into the empty parking lot on Sunday afternoon, I realized I could have just as well waited a week. It was only the second day of the season, temperatures were in the teens, and everyone was still out hunting. A few dozen deer had been dropped off, but things were still fairly quiet.

Since I was already here, I stayed for an hour or so to watch and learn. As an amateur who's butchered a few deer of my own, I had to admire the skills of these professionals. First I watched the skinners, whose job also involves removing each deer's head and lower legs. Next I watched Clyde reduce a carcass to boneless backstrap, steaks, and roasts. Every cut was swift and sure. I could tell this was not his first deer. Nearby a nephew trimmed a shoulder for chunks that would be ground into burger and sausage.

Despite the volume, and despite all the efficiencies, the butchers at Hursh only work on one deer at a time. After each deer they clean their table, touch up their knives, and start out fresh. At check-in, every deer receives a tag that stays with it through the entire process. Once the deer is completely butchered, the tag is affixed to the freezer tub that holds the venison from that deer and that deer alone. Any burger, sausage, or jerky made from that deer goes into the same tub.

Bucks get a second tag that stays with the head or antlers once they're separated from the rest of the carcass. (Some hunters want the head and cape for their taxidermist; others are only interested in the antlers.) The result is that every hunter knows the venison and antlers he gets back will be from his own deer and no one else's.

Anyone else could have watched the crew working that day too. Toward the front of the lobby, among the freezer cases stocked with steaks, chops, hams, and bacon, a large window allows customers to see what's happening in the skinning area. Farther back, customers standing in line at the counter can watch Clyde and the other meat cutters at work. The whole place is spotless. Clearly the Hurshes have nothing to hide.

Exactly one week later, the scene is totally different. It's Sunday afternoon, only a couple hours before the end of Wisconsin's deer season. The
parking lot is full, hunters are standing in line to complete their paperwork, and more hunters are admiring the antlers on some of the deer that
have just been dropped off.

It's sunny and in the mid-twenties—perfect weather for a little outdoor socializing after a successful hunt. In fact, one of the first sounds
I hear after opening my car door is someone else opening a beer. Scattered groups of hunters out here in the parking lot are swapping stories
and telling tales. A few are quite obviously groups of men having their
week without women. But women hunters are here too, as well as families
with teenage hunters experiencing all this for the very first time. Looking
around, I'd estimate that the hunters visiting out here in the parking lot
range in age from about eleven to eighty.

When they drive up, I can tell which hunters have never been here
before. They're the ones staring with their mouths hanging open. In a
rough semicircle all around us, stacked neatly on a dozen or so hay wagons, are over three hundred deer. By the time I leave, it will be closer to
four hundred.

Even for hunters who were happily shooting and gutting their own
deer an hour or two earlier, the sight of so many deer stacked up in one
place can be a little disconcerting. As far as I know, this isn't a sight you'd
see anywhere else. It requires a secure rural location, tolerant neighbors,
and temperatures that will remain reliably below freezing.

Nor is it a sight you'll see in many hunting magazines. Like outdoor
retailers, these magazines and their advertisers sell a dream that involves
the pursuit of a noble game animal—and occasionally, in a very literal
sense, "bringing home the bacon." But when hunters do dream of venison,
they see themselves as rugged individuals being strong and self-reliant,
providing for their families one deer at a time. Images of 347 deer stacked
on hay wagons are not part of this dream.

Later I'll get photos like that. But first I have to hear a few stories. In
between I'll get a few more shots of skinning, butchering, and wrapping;

a "souvenir" jar filled with recently discovered bullets and broadheads; orange-clad hunters standing in line to complete their paperwork; hunters swapping stories in the parking lot; employees helping unload deer from pickups, minivans, and even a few Subarus and Toyotas—but mostly pickups.

One pickup is hauling five deer: a buck and four does. Until I get close enough to peer over the side and into the bed, I can only see a forest of frozen legs protruding at various odd angles. Later I learn that these two hunters, both in their twenties, are giving four of their five deer to the state's venison donation program. Like many states, Wisconsin uses a small portion of license revenues to reimburse processors and pay for distribution. Since the program began in 2000, hunters' donations have added up to over 3.5 million pounds of ground venison for area food banks.

Finally I take those other photos too: wagonloads of deer; more wagonloads of deer; hundreds of frozen, neatly stacked deer carcasses silhouetted against the sunset.

Out here in the parking lot, the temperature is dropping fast. The sun is setting. In a few moments, when the sun dips a bit lower, this year's deer season will be officially over. Back inside, the work is only beginning.

DEER DIY

If you're the self-reliant type and would prefer to butcher your own deer, it's not really all that difficult. Here's the short version, minus most of the gory details.

Let's begin at the beginning. You've pulled the trigger, you've made a good shot, your deer is down, and you're very sure it's very dead. If this is your first time, I suggest you pause right now. Take a deep breath, exhale, and relax. Repeat.

Whether you're experiencing this moment for the first time or the hundredth, you'll feel feelings. This is not the same as killing and cutting up a fish or a pheasant. It's a warm-blooded mammal that's nearly as large as you are. Maybe even larger. In a few moments, when you reach inside it, its blood will feel very warm.

If you've made a good shot, your deer's transition from mammal to meat will be brief and humane. For you the psychological transition from hunter to butcher may take a bit longer. Although I'm slowly becoming accustomed to this experience, I hope I never come to feel nothing at all. Some but not all of the feelings washing over me at these moments have actually been quite positive. Satisfaction at a well-placed shot. Relief that an animal's death has been quick, humane, and painless. Even delight that an empty freezer will soon be empty no longer.

Once, although a longtime practicing agnostic, I knelt beside a fallen doe at the far edge of a rolling, eighty-acre alfalfa field that stretched out into the distance behind a backwoods Baptist church. As I opened my knife, I gave a brief and wordless prayer of thanksgiving for the blessings our freezer was about to receive. I have yet to jump up and down excitedly, whoop and holler, and high-five my cameraman like those guys on the TV hunting shows always do. But that's just me.

As you're collecting your thoughts, remember to "tag" your deer so that it's officially yours. Although the regulations and details vary by state, you'll typically do this by tying a small square of plasticized paperwork to the deer's antlers. If your deer has no antlers, you'll need to make a small slit in one of its ears. Then you can poke a zip-tie or piece of string through the slit—unpleasant, but a small warm-up for what's coming next.

It's time. Tag it. Remember that whole "public trust doctrine"? The act you've just completed has officially transferred the deer's ownership from the state to you. You have now, to use the proper legal term, "taken" your deer.

The next thing you'll need to do is field-dress your deer. This is a rather euphemistic term for the process of removing a deer's insides before removing the deer from the woods. Hunters usually do this immediately. It gets rid of any blood or other fluids that could hasten spoilage, allows the carcass to cool more quickly, and greatly lightens the load you'll need to drag from the woods. If you like, save the heart and liver. (Assuming of course that both are undamaged.) But unless you're really into offal, you're not going to need any of that other stuff.

Nor is there any need for further euphemisms. The part that's left behind is generally referred to as a "gutpile." Depending on where you're hunting, some combination of wolves, coyotes, raccoons, possums, eagles, vultures, or ravens will take care of the cleanup within hours. If you shoot a deer late in the day, the entire gutpile, including the contents of the deer's stomach and intestines, will almost invariably be gone by morning. All that will remain is a greasy stain in the grass.

—◦—

Although I've spared you the gory details, I hope you didn't just read that last bit during your lunch break. If so, I apologize. Field-dressing is a dirty job, but someone's got to do it—probably you if you're a hunter. Even if you take your deer to a butcher, you'll still have to do this part yourself. It's an unpleasant but unavoidable part of deer hunting.

And here's the thing: The rest of the job, all the skinning and butchering that most hunters pay someone else to do? It's not nearly as messy, bloody, and unpleasant as field-dressing was. True, it does have its moments. When you get your deer home, you'll need to remove its head and lower legs. This, especially the beheading part, can feel a bit harsh. But by now you'll be getting used to the idea that this is a very dead deer.

A few minutes later, when your deer is headless, footless, and hanging from the rafters in your garage, the transformation is nearly complete. It's not an animal, it's a carcass. Later still, when you've finished skinning that carcass, it will very much begin to resemble venison. All that remains is a few more hours of disassembly, packaging, and cleanup.

Today most home butchers use a process yielding lean, boneless venison that looks very different from the traditional cuts of beef or pork you'd find at the grocery store. By leaving out the bones, fat, and gristle, you'll save freezer space and enjoy a healthier, better tasting dinner. Best of all, you won't be sawing through bones and spraying sawdust and bone chips all over your venison. Instead you'll use a sharp knife to slice through the spaces between bones.

The first time you remove a deer's front leg, it's a revelation. There's no bone-to-bone connection, only tendons and ligaments. This gives deer extra flexibility, which in turn gives them extra speed and agility. By chance, it also makes for easier butchering. Two quick sweeps of a knife, and a front leg is free. Two more cuts, and so is the other.

They're the first of several pieces you'll stack on a garage workbench, one you've first made spotless and sanitary by covering it with multiple layers of white freezer paper. There, you'll break these chunks down into smaller pieces, finish any further deboning, and trim away every last bit of gristle and fat. Deer, unlike cows or pigs, have very little intramuscular fat that's marbled right into the meat. When you're done trimming away the fat, you'll be left with nothing but lean, luscious, dark red meat.

Finally it's almost time to wrap and label all those packages for your freezer. And don't forget . . . If you'll be grinding some of your venison into deerburger, you'll need to do that now too. Or if you're an optimist who hopes to shoot another deer later in the season, you can freeze all those leftover trimmings and burger chunks in gallon-size resealable bags. With luck you'll be able to thaw them, add more from a subsequent deer, and then grind and package an even larger batch sometime the week after deer season.

Yesterday afternoon my wife and I completed this end-of-season project in just over an hour. As I fed partially frozen chunks into our half-horsepower electric meat grinder, she did the packaging and labeling. A layer of plastic, a layer of freezer paper, and a few bits of tape to seal it. Then a neat label with the month and year: deerburger. Last night we enjoyed our first meatloaf of the winter.

—— ~ ——

As you might guess, butchering one deer at a time can be a very labor-intensive process. Even after we've done it a few times, we amateurs need to set aside at least half a day. If you ever hear some hunter boast of completing the job in an hour, he—and it will be a he—is probably not including prep time, packaging, disposal of bones and scraps, resharpening of knifes, and cleanup—*all* the cleanup. Ask his wife how long it really takes.

If the process is different for us beginners, so is the product. As we finish, we often find ourselves packaging up rough-hewn roasts and noticeably asymmetrical steaks. We may have inadvertently turned some of the very best cuts into a heap of ragged scraps and shreds. No matter; these tender trimmings will be delicious in less traditional venison dishes like fajitas, curries, and stir-fries.

Which brings to mind a favorite quote. In context it's a metaphor, a sort of Taoist parable. More literally it reminds me of how I often find myself probing repeatedly with the tip of my knife, searching the entire neighborhood of that ball-and-socket joint where the deer's rear leg is attached. Eventually I find and sever the single tendon that will release it.

A more skilled butcher, like the one Chuang Tzu described in the third century BC, would know fully the Tao of deer disassembly:

Trusting in the Tao, I send my knife slicing through cavernous crevices; it touches neither joint nor bone. A good cook needs a new knife once a year; he chops. A poor cook needs a new knife once a month; he hacks. I've used this same knife nineteen years. It has butchered a thousand oxen, and it's still like new.

There are spaces in the joints; a sharp, thin blade can slide right through. When I reach a more difficult joint, I pause to consider it. Then I move my knife slowly and carefully, and bam! The part falls away, landing like a clod of earth.

MINDFUL NEW CARNIVORES

In the typical American deer camp, hunters rarely quote Taoist or Buddhist scriptures. Even biblical references to venison are quite scarce. Hunters mostly quote the verse from Genesis that began this chapter. In other Old Testament news, when Deuteronomy lists "the beasts which ye shall eat," deer do indeed make the list. They also made King Solomon's table. Venison—a dish fit for a king.[18]

But these topics rarely come up around the campfire. And as much as hunters might value venison, they rarely speak aloud of the meaning and metaphysics of meat. To do so would be unseemly. It's just not done.

At this very moment other hunters are bringing to the sport new traditions and cultural norms of their own. They're mindful, self-aware, and more than a little self-conscious about what all this means. They ask "How?" but also ask "Why?" They don't come from hunting families, and their beliefs, values, and motives are often entirely different. To start with, most of them couldn't care less about antlers.

But venison, they've discovered, is naturally lean, local, organic, and delicious; that alone is motivating many people to try hunting. Since there's more meat on a deer than on a squirrel or a quail, these newcomers are especially interested in deer hunting. And for those who think just a little too much about where their food comes from, eating venison feels more morally defensible than eating beef or pork from the grocery store. Deer aren't raised on huge factory farms. They live wild and free. New hunters hope their aim will be true and their quarry's death quick and painless.

One person I talked with is Tovar Cerulli, author of *The Mindful Carnivore: A Vegetarian's Hunt for Sustenance.* His book is in every sense a meaty memoir. As he tells a deeply personal story, he connects his own experiences to larger themes having to do with meat, meaning, and the karmic costs of every food on his table—including the brown rice, tofu, and organic vegetables. Today Cerulli views such choices far less simply than he once did.

After reflecting on the compassionate words of Buddhist teacher Thich Nhat Hanh, he became a vegetarian at age twenty. Eventually though, after learning more about the modern egg and dairy industries, he went vegan. Eventually he began to have second thoughts. Initially for health reasons, he and his wife returned first to eggs and dairy products and then to fish and poultry.

When Cerulli next picked up a rifle and stepped into the deer woods, he brought with him a vegetarian's values and sensibilities. "I was concerned," he told me, "about two things: animal welfare and the ecological impacts of food production. Hunting was a way to get at least some of my food in a way that's ecologically sound—and, if done well, more humanely. After being a vegetarian for so long, beginning to eat other creatures again was a big deal for me. Hunting was a way to confront the reality of what that meant."

This was not a decision he made lightly, and it's one he still thinks about quite a lot. He is indeed a mindful carnivore.

Cerulli is also the writer who first coined a delightful neologism that appears to be sticking: the "adult-onset hunter." The term is appearing more often, and so are the hunters it describes. Cerulli is one, and I am myself. And finally, all across the United States and Canada, the right people are beginning to notice and nurture us.

Faced with rising deer numbers and falling hunter numbers, state and provincial wildlife agencies are finally looking for new hunters in some new places. Traditionally their retention and recruitment specialists used the term "recruitment" the same way wildlife biologists do. Just as fawn recruitment rates measure the percentage of fawns surviving their first year to become adult deer, hunter recruitment rates have measured the percentage of hunters' children growing up to become adult hunters.

True, recent years have seen a new emphasis on recruiting women and girls. But all too often we've widened our search just enough to include the daughters of hunters rather than only their sons. Hunters have rarely presumed to proselytize, and adult converts were once rare. Even when those converts were willing, they found the barriers to entry were high.

As Lily Raff McCaulou writes in her memoir, *Call of the Mild: Learning to Hunt My Own Dinner,* "Hunting is a twenty-first century rarity—something you can't learn online or in a book. There's no *Hunting for Dummies.* There are no intro classes at the local community college. Most hunters would have you believe that theirs is the sport of the everyman. But I'm finding it to be oddly exclusive. Hunting isn't so much a hobby as an inheritance, passed from one generation to the next. You have to learn from someone, and that someone is usually your dad. But where does that leave me—an adult whose parents are openly disgusted by the idea of killing an animal in the wild?"

Today all that is changing, and adult-onset hunters are becoming more common every year. To meet a few of them, I recently attended an event called, quite simply, "Deer Day." Sponsored by the Minnesota DNR, the event began several years ago as part of the popular Becoming an Outdoors Woman (BOW) program. Since then the program's been broadened to include men, young people, and whole families. It's held at the central Minnesota farm of Betty and Dan Wilkens, who have graciously hosted the event every August for the past several years. It takes a fair amount of acreage to host an event like this, as well as some good backstops for the various rifle, shotgun, and archery ranges.

Apart from a brief opening and closing, most of the program consisted of breakout sessions held at various stations that participants rotated among throughout the day. In addition to all the shooting, there were sessions on topics like treestand safety and blood tracking for bowhunters.

The treestand safety session was an important one, since far more hunters are now injured by falls from treestands than by gunshot wounds.

The two conservation officers leading this session ended by demonstrating a small but comfortable ground blind. For those of us afraid of heights, these camo tents with convenient shooting windows were beginning to seem like a very appealing alternative.

Next up for my group was the blood-trailing lesson. Earlier that morning our instructors had prepared simulated blood trails that were disturbingly realistic. They'd done this by dipping a large brush into a pail of pig blood and then artistically applying various spatters and droplets to the vegetation beside paths leading into the woods from Station #3. To my untrained eye it seemed like a pretty convincing imitation of what you'd see after a lung, liver, or gut shot. This helped persuade everyone to spend the afternoon on more target practice.

But first it was time to break for lunch, which featured an all-American menu of potato salad, brownies, beans, and plenty of barbecue sandwiches made with ground venison (known as "sloppy does" rather than "sloppy joes"). Delicious. Then it was time for more shooting. I saw impressive sunburns getting under way, but everyone seemed to be having a good time and learning a lot.

That day I talked with several adult-onset hunters and heard their stories: the mother with her grown daughter; the father with his young son; the couples; the single men and women of every age; the families. Some, like the family of Russian immigrants, spoke English as their second language. The Cold War had ended long ago. No one, not even the rifle instructor in his black and red NRA cap, seemed at all concerned about hearing Russian spoken on the firing line.

I remembered that Minnesota is home to many other immigrants, including more than fifty thousand Hmong whose families arrived after the Vietnam War as refugees from Laos. Their own culture has a long tradition of true subsistence hunting and gathering, and it's one that doesn't always dovetail neatly with mainstream American hunting culture. Today an estimated ten thousand Minnesota Hmong hunt deer every year.

One of the instructors I met at the range that day was Erik Jensen, who had recently begun blogging as The Progressive Outdoorsman. A few months later he led his first "Deer Hunting for Beginners" class at a Minneapolis health-food co-op. He tells me others have held similar workshops at co-ops all over the country, and he's already scheduled more sessions for later in the year—just in time for hunting season.

Whether they come from the other side of the globe or the other side of town, America's future hunters won't necessarily look, think, or vote like those of the past or present. As they begin venturing out into the woods, their fresh new voices will transform our dialogue about what hunting means in twenty-first-century America.

And whether they hunt or not, the next generation of Americans will still love deer. A few will continue to be obsessed with deer, and some small number will still hunt and eat them. Let's hope these hunters of the future are hungry and own large freezers.

It's easy to forget that by 1900 we'd nearly extirpated deer from North America. We've brought them back from the brink, and we now have a hundred times more deer than we did a century ago. Having thirty million deer is a wonderful thing. It does, however, have consequences.

II. Consequences

CHAPTER 6

Why the Mountain Fears Its Deer

Just as a deer herd lives in mortal fear of its wolves, so does a mountain live in mortal fear of its deer. And perhaps with better cause, for while a buck pulled down by wolves can be replaced in two or three years, a range pulled down by too many deer may fail of replacement in as many decades.

—ALDO LEOPOLD, FROM HIS ESSAY "THINKING LIKE A MOUNTAIN"

Exclosure.

It's an odd word. The first time I saw it in print, it just looked wrong. Still, I knew exactly what it must mean. If an *enclosure* keeps deer in, then an *exclosure* must keep them out.

Today I'd see several of them. Each would tell a story about what happens when deer densities approach levels that are becoming increasingly common in America's parks and suburbs—levels five, ten, or even twenty times what most biologists would consider normal and sustainable. Inside each exclosure I'd see something approximating a normal, healthy forest. On the outside I'd see an extreme example of the ecological havoc deer can wreak when there are way too many of them for the land to support. I'd see browse lines, a forest understory that was completely missing, and even the sad spectacle of a lollipop tree. As sweet as it may sound, it's not called that because lollipops grow on it.

My guide was Dr. Tom Rooney, a botanist from Ohio's Wright State University. He's one of the world's leading experts on the effects of overabundant deer on the forest ecosystem. Today we were on our way to one of his experimental sites just outside Boulder Junction, a small town in northeastern Wisconsin. To be precise, we were on our way to Dairymen's.

THE DEER OF DAIRYMEN'S

As we headed out of town that morning, Tom explained that Dairymen's maintains a fairly low profile. It's a private club with its own lodge, cabins, tennis courts, trails, six medium-size lakes, and access to four more lakes on the edge of the property. Back in the 1920s the club was started by a small group of wealthy dairy magnates who wanted their own private playground in the north woods. From the very beginning they decided that its entire six thousand acres would be a wildlife refuge where no hunting was allowed. Back then this unusual move was considered quite progressive and enlightened.

Deer had been almost totally eliminated from northern Wisconsin, and they pretty much had been eliminated from the southern part of the state. Other game was scarce too. So at the time, creating a wildlife refuge was a great idea. Soon members began to hear grouse drumming. One or two claimed they'd glimpsed a deer. One year someone put a feeder outside the lodge and filled it with corn. It wasn't long before dairymen and their families could watch through the window at dinnertime as deer ate their own dinners.

By the late 1940s, however, Dairymen's had a new problem. It now had too many deer. Looking for answers, the club's Conservation Committee turned to the Wisconsin Conservation Department, the precursor to what's now the Department of Natural Resources. The department told them they had far more deer than the land could support and advised them to open Dairymen's to hunting.

The committee initially planned to follow the department's advice, but the issue quickly became contentious among club members. As a compromise, they decided to solve the problem by feeding the deer in a more serious way—not just a couple gallons every night at a feeder outside the lodge but on a larger scale at various spots around the property. That way, they figured, the land could easily support more deer.

In response, the deer were fruitful and multiplied. More wandered in from nearby. Eventually their densities exceeded one hundred per square mile, a number that's unusual but not unique. The United States now has over thirty million deer, a hundred times more than were here just a century ago. Their densities per square mile in America's suburbs and parks have at times reached 207 in Kansas City,[1] 241 in Philadelphia,[2] 300 in parts of New Jersey,[3] and 400 in Washington, D.C.[4] Clearly, cervids are invading our suburbs.

Meanwhile, back at Dairymen's you didn't have to be a botanist to notice that things were looking different. The deer ate every kernel of corn they were fed, but they also ate every bit of vegetation they could reach. The closer to the lodge, the worse the damage. Clear browse lines were now visible everywhere. The understory was disappearing. The forest was still filled with towering hemlocks; their beauty was one of the reasons the founding dairymen choose this site for their summer getaway. But no seedlings or saplings were waiting in line to replace them. The forest floor was bare.

In the late 1990s, half a century after ignoring the Conservation Department's advice, the Dairymen's Conservation Committee resolved to hire a consultant. They eventually chose Dr. Rooney, who by then was already recognized as an expert in his field. For him the invitation meant a unique opportunity to study the healing of a forest that had been hammered hard for half a century.

Real recovery will take time, and fifteen years later Rooney continues to measure its progress with painstaking analysis and sophisticated sampling techniques. When he first arrived, however, his immediate advice was quite simple: Stop feeding the deer. Because they'd find better cover and forage elsewhere, the deer would soon begin dispersing. In time Dairymen's might even have *fewer* deer than the surrounding area. Still, one question remained: Now that the forest understory was completely gone, how much would a smaller residual population of deer slow its recovery? For that matter, would the hardest-hit areas ever recover?

I was about to see for myself. When Tom turned onto the unmarked but well-paved road into Dairymen's, we drove another quarter mile before reaching the sign that read WILDLIFE SANCTUARY. Just a hundred yards later, I began to see the consequences.

The forest understory grew more sparse. The farther we drove, the more the forest on either side of the road began to look like a city park that had just been mown. "Holy—Look at that! It's gone," I said. "There's nothing left."

"Just wait," Tom said. "It gets worse. Wait until we get closer to the lodge."

In another half mile or so, I spotted the first exclosure. A short distance off the road, it was an isolated, perfectly square block of fenced-in underbrush about a hundred feet across. It hadn't been difficult to spot; it was a lonely cube of green standing in an open, parklike area. All around it, the forest floor was brown and bare.

"Interesting you used that expression," said Tom. "I hear the term 'parklike' quite a bit when people are describing an area with too many deer. We see parks as positive. It's more than cultural; it's hardwired into us. That kind of scene is just naturally pleasing to the human eye—unless you're a botanist. And in this park no one's been mowing. Only the deer."

The moment we pulled over and stepped out, we were greeted by a horde of mosquitoes. It had rained during the night, and the air was thick with humidity. Before we walked over to the exclosure, we sprayed ourselves down with DEET. That helped, but it still looked as though we were about to become part of the food web.

As we headed for the exclosure, I could see that that the areas on either side of the fence looked very different. Outside the exclosure we saw only scattered ferns and sedges growing beneath the hemlocks. These were the rare plants that either tolerated or resisted browsing.

On the inside we saw lush new growth. This was closer to what a normal, healthy forest looks like—a forest, that is, with a normal, healthy number of deer. There were seedlings, saplings, and even small trees. Beneath them were other plants that might be less noticeable to the casual observer. But there's more to a forest than its trees.

Tom opened the gate so I could get a closer look. Some of the plants I recognized—hemlock seedlings, maple seedlings, and new raspberry plants whose stalks were still green and tender. Tom told me the common and scientific names of at least a dozen more. Each time he explained the plant's role in the forest ecosystem. Food, cover, shelter, nesting sites . . . I can't remember everything he told me that morning, but I do remember this: All these plants matter, and not just to hungry deer.

Tom explained that the exclosure was built over ten years ago, and the area inside still isn't quite back to normal. Already, however, it looks very different from what's on the outside. And that's the problem. Outside the exclosure this forest is healing slowly. Very slowly. Although the deer of Dairymen's are far less numerous than they once were, there are still enough to keep this area from making a quick recovery. At best it's going to take a long, long time.

When plants eventually do recolonize this corner of Dairymen's and form a new understory, some will arrive in the form of seeds dispersed by birds over a wide area. Maple seeds get a short ride on the wind. Conifers and oaks rely on gravity and forgetful squirrels. Other plants, like many of those in the exclosure, are tiny shoots that remain alive beneath the ground and stubbornly keep emerging year after year. Every year deer snip them off at ground level, and every year they emerge again. One surprising spring, the shoots inside this newly erected exclosure were suddenly safe.

Some plants will return by slowly, inexorably marching in from outer edges and hidden refuges. (Indeed, botanists refer to these isolated pockets, often found amid jagged boulders or halfway up a cliff, as "refugia.") This exclosure has become one of those sanctuaries, a tiny oasis of biodiversity in the middle of a green desert.

As we left the exclosure, Tom explained how he measures these patterns of change. Along each side of the exclosure, at ten-meter intervals, were faded plastic flags marking the ends of his transects. They'd once been bright orange but by now had faded to gray. On the same date every summer, Tom places one end of a ten-meter measuring tape against the fence at each of these points. He extends it directly outward from the exclosure and then takes careful notes about what's growing along every centimeter of the entire ten-meter transect.

The news is encouraging. It's happening slowly, but this forest is recovering.

Tom's doing the same thing at other sites around Dairymen's, and he showed me more exclosures over the next couple hours. None looked exactly the same. Tom emphasized that there are more variables here than just the deer. One exclosure was more shaded; the canopy overhead was much thicker than it had been at the first site. The forest floor was bare. Even inside the exclosure, new growth was sparse.

"There's not much light here," he explained. "Any seedlings that make it past the deer are going to grow very slowly. That sapling over there, the one that's about your height? Its trunk is less than an inch in diameter, but it's probably about seventy years old. If one or two of these older hemlocks came down, it would have all the light it needs. Instant growth spurt."

"So it's just waiting, biding its time?" I asked.

"Exactly. These hemlocks can be very patient."

Outside one exclosure Tom showed me my first lollipop tree. Disappointingly, lollipops weren't actually growing on it. The term merely describes the shape of a small tree that's been heavily browsed by deer and is just now escaping above the browse line.

Very few hemlock seedlings outside this exclosure are making it past their first year or two. This particular survivor is on of the rare exceptions. It's a seven-foot eastern hemlock that appears to have just hopped out of a Dr. Seuss story. Its long, pencil-thin trunk has a single, gangly tuft of needles at the top.

After a clear-cut, an aspen sapling might reach this height over a single summer. This lollipop tree, however, is probably sixty or seventy years old. Every winter, hungry deer have been hitting it hard. Now it's finally about to break free and begin growing normally. Over the next few decades, it will morph from lollipop to cartoon palm tree to normal-looking hemlock.

◦—◦

At another stop the cedars on the far shore of a small lake showed a visible browse line. "You can still see it," said Tom. "But it's not as clear and distinct as it was ten years ago. Every year the browse line gets a little softer."

Straight horizontal lines are remarkably rare in nature. The browse line is one of those rare exceptions; it marks the highest branch a deer can reach. If deer are hungry enough, it marks the highest branch a deer can reach while momentarily standing on its hind legs. Everything below the browse line is gone; everything above it is safe and untouched.

Because most adult deer are roughly the same size, the browse line is often impossibly neat and well defined. A team of patient human gardeners with hedge trimmers couldn't have pruned more precisely. It looks too uniform to be natural—and in one sense, it's not. When deer populations are in balance, clearly defined browse lines are rare. When you see one, it's usually a sign that something's wrong.

—— ——

Elsewhere the scene was green and, well, parklike. There was no understory, and the forest floor was covered with an emerald green carpet of sedges, mostly Pennsylvania sedge (*Carex pennsylvanica*). Sedges, I learned, are a family of plants that superficially resemble grasses or rushes, but have stems that are usually triangular in cross section and leaves that are spirally arranged in three ranks rather than two. If you're not a botanist, you'll notice them as simply a grassy plant that's especially tough and fibrous. Once they're established, they form a dense root mat that doesn't allow other plants to get a toehold. And whether it's because of the taste, the texture, or both, deer don't eat them.

In the Northeast, hay-scented ferns are also likely to fill this same ecological niche. If you see a forest with a missing understory and what looks like an open "fern park," chances are good it's an area with too many deer. Chances are also good that when you look out over a scene like this, you'll be standing within an actual park. All too often suburban parks where deer are safe from hunters can end up looking a lot like Dairymen's.

Once, not far from the road, we spotted another clue. There, tipped on its side, was the rusted half of a fifty-five-gallon drum. Undoubtedly it had once been filled with corn for the deer. As is so often the case, feeding was a key part of the Dairymen's story.

As we walked farther, Tom pointed out a few more types of plants that for one reason or another don't interest deer. Everything else was gone. Still, if I didn't know what I was seeing, it would have looked lovely. Green and parklike.

True, it was green. But there was no cover for small mammals or ground-nesting birds. There was no understory or midstory where other songbirds would be nesting—no grouse, no turkeys, no finches, no warblers, no squirrels, no chipmunks, no nothing. It was a still, humid day in June. Nothing moved, and the forest was strangely silent. Once or twice I heard a robin off in the distance. That was all.

But with enough time, who knows? Although Dairymen's still doesn't allow hunting, its members have stopped feeding the deer. A couple years ago a pack of wolves moved in. Things are looking up.

SILENT SUMMER

It doesn't take a botanist to notice that something isn't quite right in the open, parklike expanses of Dairymen's. Elsewhere, even when the impacts of overabundant deer are less visible and obvious, they're still easy enough to understand. They're also surprisingly long lasting.

It's a matter of both quantity and quality. Deer reduce the total density of plants in the understory, but they also alter species composition and diversity. This happens for three reasons. First, deer browse preferentially, eating some species first. Second, even when deer do relish a particular species, it may tolerate browsing better than others that deer find equally tasty. Third, the plants deer don't prefer are suddenly released from competition and begin to take over. For all these reasons, a forest with too many deer has both fewer and different plants.

Deer can also increase the rates of foliage decomposition, disperse seeds, and help or hinder plant growth through soil compaction and trampling. But most of all, deer affect forests simply by eating them. They eat seedlings and saplings that will never become trees, and they eat other plants whose absence, although rarely noticed by us, definitely does matter somehow.

Scientists don't understand these indirect effects of overabundant deer as clearly as they do the more simple, direct ones. A search of the literature turns up hundreds of papers by botanists but far fewer by ecologists, entomologists, or ornithologists. Hypotheses, however, do come easily. If the forest understory is gone completely, it stands to reason that ground-nesting birds will be more exposed to predators and the elements. If they survive, they'll soon be looking for a new home. As plants in the midstory die or graduate into the canopy, birds that nest and forage there will be homeless too. Even spiders will be affected when they have fewer places to attach a web. And what about the insects they were hoping to catch in those webs? As any ecologist will tell you, this whole food web can get complicated in a hurry.

One landmark study of these indirect effects involved enclosures rather than exclosures. Back in the 1980s, biologist David deCalesta used four of them as deer pens to simulate deer densities of ten, twenty, forty, and sixty-five per square mile. (Keep in mind that Dairymen's had over one hundred deer per square mile for a much longer duration. So have the suburbs of many major American cities.) Within each enclosure, 10 percent of the area was clear-cut and 30 percent was thinned. Deer were kept in these enclosures for an entire decade, from 1979 until 1990. That's when the deer were released and the fences came down.

In 1991 deCalesta counted birds at the locations where each enclosure had been. He didn't find much difference in the ground- or upper canopy–nesting species. But when it came to birds that nest in the mid-story, he found significant differences between the areas with the lowest and highest deer densities. The pen with the most deer had 37 percent fewer birds and 27 percent less species diversity. Some species disappeared as soon as deer reached densities of twenty per square mile. Even phoebes and robins had gone missing at sixty-five deer per square mile. DeCalesta concluded that the "threshold deer density for effect on habitat and song-birds within managed (100-year rotation) forests was between 20 and 40 deer per square mile."[5] This isn't anywhere near the one hundred deer per square mile that once roamed Dairymen's, and chances are quite good that more deer per square mile live in the neighborhood where you're sitting right now as you read this.

The experiment was over when deCalesta finished counting his birds in 1991. Since then, the plants and trees in these experimental plots have only had to contend with a lower ambient population of deer that's now at more "normal" levels. But what if an ecologist with a discerning eye returned to this same patch of woods twenty years later—thirty years after the original experiment began? All these years later, would the effects of a decade's extra deer somehow still be echoing and reverberating through the ecosystem?

The answer, of course, is yes. The ecologist was Dr. Timothy Nuttle from Indiana University of Pennsylvania. In 2011 he and his collaborators

published a groundbreaking study that sheds new light on these questions. Its title was "Legacy of Top-down Herbivore Pressure Ricochets
Back Up Multiple Trophic Levels in Forest Canopies over 30 Years."[6]

I knew deer were the herbivore in question, that "trophic" had to do
with eating, and that a ricochet lasting thirty years was probably not a
good thing. To learn more, I asked Nuttle to walk me through the experiment and its results. Here's a greatly simplified version.

"Short term," he told me, "we know that too many hungry deer can
eliminate the habitat where ground-nesting and midstory birds eat, nest,
and rest. But here's the question: How does herbivory by whitetails affect
bird communities in the long term? As whatever trees are left behind by
deer eventually grow and mature, how do those effects extend to birds in
the canopy?"

"To find out," he said, "we went back to deCalesta's original study
site. It was the perfect place for a brand-new experiment. Back then, he
manipulated deer densities for ten years. Since then, deer densities have
been lower—and also roughly similar all across the area where the four
enclosures used to be. We knew that any effects we found would be a
direct result of what happened during those ten years. It wouldn't just be
correlation; it would be causal. And if there were differences, we needed
to figure out what the mechanism was. How did all this work?"

To learn the answer, Nuttle and his team focused on the areas within
each enclosure that had been clear-cut. They were especially curious about
what happens in a young forest that's starting over after logging, a fire,
or a storm. Within these areas they measured several different variables
and analyzed their relationships. To determine trees' number and size,
they counted them and then estimated their basal area by calculating each
tree's areal cross section at about chest height. Other variables included
tree diversity and composition, foliage density in the canopy, insect abun-
dance and composition, and bird number and composition.

The study involved much careful measuring and counting of trees,
caterpillars, and birds. The only exception to all this low-tech data collection was an ingenious technique botanists have developed to measure
canopy foliage density and leaf area indices. Using a specialized digital
camera with an ultra-wide-angle lens that covers a full 180 degrees, they

aim straight up from the forest floor and take hundreds of hemispheric canopy photos. When captured on a cloudless day with bright sunlight filtering through the canopy, these photos can be quite beautiful. But as much as one might enjoy their aesthetic value, they're studied most closely by a piece of software that analyzes the light patterns and uses certain mathematical relationships to obtain a measure of foliage density at that particular location. Average out the results for multiple photos, and you get a single foliage density value for each stand.

And the result? "The details are complicated," Nuttle said. "But we found that one simple relationship seems key. Both deer and caterpillars like to eat leaves from the same trees, and for the same reasons. They're more delicious and digestible than the leaves on other trees. If deer eat those leaves first, before the seedling or saplings can even turn into trees, then caterpillars don't get them. Fewer caterpillars in the canopy, fewer birds. So apart from deer eating the places where birds would nest and rest, the closest link between deer and birds is caterpillars."

In their paper Nuttle and his coauthors describe "a five-step trophic ricochet: top-down release of ungulates has shifted forest tree communities to less-palatable species that present a less-dense food resource (foliage) for canopy herbivores (caterpillars) and their predators (insectivorous birds). Furthermore, this browsing legacy persists long after ungulate density has been equalized and trees have escaped browsing by growing into the canopy."

How long does the legacy persist? In the paper's abstract Nuttle and his coauthors write, "Because recruitment of trees from seedlings to the canopy occurs over a relatively brief period (ca. 10 yr), with membership in the canopy lasting an order of magnitude longer, our results show that even short-term perturbations in ungulate density may cause centuries-long disruptions to forest ecosystem structure and function.... As predators decline and ungulate herbivores increase worldwide, similar impacts may result that persist long after herbivore density becomes effectively managed."

The answer is that these dubious "legacies" can last decades and even centuries. Even though deer densities were lower than at Dairymen's, and even though the damage was less severe, disruptions to the forest ecosystem were still significant. And they were going to last a long, long time.

A skeptic might feel we're being a little too hard on the deer. And were the study's deer densities of ten, twenty, forty, and sixty-five per square mile even all that high? After all, when populations across large swaths of the landscape dip to ten and twenty per square mile, state wildlife agencies receive floods of complaints from angry deer hunters. Even deer densities of forty and sixty-five per square mile are much lower than those now taken for granted in many American suburbs and exurbs. For those who feel we should leave those deer alone and let nature take its course, I include one more part of this story that's rarely told.

As Nuttle walked me through dozens of charts and graphs, he pointed out a detail I might never have noticed. "See these numbers along the X axis? Back during the original study, the experimenters tried to maintain their simulated deer densities within each enclosure at ten, twenty, forty, and eighty deer per square mile. But the numbers weren't perfectly constant. It was a ten-year experiment, and most deer don't live that long. Since all the deer were does, no fawns were born inside the enclosures. So during that decade, dozens of deer died and new ones were put into replace them.

"The ones that died," he said, "especially in the high-density enclosures? It mostly happened during hard winters when there wasn't enough browse to go around. So the data in that study, and now in ours, wasn't perfectly tidy—particularly in the high-density enclosures. The one that was supposed to be at eighty deer per square mile? In the end the researchers settled for sixty-five and reported that number. When a deer in one of those enclosures starved, it didn't seem like a good idea to immediately add another one."

Grow Deer or Grow Trees

The conflict is a simple one: A forester's job is to plant seedlings and grow more trees. A deer's job is to eat seedlings and make more deer.

Some days the deer win; some days the foresters win. The deer are hungry, but hungry foresters need their paychecks too—paychecks that depend on revenue from timber sales, which in the long run depends on new seedlings growing up to replace trees that have been harvested.

Both deer and foresters are highly motivated. So far, at least, the foresters seem to be learning faster than the deer. They're learning the hard way how overabundant deer impact the forest. They're also learning to mitigate those impacts. True, their goals are different from those of botanists or ecologists, and their solutions may not always fit a less managed, industrial forest. Still, they have their own unique insights into some of the very same problems.

Like the botanists I'd already talked with, foresters are learning about deer impacts through careful study and analysis. The difference is that the foresters' experimental plots are a bit larger, they can't build an exclosure big enough to exclude deer from an entire forest, and their paychecks depend on their ability to defeat deer. Here in northern Wisconsin, so do our property taxes.

My wife and I live in Douglas County. A third larger than Rhode Island, it has about 4 percent of the population. To support even our minimal infrastructure, we'd all be paying a lot more in taxes if the county weren't able to generate an annual three million to four million dollars through timber sales. At 273,000 acres, ours is the largest county forest in the state and the fourth largest in the nation. If it's managed carefully and sustainably, timber sales can continue producing those kind of revenues just about indefinitely.

To learn more about how deer make the job more challenging, I talked with Craig Golembiewski, one of our four county foresters. It's his job to manage seventy-three thousand acres of forest for recreation, wildlife, and a profitable but sustainable yield of timber. For him, long-term sustainability is part of the job description.

"It's like being a farmer," he said, "only you have to plan way ahead and be very patient. The trees we plant this year won't be harvested for another forty to eighty years. The ones we're cutting today were planted a while back. We cut a few stands every year, but only what we can sustain at the same level indefinitely. At least that's the plan."

Craig manages a patchwork mosaic of hardwoods and softwoods that are all maturing at different times and different rates. Every time a stand is harvested, it needs to be replaced with new seedlings. Aspen, oak, and maple regenerate naturally; jack pine and red pine are replanted by hand-planted seedlings or by aerial seeding. Some stands are thousands of acres, others less than a hundred. For each of them, Craig has a plan. Unfortunately, so do the deer.

Back at the office, Craig has already explained what he's up against. For the rest of the day, he's going to actually show me. We'll stop at half a dozen different plantings. Each will tell its own story about deer and forests, and each will be instructive in its own way. At some of those stands, Craig is winning. At others, at least for now, the deer are winning.

That was definitely the case at our first stop. Three years earlier this stand had been planted with rows of two-year-old root stock, red pine seedlings that were already off to a good start. Deer were waiting to welcome them.

"Deer really love freshly planted nursery stock," said Craig. "They'll browse on it preferentially, over anything else that's growing out here. I've seen places, and this was one of them, where deer went right down the row and took a bite out of every single seedling. Some survived, and some didn't. Take a look over here. I'll show you what I mean."

Craig pointed to some seedlings that were a foot high. Others were still only a few inches tall. We could see where they'd been, quite literally, nipped in the bud. Others were brown and dead, with their topmost terminal bud missing entirely.

Later I heard similar stories from foresters in British Columbia, Maine, and everywhere in between. No one was certain exactly how deer could smell, taste, or see the difference. One crew of planters in Pennsylvania was even instructed to plant seedlings in brushy areas where they'd be hidden from deer. They'd grow more slowly, the forester reasoned, but at least they'd be safe from deer. It didn't work. Even though the seedlings were hidden from view, the deer found them almost immediately.

Somehow deer are able to zero in on transplanted seedlings that have been carefully watered and fertilized back at the nursery. These seedlings are measurably more nutritious and higher in protein, and deer can tell the difference without using lab equipment. One possibility is that these seedlings actually have a different, more appetizing scent. Or, the deer may just be seeing differences we're unable to discern. They can see farther into the UV spectrum than we can, and they may also be able to differentiate better between shades of green and blue that look identical to us.

—◦—

Our second stop was at a plot about five years farther along. There, a few scattered trees were almost six feet tall. Most, however, were only waist high. Others were little more than seedlings. Nearly all of these trees had been nibbled on by deer. Were it not for that, they'd be much taller by now.

"If you know what to look for," said Craig, "you can still see the scars." He got down on one knee and gently bent the broomstick-size trunk to one side. Then he pointed to a sharp bend at the base of the trunk. "Right here. That's where this one got nipped off when it was just a seedling. See the brown spot? But then the trunk grew out this way instead, with a sharp bend until it found its way back to vertical."

Craig showed me similar scars and crooked trunks on three or four more trees. This was definitely a dangerous place to be a pine seedling. He also pointed out one more thing that has disturbing implications for nonmanaged forests that have been damaged by overabundant deer.

"Remember," Craig asked, "how ferns and sedges that take over when deer have browsed everything else? Deer don't eat them, they get established, and nothing else has a chance. That's one reason we scarify the ground so heavily before we plant these stands. Otherwise the trees would never get a toehold."

(By scarifying, Craig meant using a bulldozer with a giant plowlike implement to rip a swath of two-foot furrows across the entire surface of a pine plantation that's just been harvested. This would not be an ideal solution for most forests—or indeed for most suburban parks.)

"Around here," said Craig, "it's mainly Pennsylvania sedge that takes over. This stuff right here. Looks like grass, but its root system is incredible. Watch this." With that he began stomping and scraping the ground with his heavy work boots. Next he slammed one heel into the ground as hard as he could . . . and again. And then he slammed the other. This demented dance continued for several seconds. Even forewarned, I found it a bit alarming.

When Craig stopped, he'd barely made a dent. The wet ground was soft, and he had managed to scrape away the aboveground portion of the sedges. But then he pointed to the thick, fibrous root mat he'd just revealed. "See that? That's not going to let any other plant get a start. Here we're in a pine plantation. We can use bulldozers and scarifiers to tear all this up when we replant. But way out in the woods somewhere? If there are too many deer, that forest is going to be changed for a long time."

After climbing out of the truck at our third stop, we saw thousands of small saplings, none of them more than a foot high. They were scattered randomly, and most of them seemed to be doing okay.

Craig explained that this stand had been harvested a few years back. The ground was torn up from the logging operation, and was then scraped and scarified even further to take care of the sedges. The very next spring these trees were planted by aerial seeding. They'll take longer to reach maturity than seedlings would, but this time there's less up-front labor and expense. Even if the deer get some of them, Craig hopes plenty will remain.

Craig showed me, however, why these seedlings are still in danger. "Brush the palm of your hand across this one," he instructed. I reached for the three-inch seedling and gently caressed it. Soft and feathery—and to a deer, delicious.

"Now do the same with the bud tip on that tree over here. This one is left over from an earlier planting. It's only about four feet high, but it's escaping. A deer would have to be starving before it would go after that one."

I dragged my palm across the sapling's highest terminal bud. A wire brush. Same with the bud I tried on one of the branches. This tree was finally safe.

At our fourth stop I learned the bizarre lengths to which foresters will go in an effort to protect vulnerable seedlings. Here a thick stand of healthy-looking red pines had all reached a uniform height of four to five feet. Strangely, each red pine seemed to be sprouting a half-dozen large white flowers.

Red pines, however, don't actually grow white flowers. On closer inspection these "blossoms" were actually small scraps of paper that had been carefully stapled to thousands of seedlings. The technique is called "bud-capping," and it's a desperate, last-ditch strategy to protect a tree's tender new growth.

These bud caps are made from special paper that's permeable but still quite durable. They've been applied in a way that doesn't harm the tree, but they're still tight enough so deer can't easily nuzzle them off. These trees received their bud caps four or five years ago, and the caps are still there.

By now the sun and rain have softened the paper. Tips of branches are poking through, and so is that all-important topmost terminal bud the tree relies on for vertical growth. Next year's spring rains will wash away what remains of these bud caps. But by now these trees are relatively safe.

Tender new seedlings without bud caps don't stand a chance, even with repeated replantings. Bud caps are a labor-intensive solution, and the labor is provided by migrant workers from Mexico—the same crews that arrive every spring to plant these seedlings in the first place.

Every April one of these crews stays at a resort just down the road from where I live. The forestry contractor gets a special rate, and it's extra business for the resort during the weeks before fishing season. Occasionally these crews arrive at other times of year. They arrive in the night, quietly and unannounced. Their secret mission: to protect vulnerable pine seedlings by battling deer with office supplies. Instead of being issued a shovel, each worker is given small scraps of paper and a loaded stapler. And thus the war continues.

If you're ever looking for a good hunting spot on public land, you might want to ask someone like Craig. He knows where the deer are; he can even send you to areas where the herd could use a little thinning. He sees things you or I wouldn't notice. Like the botanists I've met, he can probably spot the clues from behind the wheel when he's driving down the highway at sixty miles an hour.

I'm not a forester or a botanist, and I'm only beginning to see these clues. Still, every now and then I see them when I'm not even looking. If you want to find a hunting spot where deer will be especially numerous, and if you know what to look for, just ask the trees.

❧

At our last two stops of the day, it was easy, even for me, to read these tree stories. One was a hardwood stand that had been harvested a couple years earlier. It turns out hardwoods aren't so hard when they're young. These tender oak shoots were only a foot or two high, and nearly all of them had been nibbled by deer.

Some would survive, but many would not. Craig pointed to the tender new growth at the end of one shoot. Even in August these succulent one- and two-inch oak leaves were still unfurling. "This is what they're after" he told me. "To a deer this is delicious. They've already been here. They'll be back. Who knows? Maybe tonight."

At our final stop we saw small, stunted jack pines with clear browse lines that nearly matched some of those I'd seen at Dairymen's. There were no lollipop trees here, but there were some definite umbrellas. Hundreds of them.

"This is all county forest back in here," Craig explained. "But there are a couple houses just over that hill. Every winter those people feed the deer. Down the road are half a dozen more houses, all on little lots over by the lake. Some of those people feed deer too. They love living out here, and they love nature, but unfortunately none of them are hunters."

Craig explained that their feeding, probably in amounts well over Wisconsin's two-gallon legal limit, keeps the deer concentrated in this small area all winter long. They bed down somewhere nearby, head over to the feeders every night, and then return here to browse on whatever they find. "Basically," he said, "they come for the corn and stay for the salad."

Craig told me this is a familiar pattern. Whenever someone's feeding deer, he can see clear evidence in the adjacent county forest. A few years back he harvested a good-size stand of red pine, and then had an especially difficult time getting new seedlings started the next spring. Deer ate almost every single one. The next year he tried bud caps, but even then he lost a lot of seedlings.

"The whole time," he told me, "I knew exactly what was going on. One house—just one house, right across the road from there. They were feeding the deer, and the deer stuck around all winter. Lots of them."

Thanks to baiting, Craig has observed these same patterns way out in the woods, miles from the nearest house. "You wouldn't believe some of the corn piles we find out there. Whenever I spot anything especially interesting, I pass the GPS coordinates along to the game warden.

"Don't get me wrong," says Craig. "I wouldn't want his job. But I am getting good at finding bait piles. You don't even have to look for browse lines. Just walk around in the woods and listen for blue jays. Find the blue jays, you'll find the corn."

Craig explained why a little baiting can lead to a lot of damage: "The bowhunters might only be baiting in October, November, and maybe a little bit of December. Gun hunters, maybe only a couple weeks in November. That's enough. It draws in deer and concentrates them in one spot, and at just the wrong time. Most other plants are done. They're brown and dead, or at least dormant. But the new growth on those pine seedlings is still green and tender. When the corn is gone, the deer start in on their salad course."

⚬⚬⚬

The peanut butter sandwiches I wolfed down in Craig's truck between stops were OK. Maybe a little dry. But later, after Craig dropped me off and I was driving home from the county forestry building, I found myself craving salad. I remembered what those tiny jack pine seedlings had felt like beneath my fingertips. Soft, feathery tendrils. And there was some-thing vaguely familiar about that shape. Dill. Yes. That's it. They looked almost like dill. Or maybe the late-summer asparagus in the back corner of our garden, after we stop cutting it every July and let it grow.

But these seedlings wouldn't taste like anything else. They'd have a flavor all their own. Tart. Tangy. Piney. And would the tender terminal buds on those maple and oak seedlings be as sweet as the buds of any artichoke or asparagus? Would the maple buds taste like maple syrup? Would the oak seedlings have a mild, nutty sweetness? Would they taste like acorns, or more like those bright green pistachios?

CHAPTER 7

We Get the Leftovers

Hunting is no less important than is the plow. Tracing our connections to deer can reveal disquieting realities and unexpected dilemmas. . . . Deer are not merely part of the scenery, not just works of natural artistry carrying on lives remote and disconnected from our own. We are bound together with deer in an intricate relationship centered around cultivated crops.

—RICHARD NELSON IN *HEART AND BLOOD*

It's a warm, sunny March afternoon. I'm looking out over an eighty-acre alfalfa field that was seeded last fall. Tender green shoots are just beginning to appear. The ground is still damp from melting snow. It's been a long winter. Out in the dense woods that surround this field, hungry deer are waiting. Already, hoofprints from last night are everywhere.

It will be a perfect evening for deer hunting. True, deer season won't be here for six more months, but our freezer is almost empty, and tonight I'm here with a special "agricultural damage mitigation shooting permit" that allows me to harvest deer outside the regular season. More informally, it's known as an "ag tag."

When I called this farmer a couple nights ago, he told me he'd seen over seventy deer out here the night before. A neighbor driving by claimed to have seen two hundred. I assumed these were wild exaggerations. I also assumed that no deer would appear until just before dusk—if then. It would turn out that I was wrong on both counts.

By the time the first deer was in range, dozens more were arriving from the far edge of the field. I had never in my life seen so many deer in one place. When I pulled the trigger, all but one stampeded toward the woods. Hearing more hoofbeats behind me, I turned to see a dozen more deer fleeing in the other direction.

Tomorrow will bring a long morning of amateur butchering out in the garage. By afternoon one deer will be in the freezer. Meanwhile, later tonight, before I'm more than a few miles down the road, the other 199 will be back out in this field.

The Angel's Share

Tonight and every night, hungry deer are trickling out into farm fields all across America. Collectively this nightly buffet costs farmers billions of dollars every year. For some individual farmers, it can be a serious threat to their livelihood.

In one New Jersey study, researchers used exclosures, comparative yield measurements, and other techniques to measure deer damage on 1,410 acres of agricultural crops spread across 111 different farms. They calculated that the season's average economic loss directly attributable to deer was $1,253.48 per acre. Similarly, after surveying 583 acres in vegetable production, they calculated deer-related losses at $2,443 per acre.[1]

Another New Jersey study found that 25 percent of responding farmers had abandoned a parcel of tillable ground because of excessive deer damage, and that 36 percent had for the same reason ceased growing their preferred crop. Some attempted to address the problem by hunting themselves, inviting others to hunt their lands, or taking advantage of special shooting permits like the one I was using as this chapter began. Other farmers, however, had little recourse. A full 50 percent of respondents owned less than eight acres of deer cover and typically rented or leased at least a quarter of their land. They reported being unable to use shooting permits on 40 percent of rented land, and that 20 percent of their rented land was closed to all hunting.

They also of course had no control over what happened on adjacent land. Forty-three percent of respondents indicated the presence of a hundred-acre or greater parcel of land serving as a deer refuge within one mile of their most severe crop losses. In a sign that many of those de facto deer refuges might be in places where sprawling suburbs and exurbs butt up against farmers' fields, 32 percent of respondents stated that firearms discharge ordinances were impacting their ability to reduce deer numbers.[2]

In an Illinois survey, 65 percent of farmers stated they'd experienced wildlife damage during the preceding twelve months. Of those, 91 percent reported deer damage. On average, they estimated that deer had damaged twenty acres.[3]

Deer are hungry, and the numbers add up quickly. A typical deer consumes eight to ten pounds of vegetation per day. Since a deer's metabolism slows in the winter, and since sometimes there's just plain less food available, let's round down and estimate that each of America's thirty million deer eats around three thousand pounds of vegetation per year. (This "three thousand pounds per year" figure is the one most often quoted by biologists, agronomists, and wildlife managers.) A lot of those deer live in farm country, where for several months of the year they subsist largely on crops like soybeans, corn, and alfalfa. Although precise statistics for the United States as a whole are difficult to come by, one researcher very conservatively estimated farmers' annual losses at two billion dollars. The same researcher found that 80 percent of farmers had experienced wildlife damage to their crops, and that 53 percent indicated the damage exceeded their tolerance.[4]

For most crops, however, deer-proof fences just aren't affordable or practical. Deer can easily leap a five-strand barbwire fence that keeps out cattle. On open ground, a deer-proof fence needs to be at least eight feet high. That's not affordable or practical for anything but high-value, low-acreage deer candy crops like cranberries, apples, or strawberries. Most farmers just resign themselves to sharing with deer.

Vintners and distillers sometimes call the amount lost from their barrels due to evaporation the "angel's share." For farmers the situation isn't so different. *Angels,* however, is not one of the many words I've heard them use to describe deer.

Although the impacts of deer on agriculture are tough to measure for our nation as a whole, they definitely can be measured, as in that New Jersey study, one field at a time. To learn more, I was about to head out into the field.

IN THE FIELD

An hour before sunrise I climbed into an unmarked pickup with US government plates. It happened to be driven by my friend Eric Fromm. He helped me get started deer hunting, and together we wrote a book about how to butcher your own deer. But even if we'd never met until now, I'd still be interviewing him for this chapter. This is his day job.

He's a US Department of Agriculture–Animal and Plant Health Inspection Service (USDA-APHIS) Wildlife Specialist who covers a big chunk of northwestern Wisconsin. All spring and summer he and his colleagues have put in long days clearing beaver dams from trout streams, investigating wolf depredation complaints, and relocating troublesome bears to new zip codes. Now, in October and November, they'll work even longer days appraising deer damage in corn and soybean fields.

Eric explained why these appraisals have to be completed during such a narrow window. "The farmers all want to wait until the last minute so that the deer have time to do as much damage as possible. If we went out sooner, we'd see less damage and they'd get a smaller check. But when the corn or beans are ready, and when the moisture content gets down to where it should be, they want to get out there with a combine and start harvesting so they can get those crops in before they're rained on."

Some farmers hardly wait for him to finish. "I'll walk out one end of the field," he told me, "and hear the combine behind me, starting in at the other end. When the weather's good, farmers can't afford to wait."

For both corn and beans, the appraisal process takes a sharp eye, a sharp pencil, and some sizable spreadsheets back at the office. The general concept is simple enough: Start by knowing how big the whole field is. Then measure the areas that have been eaten completely or damaged partially.

For now, set aside the areas that are totally gone. Then use carefully chosen samples to calculate the expected yield from both the damaged and undamaged areas. To do that, test the samples' moisture levels, weigh them, and do a little calculating. Actually, a lot of calculating.

Depending on how the numbers add up, these farmers could receive a sizable check compensating them for part of the damage. In return they're asked to open their land to hunting. They may even receive shooting permits that can be used outside the regular season. (That's how I ended up on the springtime hunt that began this chapter.) Although the details vary, Wisconsin is just one of several states with programs like this. Wisconsin's program, however, is one of the few that also includes bears, geese, and turkeys.

I was curious to see firsthand how all this works. To be honest, I was less interested in the math than in what all this deer damage would actually look like out in the field. I was about to find out.

As the eastern sky turned gray and the sun finally rose, we drove for over an hour before reaching our first farm. These fields, like most of the others I'd see, were rented from another landowner several miles down the road from where our farmer lived. We planned to stop and say hello if the fields were near a farmhouse, but this time there was no farmhouse in sight. We pulled off the two-lane blacktop and followed a two-track farm road out along the edge of the field.

The trail ended where the field farthest from the road began. Before we even got out of the truck, Eric spread out an aerial photo so we could get oriented. This one was black and white, and the two fields we'd be appraising were identified with color-coded highlighting: yellow for corn, orange for beans.

Eric pointed to the fields we'd be appraising. "I remember these fields from previous years," he said. "But even if I'd never been here before, we could look at this aerial and have a pretty good idea of where the worst damage will be. See these lighter spots out in the middle, here and here? That's probably bear damage. We'll need to keep track of that too."

Eric explained that these aerials, taken just a couple weeks earlier, are pretty much the only way to spot most bear damage. There could be a clearing the size of a football field out there and you'd never be able to see it from the edge of the field. A farmer would not be happy to discover this while combining.

Next he pointed to the corner of the bean field we were about to enter. "Over here, with the woods on both sides? The deer will be hammering that corner hard. Along the south side, right next to that swampy area? Same thing. Deer like to stay close to cover. We'll see the most damage along the edge, especially by the corners. Let's go check it out."

It only took Eric a moment to grab his equipment from the back of the truck. We'd be traveling light. First came a long-handled, walk-behind measuring wheel and a white plastic five-gallon pail. Into the pail went a tape measure, a scale, an odd-looking serrated metal ring, and a mysterious electronic device. Eric explained that the first gadget was for shelling corn, the second for testing moisture. Soon I'd see both in action.

Our first field was a bean field. Even I could tell that this one was worth a look. The ground beneath our feet was covered with deer tracks. It looked like a cow path. I could see deer droppings here and there, and the outer two rows of beans were pretty much a total loss. Nothing but stubble. As we approached the corner, the damage extended farther and farther out into the field.

It was time to do some measuring. Eric reset his measuring wheel to zero and began wheeling it ahead of him. When we reached the corner, Eric pulled the notepad from his pocket and scribbled some numbers on his sketch. Then he pointed along the next fencerow we'd be walking. "The damage goes about the same distance the other direction," he explained. "We'll measure, but it's going to be about the same. And we'll just subtract the two outer rows along this whole side of the field. They're a total loss."

More hiking, more sketching and scribbling, and it was time to take a few samples. With beans it's as simple as pulling up a plant and counting the pods. If you know how many pods to a plant, how far apart the plants are, and how far apart the rows are, you're pretty close to knowing how many bushels per acre. All that remained was to open some pods and harvest a few tablespoons of beans for Eric's handheld moisture tester.

While Eric was doing all this, he also sampled a few beans more directly. It looked like he was chewing pretty hard. "Mmmmm. Try some," he told me. "They're not bad. But they're not quite ready to harvest. Later they'll have a nice nutty texture, just like those raw soybeans at the health food store. These are still a little gummy when you bite down. Tasty, but they stick to your molars."

I tried a pod full to see for myself. It was true. Gummy and chewy—but sweet. A moment later, the electronic moisture tester agreed with his assessment. Not quite ready for harvest. A nice flavor though.

"Don't start eating too many," cautioned Eric. "You won't be able to stop. That's what happens to the deer. Loosens 'em right up. See over there?"

I looked on the ground where he was pointing. No dry, discrete pellets this time. It looked like an extra-soupy cow pie, and it's what happens when a deer that's been enjoying its usual high-fiber diet suddenly switches to straight soybeans, which are about 50 percent protein and 50 percent fat. I could still identify dozens of pale seed hulls that were about the size of a soybean. (Later that week I observed signs of these same digestive symptoms near a stand of oak trees where gluttonous deer had eaten way too many acorns. Absent our bean fields, acorns are probably the closest nutritional equivalent that deer would ever encounter.)

Next we were on to our first cornfield. To reach it, we'd first cut a corner through an area thick with waist-high grass. It was easy walking, though. We just followed the deer trail. As we entered the field, Eric told me we'd probably see more damage when we got a little farther from the beans. "Corn has less protein and fat. It's mostly carbohydrates. Deer love that too. But when they can choose between corn and beans, they'll almost always go for the beans first."

Still, we hadn't walked far before I saw corn that looked like it had been hit hard. Nearly all the stalks were broken off near ground level. They were lying in random directions, one on top of the other. Obviously not wind. The cobs were still attached to the stalks, but every single one was stripped clean.

"Is this what deer damage looks like?" I asked.

"Ah ... No. Sorry," he said. "Raccoons. Not part of the program."

Eric then explained how raccoons usually go for the corn at an earlier stage, when even field corn is sweet and tender. At that stage it probably tastes a lot like the corn on the cob you ate last August, except without the butter and salt. To reach it, raccoons climb up a stalk until it breaks. They ride down with the stalk, sit on the ground while eating the corn that's now within easy reach, and repeat. One can almost imagine them out there in the darkness, squealing and chirping with delight. It must be great fun—for raccoons, if not for farmers. In a single night a small band of masked, marauding raccoons can do some serious damage.

These raccoons had been here more than once though. Eric pointed to the trail over at the edge of the field. It was narrower and fainter than a deer trail, but obvious now that I knew what it was. "You'll see that a lot in spots like this. It's a little low here. We've got a swampy area over on the other side of the fence. Raccoon heaven."

After walking only a few more yards, we came to a part of the corn field where deer had been dining regularly for the past two or three months. Within a twenty-yard radius, Eric was able to show me all three types of deer damage you'd see in a cornfield. He explained that deer damage can look different, depending on whether it occurred as the corn was still growing, a little later as the cob was forming, or after the corn was mature and the kernels fully formed.

He then showed me examples of each. First a patch of slender stalks that were bitten off about waist high. This happened a few months ago, back last summer. Now these stalks were dry and fibrous, almost woody. Back then they would have been green and succulent. Every single one was snipped off within inches of the same height—about the same level as a deer's upper lip.

Next Eric pointed out a small cob, roughly half the usual size, that had been bitten clean in half. This had happened more recently, probably September, when the cob was still tender and not yet fully formed.

A few yards farther down the row, he pointed to an ear that had its husk pulled back and about a quarter of its kernels missing. Some were still lying in the dust. A deer had been here very recently, maybe even last night. It had also been a very messy eater.

Bears, I would soon learn, are different. From their perspective, at least, they waste very little. It wasn't much longer before I saw my first example.

"Here's some bear damage from about a month ago," Eric told me. "Later we might see fresher damage. But mostly bears like to get in here earlier, when the corn is still tender and sweet."

Just in from the edge of the field was a ten-yard circle without a single stalk of corn still standing. They were lying flat on the ground in oddly symmetrical patterns. All the cobs had been stripped from the stalks, and every single cob was stripped clean.

Eric explained that bears tend to waddle out into the cornfield, sit upright like a giant furry sumo wrestler, and begin raking in huge armfuls of corn. Next they pick cobs off and chew on them one at a time. They then shift a bit to the left or right, and do it again. And again. This leaves characteristic bundles of stalks all laid down in the same direction, but with a bit of a swirled pattern. Here and there it almost looks like giant cornstalk mattresses.

Eric paced off the clearing created last August by this particular bear's midnight snack, and then took careful notes before we continued along the edge of the cornfield. As we approached a corner near the woods, deer damage became more pronounced. Looking down, even an amateur like me could spot tracks and deer pellets. It was like following a cow path. Here and there were kernels of corn that had probably fallen from the jaws of a gluttonous deer just hours before. At the corner, unsurprisingly, a heavily traveled deer trail led into the woods.

Soon it was time to take a few samples. Eric explained that we'd measure out a thousandth of an acre, weigh our sample and test its moisture, do a little calculating, and then move the decimal point to figure out the yield for an entire acre. We'd do that a few more times in both damaged and undamaged areas. Once we knew the size of the entire field and the size of the damaged areas, all that remained would be a little more calculating. On the two sides bordered by woods, we'd subtract the outside row as a total loss. For Eric, at least, that number was easy to calculate once he knew the size and shape of the field.

To measure out a thousandth of an acre, you need to first know how far apart the rows are, then how far apart the plants are within each row. Those numbers are different than they were a generation ago. I learned that today's incredible corn yields are due only in part to better plant breeding, genetic engineering, petroleum-based pesticides and herbicides, and huge quantities of nitrogen fertilizer that's made from natural gas. A part of the secret is simply cramming more and more corn plants into every single acre.

The standard spacing for rows is now thirty inches, and some farmers are planting them even closer, while simultaneously planting individual stalks closer together within each row. But even with plenty of fertilizer, farmers are now reaching a point of diminishing returns. This also, I learned, makes cornfields a lot harder to walk through than they used to be.

Eric told me he grew up bowhunting in cornfields on windy autumn days. "The deer would be feeding, or even bedded down out there. As long as there was wind to rattle the leaves, they couldn't hear you. You could sneak right up on them. But that was when the rows were at thirty-eight inches."

The old "hide-and-seek in the cornfield" strategy wouldn't work nearly as well today. Even if you're not carrying a bow and arrows, and even if you're not trying to cross rows, it's not much fun trying to walk through a modern cornfield. Deer apparently feel the same. Nearly all the damage we found was along the edges. Once we were in eight or ten rows, there was none at all.

At our first sampling site, I watched Eric use his tape to measure out a thousandth of an acre. Then he picked every single ear of corn along that length of the row. Into the bucket, up on the scale, and then dumped back out on the ground. "Whitetail bait," he said.

Then, using an aluminum ring with jagged serrations along its tapered, corncob-size inner circumference, he shelled enough kernels from one of the ears to fill the reservoir of his electronic moisture tester. It only took a few seconds before he had a reading. "Down to 16 percent," he told me. "Just about ready to harvest. Here. Try some."

The kernels did indeed have a dry, nutlike texture. They didn't stick to my molars like the beans I'd sampled earlier. Although the texture was pleasant enough, the flavor left something to be desired. Not sweet like the beans. Definitely not sweet like sweet corn. Mealier and starchier, vaguely reminiscent of stale Fritos or Doritos. Could have used a little salt.

A week later I was back out in the field with one of Eric's colleagues, Wildlife Specialist Chad Alberg. At our first stop we parked beside a massive array of gleaming, fifty-foot-tall steel cylinders connected to a towering superstructure. From the central stack a slender stainless-steel tube extended to the center of each cylinder's conical lid. One of these giant cylinders was a propane-powered dryer; the others were all storage bins.

This farmer's operation was large enough that he'd been able to invest in his own drying and storage, right out here at the edge of the field. By drying and storing grain here, he'd have the option of selling it later if prices seemed poised to rise. And when a lot of corn needed to come off those fields in a hurry, his crew would be able to spend more time harvesting and less time driving truckloads of grain into town.

Today we'd be appraising the deer and bear damage in fields scattered all over this part of the county. All the corn belonged to this same farmer, and it would all end up in these bins. Most of the fields, however, were rented. The farmer himself lives an eight-hour drive from here, somewhere in northern Illinois.

As on my first trip, we paused in the truck for a moment to study the aerials and get oriented. Chad pointed to some areas along one edge of the field. "See these little blobs that are a paler shade of brown? I bet that's going to be bear damage."

He next pointed to a faded arc where the field was bordered by a series of lake homes. "Along where the houses are, this could be bear too. But I'm betting it's deer. Let's check it out."

Before Chad grabbed his gear from the back of the truck, we deliberated for a moment about how to dress. Although the temperature was still barely above freezing, the sun was climbing higher. We wisely decided to leave our jackets behind, and soon we were sweating. We hiked fast and covered a lot of corn that morning.

One of our first stops was the arc of deer damage Chad had predicted beside the cabins and lake homes. "These deer aren't afraid," he said. "They might even feel safer from predators here. Wouldn't be surprised if someone's feeding them corn at a couple of these houses."

The deer were also getting plenty of corn out here in the field. Over a wide area they'd snipped off every single stalk, all about waist high. Some night in late July, a small herd of deer had enjoyed a pretty solid midnight snack.

Over the next couple hours, we saw more deer damage. Some was more recent, either in the form of cobs bitten cleanly in half or cobs with every kernel freshly removed. We also saw more of those classic bear clearings with their characteristic swirl patterns and cornstalk mattresses. Later that morning we interrupted a bear that was apparently still in the process of making its mysterious ursine crop circles. Although we never actually saw it, there was no mistaking its panicked grunting and wheezing as it crashed off through the cornfield.

As we walked the far side of the field, I asked Chad to help me put all this in perspective. I told him it was hard to find solid deer damage numbers for our nation as a whole. They seemed to all be guesses, and about all I knew for sure was that we have around thirty million deer, each of which eat around three thousand pounds of vegetation a year. For deer in farm country, a lot of those three thousand pounds might be farm crops. But how does deer damage compare with hail, drought, or insects?

Chad thought for a long while before answering. "I'd say . . . It depends. And in a way, deer are just like hail. When there's a thunderstorm, the hail might hit one farm but not the next. Same with deer. For some farmers deer are a big deal. Elsewhere, less so. Same with bears. Here in northern Wisconsin they can cause as much damage as deer. Farther south they're less of a factor. It all depends. And around here we don't have plagues of locusts. So the totals? Who knows?"

Chad then answered a couple important questions I hadn't thought to ask. Around here, he said, a lot more farmers were enrolled in the program for bears than for deer. For them there was a big difference in each animal's perceived value. Bears are pests, but deer are deer.

In fact, only a tiny fraction of all eligible farmers participate in the deer portion of this program. I suspect the same is true in other states that have similar programs. From the farmers I talked with, I heard a variety of reasons.

Some don't want to bother with the paperwork. Others want to maintain more control over hunter access. In places like Buffalo County, farmers make more money leasing out hunting rights, which they can't do while simultaneously being reimbursed for deer damage.

But the biggest reason so few farmers participate in these programs is something Chad summed up neatly the day we were out walking those Wisconsin cornfields owned by the Illinois farmer. "This guy doesn't even live around here," he explained. "For him it's a simple, rational decision. Dollars and cents. But most farmers value the deer more than the dollars.

"They may hunt themselves," he said, "or they may just want to see deer. But for every farmer who gets a check to pay for those outer two rows the deer ate, dozens more farmers are going to pick their corn and leave four rows standing out there on purpose. Why? For the deer, of course."

Abatement and Claims
Both Chad and Eric work for a USDA-APHIS organization called Wildlife Services. It has a remarkable history, one that reflects Americans' changing relationship with wildlife. If you're like most people, you've never heard of it. But in the early part of the twentieth century, every rancher in the West knew and loved one government agency above all others. It was called ADC, short for Animal Damage Control.

Formed in 1895 for the express purpose of eliminating wolves and coyotes from America's West, this small agency within the USDA would eventually come close to working itself out of a job. Over the decades its mission has changed, and it now has a kinder, gentler name to reflect that. Today only a very small number of its employees continue to trap wolves or coyotes that have been depredating livestock. The agency's mission is to reduce conflicts between people and animals, and that's not nearly as simple as it once was. Today its job is to protect agriculture, people, *and* wildlife.

Other than appraising the agricultural damage caused by deer and bears, this might include trapping and relocating nuisance bears, reducing wildlife hazards at airports, removing beavers and their dams from trout streams, dealing with problems caused by huge flocks of blackbirds and starlings, thwarting invasive species, and protecting endangered species.

After a long history of government reorganizations, Wildlife Services is now part of the USDA's APHIS, which also includes organizations that focus on biotechnology, emergency preparedness and response, animal diseases, animal welfare, and even finding and quarantining smuggled plants and animals at ports of entry.

To learn more about the role Wildlife Services plays in this particular program, I met with Bob Willging at his office in Rhinelander,

Wisconsin. Bob is Wildlife Services district supervisor for the northern part of the state, and he has more than a passing interest in deer.

Apart from his day job, he's also the author of *On the Hunt: The History of Deer Hunting in Wisconsin*. This definitive work begins in pre-European-settlement days and ends in the twenty-first century. Its early chapters are filled with black-and-white photos of proud hunters posing beside sagging buck poles at old-time deer camps. Some show entire herds of frozen deer hanging outside hunters' shanties. The hunt was unsustainable, and Bob's middle chapters tell a story of scarcity and near extirpation. His final chapters, however, tell a very different story. In many parts of the state, as is the case across much of the United States and Canada, we now have exactly the opposite problem. We have too many deer.

Which brings me back to Bob's day job and the program that takes up much of his time at the office. Its official name is the Wildlife Damage Abatement and Claims Program (WDACP). During the early-season hunt that began this chapter, I was doing my small part to help with the "abatement" part of the program. The appraisals out in all those corn and bean fields are a key step in the "claims" process.

The program is paid for in part by a surcharge on hunting licenses, and it also covers wildlife other than deer. If your farm has been ravaged by bear, geese, or turkeys, the WDACP may be able to help you too. But today I'm here to talk with Bob about deer. They account for most of the program's abatement activity, and last year they accounted for 76 percent of its appraised losses.[5]

And here's some extra perspective: Bob's office also administers a similar program that pays out compensation for livestock, pets, and bear hounds lost to Wisconsin's seven hundred or so wolves. Last year these depredation claims totaled $203,943.51. Meanwhile, appraised deer damage among the tiny percentage of eligible farmers participating in the WDACP added up to $1,201,192—six times the damage done by wolves.

Bob began by emphasizing that it's called the Abatement and Claims Program, not vice versa. Abatement comes first. "Our goal," he said, is not to get farmers a claim so they can receive a check. Our goal is for them not to have a claim in the first place."

Mostly abatement means shooting. Other measures include temporary electric fences and, on rare occasions, even permanent fences. These require extra paperwork, and the DNR studies the cost-benefit ratio very closely. Usually these projects are only approved for high-value, low-acreage crops like cranberries, strawberries, apples, or nursery stock. When they are, the WDACP covers a full 75 percent of the cost, with the landowner responsible for the remaining 25 percent.

The program is working, Bob said. On farms that have been enrolled for even just a year or two, farmers are seeing significantly less damage. When talking with Eric, Chad, and a number of farmers, I often heard anecdotal evidence of that. Bob told me that broader data for the state as a whole supports the same conclusion. Those trends are independent of whatever is happening at the moment with the state's deer population as a whole.

"The general hunting season controls deer populations on a landscape level," he noted, "but we're dealing with site-specific control. Our primary abatement method is shooting permits, and every now and then that gets controversial. Some hunters think farmers shouldn't shoot deer because the populations are too low. But in most of the state, that's not a problem. And farmers are glad to have this option. What matters to them is the size of the local deer population that's out in their corn, bean, and alfalfa fields every night.

"Plus," he said, "you need to put things in perspective. Compared with the overall harvest, the total number of deer shot under these permits is amazingly low." He has a good point. Last year that number was 2,854, compared with the 336,871 deer harvested by Wisconsin hunters during the regular seasons. (By recent standards that total was on the low side. The state's record, set in 2000, was 615,293 deer.[6])

The program is a great example of interagency cooperation that actually works. In broad outline it goes something like this: If the county chooses to participate in the program, and currently seventy of seventy-two counties do, it creates its own administrative plan. The state's DNR, however, must still approve the plan.

Here's one more place where that public trust doctrine comes into play. Remember, these deer are your deer. For now the state is holding them in public trust. That's why, once the DNR approves a county's plan, it's always the agency that issues the shooting permits. The state also processes claim payments, approves budgets, and approves permanent fence projects when they're recommended as an abatement strategy.

Once the DNR has approved a county's plan, the county is responsible for actually implementing it. They can do it themselves or else contract it out to an individual or to APHIS and its Wildlife Services division. Most counties go with APHIS. "We have a reputation for consistency, accuracy, and professionalism," Bob said. "At times counties have had issues with contractors doing appraisals that are a little shaky. We're the USDA, we know agriculture as well as we know wildlife, and we're accountable if some farmer comes before the county's Land Conservation Committee to contest his claim."

The details are complicated, and farmers can choose to enroll in different variations of the program. To maintain full eligibility they need to call within fourteen days of when damage first occurs, schedule an appraisal ten days in advance of harvest, allow hunting for enrolled species, meet certain shooting permit requirements, and follow all abatement recommendations. If farmers do all those things, and if the deer are hungry, eventually a nice check will be waiting in a mailbox at the end of a long gravel driveway.

The Food Web

None of the farms we appraised on those two days in the fall of 2011 would have any difficulty reaching the program's five-hundred-dollar deductible. One or two would surpass its ten thousand dollar annual cap. That fall, both corn and soybean prices were hitting record highs. (In 2012, after the worst drought in over fifty years, all those new records would be broken again.) Corn was selling for more than seven dollars a bushel, beans more than eleven dollars a bushel. Part of the reason was that record amounts of corn and soy were now being diverted from feedstock to fuel.

For decades American farmers have been producing far more corn and soy than we humans can eat. In response, we fed more grain and soy to our cattle, hogs, and poultry. When that no longer took care of the surplus, we began feeding corn to our cars and trucks. In 2011, for the first time in history, more American corn was used to make ethanol than was fed to livestock. The two were close: The USDA estimated 5.05 billion bushels for ethanol and 5.0 billion bushels for livestock. Each accounted for about 40 percent of the total, with another 20 percent remaining for human consumption.[7] Simultaneously we were ramping up the production of soy-based biodiesel to unprecedented levels.

Without generous taxpayer subsidies that a 2010 study by the Congressional Budget Office put at six billion dollars (which comes out to $1.78 in subsidies for every gallon of gasoline replaced by corn-based ethanol), it's likely that neither ethanol nor biodiesel would be profitable.[8] What's more, neither is a particularly good way of saving energy or reducing greenhouse gas emissions. Although biodiesel comes out a little better, ethanol takes almost as much energy to produce as it yields. When we create and burn a gallon of ethanol, we're using almost twice the energy and creating almost twice the emissions as we would if we skipped the whole exercise and just burned gasoline refined from petroleum. In fact, depending on whose calculations you believe, and depending on just how inclusive those calculations are, ethanol may actually take more energy to produce than it yields at the pump.[9] Ever since 2005, however, the US government has mandated that gasoline contain ethanol, nearly all of which is made from corn.

I didn't think much about all that while we were out walking all those cornfields and bean fields. But I do remember it crossing my mind when Eric and I stopped at a small-town gas station on our way to the next farm. There on the pump was a reminder that some of last year's corn was about to end up in our gas tank. A small decal in the corner of its LCD readout read Contains Ethanol.

Eric had brought a thermos of coffee from home, and I was feeling like I could use a little more caffeine myself. When I went inside for a Coke, I hesitated, then chose Diet. I probably didn't need the high-fructose corn syrup. On my way to the register, I walked by a long row of Doritos in many flavors. Their two main ingredients, no matter how many others may follow, are always corn and vegetable oil ("corn, soy, and/or sunflower").

Back out at the truck, I saw more corn. Eric and I had both remarked on it when we pulled into the station. Beside each pump was a tower of fifty-pound plastic sacks labeled Wildlife Corn. Bow season had begun, gun season was approaching, and bait was convenient. Locally, at least, this year's corn wasn't quite ready to harvest. The "wildlife corn" in these sacks had been harvested the previous year, possibly even earlier. Deer's leftovers left over from last year. In the end they'd get it after all.

Despite the caffeine, we both felt drowsy by the end of the day. Eric had been up since 4:00 a.m., and we'd both hiked in the wind and sun through miles of corn and beans. That afternoon, on the long road home, we both did our best to remain alert and watch for deer.

CHAPTER 8

The Deadliest Animal in North America

Thanks, and have an awesome day!
—Sign customers see as they leave Awesome Auto Body

Never mind grizzlies, wolves, rattlesnakes, or sharks. Instead, fear deer.

Statistically, car crashes make whitetail deer the deadliest animal in North America. Last year an estimated 1.1 million deer-vehicle crashes resulted in about 150 human fatalities, more than ten thousand injuries, and insurance payouts of over $3.8 billion.[1] The total cost for vehicle repairs and medical or funeral bills was undoubtedly far higher.

A disproportionate number of the fatalities involve motorcyclists. The odds are not in their favor. If you hit a deer while driving, you'll be making a trip to the body shop. If you hit one while riding, you'll probably be making a trip to the morgue.

Dan Rogers is one of the rare exceptions. He's a motorcyclist who collided with a deer and lived to tell about it—despite the fact that he wasn't wearing a helmet at the time. The lingering effects of his traumatic brain injury (TBI), however, can often make it difficult for him to tell about it in an organized, coherent way. That said, he's made incredible progress with the help of some great doctors, a couple of top-notch neurosurgeons, and a team of skilled physical, occupational, and speech therapists.

I first met Dan almost two years after the crash. That day had changed his life forever. But he beat the odds, and he's made an amazing recovery. He told me, though, that his story came very close to ending differently.

Almost an Organ Donor

Dan doesn't remember hitting the deer. He's not sure he even saw it. At that speed there wouldn't have been time to stop. He thinks he may have seen a blur of brown stepping out from the ditch. Or maybe it's just one of the dreams.

That day—and the two or three days preceding it—is pretty much gone. So are the next eighteen. It was only later that Dan learned about the farmer on a tractor who found him lying motionless in the middle of the road. If a car or truck had come over the hill first, its driver wouldn't have been able to stop in time. The farmer had a cell phone and dialed 911. That was Dan's second lucky break.

Dan doesn't remember the ambulance ride to a local hospital, the subsequent helicopter ride to a larger hospital in the city, the multiple brain surgeries, or his eighteen days in an induced coma. At times Dan's prognosis was far from certain. His doctors began serious conversations with his then-wife about the possibility of organ donation. Papers were signed and plans were made.

When Dan finally regained consciousness, he had a broken clavicle and shoulder blade, three broken ribs, severe respiratory problems, and difficulty swallowing. The top of his left ear was worn away, but the rest had been reattached. Part of his skull had been removed to relieve pressure on his injured and swollen brain. "He was quite a sight," says Dan's sister, Kathy. "At one point I counted sixteen tubes going in and out of him."

Dan continued to drift in and out of consciousness over the next several days. It would be a long road back. During the months ahead, Dan's biggest challenge would be recovering from his TBI. Depending on the part of the brain that's injured, TBI patients can experience a wide range of symptoms. Dan had most of them. It was hard for him to focus, and he had a tough time with things like organizing, planning, new learning, and memory. His balance was affected; so were his moods.

During the weeks immediately after he left the hospital, Dan was not an easy guy to be around. For a time he experienced some anger management issues that cost him his marriage. People tell me that since then he's mellowed quite a bit, and he still sees his two sons quite often.

Although I've only met Dan a couple times, I found him to be one of the most gentle, amiable, and positive people I've ever met. He has an innocent, vulnerable quality that made me feel vaguely protective, like he was that kid brother I never had.

For now he's living with his sister, Kathy, and her husband, Dave. I talked with him at their house just outside town. As we visited over a cup of coffee, he told me he sees a lot of things differently now. "I was always a nonconformist," he says, "and maybe a little bit of an outlaw. I wasn't into helmets, and I definitely wasn't into speed limits.

"I was always pushing it," he says. "Maybe ten or fifteen miles an hour over the limit. If the sign said sixty-five, I'd be going seventy-five. That doesn't give you much time to brake or maneuver. If there's a deer, you're going to be in trouble.

"When I had my last crash," says Dan, "I was on my BMW 1100. I loved that bike. But it didn't like fifty-five. It just seemed to run better at eighty or ninety. I'm not sure how fast I was going that day, but . . . maybe not fifty-five."

Dan then explained to me that those leathers often worn by motorcyclists aren't just for fashion. Without them, sliding across pavement at high speeds can cause more than just road rash. Quite often it abrades away skin and muscle tissue all the way down to the bone. Even without the pads and shields worn by racers, that thin layer of leather can provide a surprising amount of protection.

Dan knows this from experience. What's more, those leathers used to be how he made his living. Before the crash he and his wife had a small but thriving business making custom, high-end motorcycle leathers for serious riders. Depending on the style, jackets started at around four hundred dollars and went up from there. The jacket he was wearing that day was one he'd sewn himself. He'd done a good job.

At this point in his story, Dan got up from the kitchen table and walked over to the closet. He had something to show me. He reached in and pulled out a leather jacket. None of its seams were torn. Apart from very noticeable scuffmarks on the shoulder and left side, it appeared to be almost new. I wondered if it had been cleaned to remove bloodstains—either his or the deer's. I wondered if he ever wore it, and how often he took it out of the closet and studied those scuffmarks.

Dan had defied the odds twice before. This was actually his third and final encounter with a deer. The first was a ten-point mule deer near Grey Bull, Wyoming. He escaped that crash with only a broken arm, a broken thumb, and some minor abrasions. The second was a medium-size doe just outside Torrington, Connecticut. That one only got him a sprained ankle and sixteen stitches below one eye. This time was different.

It's great Dan was wearing leathers that day. Too bad he wasn't also wearing a helmet. Sure, he was lucky to survive. But for him, nothing will ever be the same.

Some days are better than others. At times, however, it's hard for Dan to focus. He often forgets appointments, and he has trouble with tasks that require concentration, planning, or organizational skills. He still does some house-painting jobs, but after his last seizure, he's once again under doctor's orders to stay off ladders for a while.

Almost every day he volunteers at the local Humane Society. He's one of their best, most consistent, long-term dog walkers. His balance has improved, and he's in great shape. He snowshoes in the winter, and he gets around by bicycle most of the year. Every time he rides, he wears a helmet.

When I asked Dan about motorcyclists who see mandatory helmet laws as an attack on their personal freedoms, he was clearly frustrated. I could tell the question had come up before. "Freedom? OK. Well, freedom's great. But what about responsibilities? And what about consequences? If you crash without a helmet, it's going to have consequences—not just for you, for everyone around you. Believe me. I know."

His other advice for fellow motorcyclists? "First, slow down. You'll have more time to react. Second, get to know your limits. Practice. Get out in the country somewhere, get up some speed, make sure no one's behind you, and then hit the brakes. Then try it again, this time braking a little harder. And again, a little harder still. But not too hard. You'll start to understand what happens in a panic stop—how fast you can react and how long it actually takes to stop. If that doesn't get you to slow down, I don't know what will.

"I used to be very active in ABATE," says Dan. "It's sort of a motor-cycle education group. As part of our motorcycle safety program, we held advanced bike-handling workshops where you could practice evasive maneuvers and hard braking. It was a real eye-opener. We usually had a dozen riders sign up, sixteen at the most. At pretty much every session, at least one person was bound to drop a bike."

—◆—

I'd heard of ABATE before, but I didn't know much about it. I wasn't even quite sure what the acronym stood for. When I got home from my visit with Dan, I sat down at my computer to do a little research.

I learned that ABATE isn't a single national organization like, say, the American Motorcyclist Association or the Motorcycle Riders Foundation. Instead it's a number of independent, very loosely affiliated chapters that are currently present in forty-one states. A few states even have more than one chapter. This all makes sense, since the ABATE organizations are heavily involved in state-level legislative issues that affect motorcyclists.

Each chapter has its own mission, focus, and legislative priorities. Some chapters place more emphasis than others on safety, education, or charitable donations. All seem to support personal liberty. One chapter's website sums it up nicely: "ABATE stands for many things, but most of all it stands for FREEDOM!"

ABATE does indeed stand for many things. After visiting a few websites, I found at least a dozen variations, including A Brotherhood Aiming Toward Education, American Bikers Aiming Toward Education, and American Bikers for Awareness, Training, and Education. Several states, however, have chosen the same version: A Brotherhood Against Totalitarian Enactments.

The "totalitarian enactments" feared by ABATE members are many. They include laws that prohibit noisy exhaust systems, mandate "unnecessary safety equipment," or promote "discrimination in health insurance." But in every state where it has a presence, ABATE's number-one legislative priority is to block the passage of mandatory helmet laws.

ON PATROL

"I've never been to a deer-motorcycle crash that turned out well," said Wisconsin state trooper Dean Luhman. "Even if you're wearing a helmet, you're going to be in trouble. I've been at three, and all were fatal.

"About eight years ago," he said," I saw one happen while I was driving down the road. The guy was less than a quarter mile ahead of me. I saw the deer come out of the ditch, but he probably never did. It pretty much tackled him off the bike. He had no license, no helmet . . . and no chance."

To learn more about deer-vehicle crashes, I'd arranged to spend an entire eight-hour shift riding along with Dean. Although we didn't exactly end up working any deer crashes that night, I was able to ask questions and learn a lot about just what actually happens at the scene.

The only true deer crash that night was on the far side of the county, and another trooper was much closer. We started heading over anyway, but only seconds later a backup call came in from a sheriff's deputy at a routine traffic stop that might not have stayed routine. When he ran the plates, the driver turned out to be a known gang member who was up from the city "visiting friends." That took priority over me seeing my deer crash.

Please understand. I didn't want anyone to get hurt. I didn't even want a deer to get hurt. But if it were going to happen anyway, I was curious to see firsthand how troopers work a deer crash. As the night went on, it began to look less likely all the time. Expired plates, expired licenses, but no expired deer.

I did, however, get a fascinating look behind the scenes. Even on a weeknight in a relatively rural area, business was surprisingly good. By the end of the shift, I'd decided that if I were younger and exploring new career options, I would not want to be a state trooper. Not everyone is happy to see you when you pull him or her over to say hello, and over the years Dean has been called to more than one "active shooter" incident. It's definitely not a job for just anyone. But I'm glad people like Dean are out there doing it.

During his entire eight-hour shift, the closest we came to a deer crash was when we were called to a car fire. We were only five miles away, and we'd be there in way less than five minutes. We could already see a tall plume of black smoke on the horizon.

Apart from the neighbor who dialed 911, we were first on the scene. The eighty-three-year-old driver was unharmed and had escaped in plenty of time to go sit on the embankment and watch from a safe distance as his car burned. He did, however, seem rather unsteady on his feet. The Breathalyzer test took awhile. He told us he sometimes had difficulty breathing—and then asked if we had any oxygen. Once he was finally able to puff into the Breathalyzer hard enough, he turned out to be at around twice the legal limit. Later we gave him a ride into town for a blood-alcohol test at the closest hospital. That night would turn out to be his last time behind the wheel.

Technically this was not a deer-vehicle crash. It was, however, deer related. The driver had enjoyed a few too many drinks before dinner on an empty stomach, and then decided to check out a couple cornfields where neighbors had been seeing a lot of deer this time of evening. Once or twice they'd even seen a bear. Apparently he'd been watching the cornfield too closely, and somehow didn't notice he was off the shoulder and into the ditch until it was too late. The grass and cornstalks were dry, his muffler and exhaust pipe were hot, and one thing led to another.

Not certain how long he'd be gone, he'd brought along his small, portable oxygen tank. Just in case. Somewhere in the car he also had a couple boxes of shotgun shells. Even if they're not going hunting on any given day, a large percentage of the drivers in this neighborhood just naturally would. Shortly after we arrived, and just as I was taking a few photos that later ended up in the local paper, the oxygen and the shotgun shells both went off at about the same time. The flames were suddenly an indescribable new color, and beautiful sparks flew in every direction. The sound was loud enough to feel, and at that same moment I was buffeted by a wall of heat. I lowered my camera and took two very quick steps backward.

From Dean I later learned two helpful things. First, we should be skeptical of all those TV cop shows in which every car that hits a tree or rolls down an embankment invariably explodes and instantly bursts into flames. In real life, even when the whole car is on fire, gas tanks almost never explode. But if the driver left his oxygen tank and a couple boxes of shotgun shells in the back seat, that's different.

Second, Dean told me that loose, unchambered rounds cooking off in a fire aren't really all that dangerous. That's especially true for shotgun shells. As long as the pellets don't hit you in the eye, it's nothing to worry about. They only sting a little.

That night I also learned a lot more from Dean about what happens at the scene of deer-car crashes. He told me his first priority is always to ensure that no further crashes occur. When he arrives on scene, he first looks for vehicles or debris—including, possibly, the deer itself—in the roadway. Then he positions his cruiser with its emergency lights on. Later he may also put out flares, traffic cones, or both. Depending on the situation, he might even call in more units or close the roadway.

Next, he talks with the driver to check for injuries. As he does, he sizes up the situation to see what needs to happen next. He might need to move the driver and passengers to a safer location, or call for an ambulance or tow truck. Assuming everyone's unharmed, the next question he'll ask is about the deer. If it's injured but still alive, it will need to be euthanized. Until that happens, there's a very real risk that it might still be able to get back up and stumble out into traffic.

Even when a deer is down and safely off in the ditch, roadkill is the gift that keeps on giving. "More than once," Dean said, "I've been to a crash where someone stopped to illegally saw the antlers off a roadkill buck. He's at a spot where he can't pull all the way off the road, and then someone else comes along and slams into the pickup from behind. Expensive antlers."

Other secondary crashes happen when drivers slow to gawk at scavengers. "It happens with coyotes," Dean said, "but mostly with eagles perched on deer carcasses. We get people up from the city who have never seen an eagle that close. They hit the brakes to get a better look, someone else is tailgating, and there you go." On rare occasions other drivers collide with gluttonous, overloaded eagles struggling desperately to gain altitude as they flap out into the road.

If vehicles at the crash site are badly damaged, Dean takes plenty of photos. To help drivers prove to their insurance company that a deer was involved, he always tries to get a few shots of evidence that's still visible on the vehicle itself—usually in the form of hair, blood, or "other bodily fluids." Then, assuming the driver and passengers are unharmed, it's time for a little paperwork. If there's only one vehicle involved and no injuries, troopers can use an abbreviated form. That's always a relief for everyone concerned. The long form requires Dean to collect more information, describe the situation in more detail, and even sketch a diagram of the scene.

Here in Wisconsin there's also a special roadkill possession form. The law states that when drivers are still on the scene, they have first chance at the deer. Dean always offers, and he never makes assumptions based on drivers' age or gender—or, for that matter, the age and type of vehicle. Although some deer do end up splattered, splintered, or smeared, most are surprisingly intact. And even if the front of the deer is in rough shape, there could be a lot of good meat left on the hindquarters.

"I hate to see a deer go to waste," Dean said, "and they rarely do." Dean patrols a county that's not especially prosperous. That was true long before the recession arrived; it's even truer now. While Dean's still at the scene, it's common for other drivers to pull over and ask if there's a chance the deer might still be available. Or, if the county has dispatched him to the scene of a deer crash, chances are good that someone listening to a police scanner will call the sheriff's department to ask if the driver is planning to keep the deer. The county often receives one or two of these calls before Dean even arrives at the scene.

After the driver, Dean always gives first priority to people on a list he carries in his pocket. It's a list of names and phone numbers that have been given to him by people who are out of work and having a tough time making ends meet. "They usually come up to me when I'm stopped at the gas station," he said. "It's not like they have many other opportunities. They'll look to make sure no one else is nearby, and then they'll walk over and hand me a phone number. I talk with them for a minute, but only if they want. Sometimes they'll tell me about their situation. I put them on my list."

Assuming there are no injuries, most drivers can leave on their own as soon as they're done with the paperwork. For everyone else, Dean has all four of the county's tow truck operators on speed dial. If he can, he'll call one directly so he can describe the location and what to expect. If there's a lot going on, he'll ask his dispatcher, a deputy, or a firefighter or first responder to make the call. If the damaged vehicle is well off the road and not hidden by a hill or a curve in the road, sometimes it stays there for a while and Dean gives the driver a ride home or into town.

The more passengers in the vehicle, the more problematic the logistics are. "For years," Dean says, "I've been asking tow operators to order trucks with four doors and a second row of seats. Finally, just the past couple years, I've been seeing more of them. One way or another, we can usually transport everyone in the tow truck and my cruiser. Sometimes I'll call a deputy to help. If all else fails, I can make several trips. It happens."

Despite the really cool hat, the uniform, the regulation haircut, the tie, and the perfectly creased trousers, Dean's job description does include cleanup. It's a dirty job, but someone's got to do it. At many crashes the roadway is littered with a fair amount of broken glass, plastic grille fragments, and ragged bits of deer carcass. The longer debris remains in the roadway, the more likely it is to trigger another accident.

When I asked Dean if back in the trunk along with his rifle and shotgun, he also carried a push broom, he told me he did—a shovel too. "Between the tow operator, firefighters, and myself," he said, "we usually get the roadway cleared pretty quickly. But if there's something major, we'll get help."

Examples? "I've seen semi-trailers dump a full load of clay pigeons, shingles, or beer," he told me. "And sticking with deer, I remember the time we had one stuck down pretty hard. It was thirty below, and what was left of the deer froze to the highway. We needed a county plow to help scrape that one off."

Working with summertime roadkill brings challenges all its own. After one stop I asked Dean about the blue nitrile gloves I'd spotted in one of the many pouches on his duty belt. They're the same type of gloves I wear when butchering deer, painting, or caulking around the bathtub. I've noticed that my dentist and dental hygienist wear the same brand. These days, with concerns over HIV and other blood-borne pathogens, I speculated that troopers might use them occasionally at other accidents too. But did Dean wear them every time he had to grab a deer by its leg and drag it off the road? Or only when he had to deal with messy chunks?

"Experience has taught me," he said, "that you can't really get a good grip with those gloves if there's blood or any other liquid. Instead I keep two pairs of heavy-duty canvas gloves under the driver's seat. They're also good protection from sharp pieces, like all the wires in tire debris." Dean also carries hand sanitizer and paper towels in his cruiser. Just in case.

"Now here's a trick," he said, "that I teach new officers. Get ten or twelve of those plastic bags from the grocery store and keep them in your trunk. Always. If you have to clean up a bad mess, put your gore-covered gloves in one of those bags and seal it shut. If it's something bad enough that you'll be using your shovel, put three or four bags over the shovel *before* you use it. When you take them off the shovel, turn them inside out and seal them inside even more bags.

"That way," he explained, "the smell will be contained inside all those layers, not perfuming the interior of your cruiser when you have seven hours and fifty-nine minutes left in your shift. When you get home, remove the gloves from the bag. Do this outdoors so that you stay married. Let them dry outside for a day or so. Then, when the wife isn't around, you can toss them in the washer with a half-cup of bleach. They'll be good as new."

Dean apparently devised these techniques after an experience that occurred early in his career. "Let me tell you some facts," he explained. "First, animals left on the pavement in the summertime tend to bloat. When some unsuspecting trooper grabs that animal to remove it, the pressure can be released with explosive or streaming force.

"Second," he advised, "do not pick up a dead skunk by its tail. Use a shovel, stay on the head side and away from the tail side, and mind the wind direction. Some smells and tastes you never forget. Third, and maybe most important, keep your mouth shut while doing this work.

"If you can't remember all three of those things, well, at least be a real trooper about whatever happens next."

Perhaps after reading all this, you're not totally certain you want to become a state trooper. Dean also has some helpful advice for the rest of us. "If you see a deer in the roadway," he says, "don't swerve; hit it. Cars can be fixed or replaced. But as long as no one's tailgating you, hit the brakes.

And if you can, slap the shifter into neutral or push in the clutch. That'll help you stop even faster.

"Here are a couple more things you can do," he added: "Adjust your headrest so it's at the right height to prevent whiplash. You'd be surprised how many people don't do that. Maintain your vehicle's lights, brakes, and tires so you can see, be seen, and stop. Wear your seat belt, don't tailgate, and slow down.

"And when you're driving," Dean said, "drive. At deer crashes, and at a lot of other crashes too, the number-one excuse I hear is 'I wasn't paying attention.'"

THE AFTERMATH

The sign out by the road isn't particularly large, and it isn't lighted. But it is awesomely hand painted.

If you're not paying attention, the sign for Awesome Auto Body is easy to miss. If you are paying attention, it's easy to find. And depending on your speed at the time of the crash, the size of the deer, the size of your vehicle, and how awesome your luck was, you may only need to worry about whether the driver of your tow truck knows how to find the place. He will.

Just outside Minong, Wisconsin, I turned at the sign and followed the narrow gravel driveway as it wound between the pines. After about a quarter of a mile, I emerged into a clearing and saw the new-looking building. The place was immaculate. No crumpled cars, no oil-stained gravel, and no snarling Rottweilers. A single courtesy car, a Buick, was parked out front for the next customer who might need it. Outside, a cold October rain was falling. Although it was almost 9:00 a.m., the sky was still dark. Inside, however, it was warm, brightly lit, and totally spotless.

Surprisingly, most body shops are. They're not to be confused with junkyards, now called "salvage yards." They're almost invariably spotless, dust free, and well lighted. Shop interiors are usually painted white for better lighting and more accurate color perception. And when new body panels are being painted to match the others, it wouldn't do to have particles of dust floating around. Strong, diffuse fluorescent lighting ensures that the smallest imperfections can be seen and remedied before a vehicle goes out the door.

Although the outdoor temperature was in the thirties that morning, I was no longer chilled when I stepped inside Awesome Auto Body, where it was around eighty. Maybe that was so the paint would cure better, or maybe just because that's the way the owner likes it. When I stepped into the small lobby, I could see him back in the shop area. He was wearing jeans, tattoos, and a sleeveless fluorescent-green shirt advertising a local lumber company. He gave me a big wave, walked over to turn off the heavy metal that had been blaring from the stereo, and came out to introduce himself.

"You must be George," I said.

"Yup. Awesome George," he confirmed. "That's me."

Before we sat down to talk, George gave me a quick tour. To break up the monotony of those four white walls, the interior of the shop was dotted with automotive logos and motivational slogans, all of them painted expertly and flawlessly. The slogan on the doors to the drive-in paint booth read: ATTITUDE IS EVERYTHING! It would turn out that Awesome George has a pretty awesome attitude. I suppose if you didn't, and if you loved cars, seeing all this automotive carnage could get a person down. But not George. He shared his philosophy with me, just as he does with his customers.

Some of them, no matter how well insured, arrive experiencing something akin to grief. But here's the wise counsel they get from Awesome George: "Don't worship your car, and don't get too attached. It's just a vehicle, a tool to get you from point A to point B. It's insured. Cars are like socks. Be ready to change them once in a while."

One of the two jobs in his shop at the moment was a trailer whose fender had just been uncrumpled and repainted after its owner experienced a little mishap backing up. Not the usual sort of work George does, but he'd thrown it in with the bodywork he did on the same guy's truck after the little "backing up not quite straight" incident.

The other vehicle was a Pontiac with a crumpled hood and front quarter panel, a broken headlight, and a cracked bumper and grille panel. Its driver had hit a deer. What are the odds I'd see such a nice example on my first visit?

Actually, they're pretty good. George tells me that more than 60 percent of his business comes from deer-car crashes. Most of the rest comes from customers who drink and drive. He tells me he owes his job security to just two things: deer and beer. When business is slow for a day or two, he goes fishing and tells his wife to stop worrying. Someone will hit a deer soon.

George has one full-time employee, and he generally hires another seasonal employee during fall and winter. The next month or two, business will be especially good. Deer will be moving a lot, and they'll be distracted during the rut.

George tells me early spring is bad too. Succulent grass is greening up along the roadside while the woods are still brown. Later in spring, does are moving with their fawns. In summer, biting insects harass deer and push them out of the woods. Come to think of it, about the only slow deer-crash months for George are December and February. Oddly, there's a spike every January.

During the winter months, icy roads are good for business. So is every stretch of road where someone is feeding deer. It's pretty much the same houses every winter, and the tow truck drivers all know the spots. Because there's such a clear link between recreational feeding and deer-vehicle collisions, Wisconsin has made it illegal to feed deer within one hundred feet of a paved road. That's difficult to enforce, and game wardens rarely reach for their tape measures. And really, would a pile of corn 102 feet from the road be any less of a hazard?

Roughly 90 percent of all vehicles damaged in deer crashes are repairable. For insurance companies the decision is a simple one: If the bill will be over 70 to 75 percent of book value, the vehicle is declared totaled. At that point insurers are better off sending the owner a check and selling the vehicle to a salvage yard. These days, the decision doesn't take long. George takes digital photos, e-mails the photos and an estimate to the insurance company, and gets an e-mailed approval within hours—sometimes within minutes.

The damage from a deer crash typically involves a lot of bodywork, but no bent frames or other structural damage of the sort you'd see from a head-on collision with another car. "It uglies up the car," says George, "but it's not as bad as it looks. Still, it can add up fast. A solid hit will take out the grille, the radiator, lights, fenders, hood, and maybe the windshield.

"An average deer hit," says George, "used to be about twelve hundred dollars. Now it's twice that. Part of the increase is due to inflation, but it also has to do with how cars are built. Now we replace parts that we would have repaired back then. And to make manufacturing more efficient, those replacement-level parts are larger and more expensive than they used to be. Airbags are another factor. The average airbag repair costs three thousand dollars. If your airbag goes off, that alone could total your vehicle."

Still, it's almost surprising the damage isn't worse. "Imagine," says George, "that you've suspended a fifty-pound bag of dog food sideways with a couple pieces of twine. It's hanging in midair, just a little higher than the center of your grille. Now slam into it at sixty miles an hour and see what happens.

"But it's not exactly the same," he says. "Parts of the deer are harder than a sack of dog food, and most deer are bigger than that. You also get a pinwheel effect if the deer starts spinning. The legs whip around, and I've actually seen dents from the hooves right in the roof of a car—just the hooves, nothing else. If it's a glancing blow, the deer can take out a fender and then do more damage all along one side of a car or truck. If deer are on the run, they can actually hit *you*. Even if you've already braked hard, they'll slam right into the side of your vehicle."

When they arrive here, many of George's shaken customers tell of deer that emerged from the ditch without warning, often at a dead run. There was no time to react. By the time they saw the deer, it was too late.

Still, George says it helps to keep vigilant, especially at dawn and dusk. If you see one deer crossing the road, slow down. Deer often travel in groups. Just when you've seen one in time and let your guard down, one or two more could be following it out onto the pavement. During the rut a lone doe could be followed by a buck in hot pursuit.

Most of all, George wants you to remember one thing: "If you're driving down the road and a deer steps out in front of you, don't swerve. Hit the damn deer."

This isn't because George wants your business. He has plenty. It's just that he'd rather not see you become earlier-than-expected business for your local funeral director.

George explains that drivers are rarely injured when they hit a deer. But when they swerve, chances are good they'll go into the ditch and roll or hit a tree. Or they may lose control and head toward a car in the other lane. "If you have time to stop," says George, "then stop. But don't swerve and risk your neck over a deer—or, worse yet, over a dog or a squirrel. Believe me, I've seen it happen."

And if you think you only need to worry about hitting deer here in the north woods, think again. George owes more than 60 percent of his business to deer because traffic is usually pretty light around here. That means fewer crashes are caused by other factors. If it weren't for beer and blizzards, George might owe nearly 100 percent of his business to deer.

Percentages are one thing. But logically, your actual risk of being involved in a deer-car crash is highest in precisely those places where deer populations are highest. If your daily commute takes you through the suburbs of states like Connecticut, New York, New Jersey, Pennsylvania, or Virginia, you're at far greater risk than someone who lives way out in the woods where deer densities are actually much lower.

As Awesome George puts it, "Don't swerve. Hit the damn deer. You're worth more than a deer or a car. And your car can be fixed. Your neck can't. Your car? That's what insurance is for." Words to live by, and many states have begun driver education campaigns with this very message. Most rely on a memorable tagline first used by the Iowa Department of Transportation: "Don't veer for deer."

On the way out of George's driveway, just before I reached the highway, I saw a small, hand-painted sign: THANKS, AND HAVE AN AWESOME DAY! I did.

Still, there's something about having just left a body shop that makes a person drive very carefully on the way home. And even at midday, this rainy, overcast weather meant that deer would be moving. I watched the roadsides warily, ready to hit the brakes. But not swerve.

WHISTLING IN THE DARK

Stay sober, stay alert, slow down at twilight and during the night, and never veer for deer. Other than that, what else can we do? Is there some way to stop the carnage?

One popular solution is those tiny plastic deer whistles so many prudent drivers affix to their vehicles' front bumper. Manufacturers typically claim that as air passes through the whistles at any speed over thirty miles per hour, they emit an ultrasonic sound far above the range of human hearing. Deer, supposedly, can hear those sounds up to a quarter mile away. When they do, they'll stop in their tracks, freeze, and not step out into the road. They may even turn and flee back into the woods. Or at least that's the theory.

These whistles were introduced in the late 1970s, and some insurance companies have even distributed them to drivers and reduced the premiums of drivers who use them. Initial claims of effectiveness were based primarily on nonscientific compilations of anecdotal evidence. Enthusiastic customers gushed that "mine work great, and I haven't hit another deer since I installed them!"

A few before-and-after studies in the 1980s seemed to confirm these testimonials. But according to a 2004 meta-analysis from Keith Knapp of the University of Wisconsin-Madison, their results were undermined by small sample sizes, a relatively brief time period considered during both the "before" and "after" phases, and a complete lack of control comparisons.[2]

Even in these before-and-after studies, the news wasn't always good. In 1993 the Insurance Institute for Highway Safety reviewed two studies that showed no discernible reduction in deer crashes.[3] One involved the Ohio State Police, the other the Georgia Game and Fish Department. The second study noted that during hundreds of deer encounters, drivers never observed a visible response to the whistles.

It was also difficult to eliminate driver bias from these studies. Once they installed deer whistles and began participating in a "scientific study," drivers couldn't help but be more aware of deer. Similarly, drivers in before-and-after studies were often a self-selecting group.

Knapp describes a Modoc County, California, study in which deer whistles were provided free of charge to 1,648 drivers who responded to a newspaper ad.[4] Anyone who took advantage of this 2001 offer would have already been aware of the hazards posed by roadside deer and thus less likely to hit one in the first place. Once they joined the study and installed their deer whistles, their awareness would have only increased. All else being equal, that alone would have made them less likely to hit a deer in 2002.

Researchers have also conducted more rigorous behavioral studies. In one 1990 study, they separately mounted two brands of air-activated whistles on the bumper of a truck. Then, in a Utah wildlife management area known to have a high population of wintering mule deer, they drove back and forth on a six-mile stretch of dirt road at a steady forty miles per hour. The first pass was without the whistle. The second, in the opposite direction, was with the whistle.

They did this repeatedly, with both brands of whistles, until they'd made three hundred behavioral observations for 150 groups of deer they encountered along the roadway. They found that 39 percent of deer responded to the truck without whistles, but only 31 percent responded to the truck with whistles. If the difference was statistically significant, it meant that drivers were actually better off without the whistles.[5]

One 2003 study measured the sounds deer whistles actually produce and then compared them with the sounds deer are able to hear. These devices are generally advertised as "ultrasonic," and some claim to produce sounds of specific frequencies—usually between 16 and 20 kHz, well above the range of human hearing. These frequencies are also, however, well above the 2 to 6 kHz range at which most deer seem to hear best.

Not surprisingly, it also turned out that most deer whistles don't actually produce sounds at the claimed frequencies. Most, even when compressed air is forced through them in the laboratory, don't make much of a sound at all. Of those that do, the open-ended designs produce sounds at around 12 kHz, audible for most humans but still above the best hearing range for deer. The closed-end designs whistle at around 3.3 kHz, which is well within the hearing range of both deer and humans.

But here's more bad news. Even if whistles do make this sound when they're mounted on the bumper of a car driving by, it's not loud enough for deer to hear it. Researchers found that the minimal sound pressure from the 3.3 kHz whistles was "totally lost" in the noise produced by a typical vehicle at forty miles per hour.[6]

If the 3.3 kHz sound is within the hearing range of both deer and humans, one could logically assume that it should be audible to both the driver and anyone standing by the side of the road. After all, if the sound were to be an effective deer deterrent, it should at least be audible at a distance of a few hundred yards. So even if human hearing is less acute, we should still be able to hear these deer whistles at a shorter range.

But no human, whether driver or bystander, seems to have ever heard this sound. It seems likely that very few deer have, either. The researchers also argued that even if deer could hear these sounds, they'd quickly become habituated to them in the same way they've become habituated to other vehicle sounds.

So before you buy a set of deer whistles and use their self-adhesive base to affix them permanently to your front bumper, you should know the answer to three questions: Do they make the sound they're supposed to make? If so, can deer hear it? And if they can, do they care? The answers to these three questions are no, no, and no.

But what safety measures do work? Transportation engineers have had some success with special wildlife crossings (picture small underpasses for deer) and with the sort of exclusionary fences usually seen along freeways. When completing new construction projects, highway departments can plant roadside vegetation that's less attractive to deer. Elsewhere they can trim back vegetation so deer approaching the roadway will be more visible.[7]

Researchers have also experimented with arrays of roadside mirrors and reflectors, and with high-tech, motion-sensing signage that alerts motorists when deer are actually present. In both cases the results were mixed.[8]

As an individual driver, your best strategy is still to stay sober, stay alert, slow down at twilight and during the night, and never veer for deer.

Collectively, all across Deerland, if we'd like to reduce the hazard in the first place, our best strategy is to reduce the deer population. Deer, however, have plans of their own. The invasion has begun.

CHAPTER 9

Invasion of the Suburban Cervids

Although other species perished, whitetails took advantage of us. Currently they exploit the urban savannah we created and the agricultural lands that sustain us. The whitetail just adjusts, fits in, and thrives. Like humans, whitetails are not habitat-specific but are great "adjusters" that do well wherever there is food and a place to hide. Humans and whitetails are a species without an ecological niche. The whitetail's current strength is its ability to thrive along with man on man-made landscapes.

—Valerius Geist

The invasion has begun.

The deer are here, and they're invading our parks, neighborhoods, backyards, and vegetable gardens. They're even invading our homes, offices, schools, and churches.

Unfortunately, it's not an exaggeration. In small towns, suburbs, and sometimes even big cities, it's a recurring news story all across America. Confused deer, not quite able to process the reflections from plate-glass windows, are crashing through them. The rest of the story usually involves a frightened, injured deer that's bleeding profusely as it searches in vain for a way out of the building—sometimes while horrified schoolchildren or parishioners look on.

A few autumns ago, a deer in Wisconsin exhibited particularly poor judgment. It crashed through the window of a small-town butcher shop, right beside a poster advertising prices for venison processing. It should have read more carefully. A few weeks later, the same thing happened at a butcher shop in Illinois. Sensing an opportunity for free advertising, the owner made sure to mention in his interview that he did, by the way, offer venison processing. He was quoted in the local paper as saying, "We're so good, they're just dying to get in."

It's usually difficult, however, to find much humor in these incidents. Some deer can be safely herded toward an exit. Most can't, and are so badly injured they must be euthanized. Still others have already bled to death by the time they're discovered the next morning. Many of these invasions and their aftermath have been captured on security cameras; of those, dozens have been posted on YouTube.[1]

THE INVASION

Already, critics of suburban sprawl have pointed to a host of unintended social and environmental consequences. In the face of rising energy prices, some have even questioned the long-term sustainability of America's sprawling suburbs. Here's one more consequence: We've created a new type of habitat that's perfect for deer, and they've adapted to this new terrain and exploited it in ways we're only now beginning to fully understand.

In their 2011 paper "Examining the Potential of Community Design to Limit Human Conflict with White-Tailed Deer," spatial ecologists Dawn Gorham and William Porter analyzed the relationship between land use, edge density, core areas, contagion and interspersion, and connectivity. They confirmed that suburban deer generally have smaller home ranges than their country cousins, and that deer are drawn to the presence of lawns, shrubs, and edge cover. Their biggest new insight, however, was this: The one variable best correlated with suburban deer density is the degree of forest canopy fragmentation and connectivity across the landscape. More cover and connectivity means better access to food and safer travel routes between food, water, and cover.[2]

A second key variable was something called "edge density." Deer love edges, and large-lot, low-density sprawl dramatically increases the amount of edge between lawns and woods. Gorham and Porter recommended that urban planners and homeowners landscape for more straight edges and fewer meandering, curvilinear ones. This change alone would greatly reduce edge density. But humans too have an instinctive craving for landscapes with gracefully curving edges. It's hardwired into our aesthetic sensibilities, and it often trumps our need for control, order, and tidy right angles. As we build our dream homes on dream lots, we dream of deer that will someday emerge from the shadows at the edge of our new lawn.

❧

They arrive in the night, silent and invisible. Once they've moved in, their numbers increase rapidly. Delighted wildlife lovers begin feeding them. Next-door neighbors, however, wonder what happened to their flowerbeds last night. Other neighbors awaken to find their vegetable gardens mown to the ground.

Arbor vitae. Balsam. Cedar. Day lily. Eastern hemlock. Fir. Geraniums. Hosta. For a deer it's the beginning of tonight's menu. They enjoy all our favorite trees and ornamentals for the exact same reasons we do: They're green, lush, and full. True, some plants are less palatable to deer, and careful landscaping choices can minimize the damage. But once deer become more numerous, all bets are off. When homeowners feed deer in hopes of luring them away from succulent shrubs, the strategy invariably backfires and lures in even more deer. They're concentrated in one small area, and they still crave salad when they've finished their corn.

Gardening books and websites offer helpful advice about repellents like ammonia, blood meal, predator urine, raw eggs, small mesh bags filled with human hair clippings, or even bars of soap hung from branches by a string. (Irish Spring is said to be deer's least favorite brand.) But if these scent-based solutions work at all, they need to be replenished every week or so—and more often still if it rains. Even the very first night, hungry deer step over or around them.

Deer seem to especially enjoy peas, beans, and broccoli. Despite rumors to the contrary, they also enjoy garlic, onions, tomatoes, potatoes, pumpkins, and squash. Come to think of it, pretty much every vegetable we eat, deer eat.

Meanwhile, residents of Lyme, Connecticut, are less than delighted that their town has become famous for a debilitating disease carried by deer ticks. The ticks, as their name suggests, are in turn carried primarily by deer. In Lyme and elsewhere, the story is the same. When deer populations increase, so does the incidence of Lyme disease. Deer themselves are unaffected.

As deer numbers increase, so do car-deer collisions. Some are fatal. Deer lose their fear of humans and sometimes even become aggressive during the rut, when defending their fawns, or simply when defending territory they now believe belongs to them. As deer become more numerous still, public parklands and green spaces are denuded. Homeowners' gardens and landscaping are subjected to even more browsing pressure. The deer are still hungry, and their welcome is wearing thin. It's time to fight back.

Resistance Is Futile

Don't want extra deer in your backyard, but don't want them dead either? How about capturing and relocating them? Unfortunately, this idea works better with mice or squirrels. Experimental "trap and translocate" programs have time and again proved the idea to be impractical, expensive, and quite often fatal for the deer that do get moved.

Some of the deaths are from "capture myopathy," a muscular condition that results from extreme exertion.[3] When deer are captured and released, they can also die from other, more mysterious causes that appear to be stress related. It may happen immediately, or even hours or days later. They're also at risk because they're unfamiliar with their new surroundings and unprepared for what one biologist called "novel mortality agents" like coyotes, highways, or hunters. In one California study, 85 percent of transplanted deer died within one year. Each of those deer had cost $431 to capture and relocate.[4]

Cost, in fact, is one of the biggest obstacles for these programs. Even before deer begin learning from the mistakes of others, it's not easy to lure a significant number of them into traps. It's a difficult, time-consuming job. Programs around the country have reported costs per deer of $400 to $2,931.[5] Most of those numbers are from the 1990s and would undoubtedly be higher today. Few deer have been relocated since then.

When they are, it's becoming increasingly difficult to find release sites that don't already have plenty deer of their own. Plus, relocated deer accustomed to suburban backyards naturally seek out similar terrain in their new home. And if they've just arrived from an area that's overpopulated and overbrowsed, it's all the more likely they'll be carrying such diseases as CWD, bovine TB, or Lyme disease.

Finally, here's one more problem with trap-and-translocate schemes: Even in a single sprawling suburb, it's extremely difficult to capture a significant percentage of all deer. As each additional deer is captured, it becomes progressively more difficult and expensive to capture the rest. The deer that remain are fruitful and multiply. More, meanwhile, wander in from the adjacent countryside. After only a year or two, despite all the effort and expense, the population is right back where it was.

This same problem is one of the many drawbacks to deer birth control. It's tough to repeatedly, right on schedule, dart, capture, and inject every single doe in a wild, free-ranging population. However futile relocation programs might be in the long run, at least some deer are removed from their original home. But when municipalities experiment with deer birth control, newly infertile deer are still present, still eating, still spreading Lyme disease, and still wandering out onto highways. Within a year or two, their fertile friends will produce enough fawns to render the entire effort meaningless.

Anti-hunters and animal rights activists are the biggest backers of deer birth control schemes, and municipalities often feel compelled to at least give them a try. The consensus among biologists, however, is that deer sterilization or contraception is only worth considering on an isolated island or peninsula that's inhabited by a very small number of relatively tame deer. At a landscape level, or even in a single suburb, it's not an effective means of controlling deer populations.[6]

Even surgical sterilization has been tried in at least half a dozen locations. This involves capturing a doe, administering a general anesthetic and performing a tubal ligation, and then safely releasing the animal after its anesthetic wears off. When sterilization was tried at Cornell University in combination with controlled hunting, it cost around a thousand dollars per deer.[7] Apparently it was also difficult to find surgeons and anesthesiologists available during the hours when most of the fifty-eight does were captured. The procedure was, however, permanent and 100 percent effective.

The same, unfortunately, cannot be said for deer contraceptives. The most effective so far is an immunocontraceptive called mammalian gonadotropin releasing hormone (GnRH). Sold under the trade name GonaCon, it's the only contraceptive vaccine approved by the Environmental Protection Agency (EPA) for use on wild whitetails. It does have a few side effects, most notably small cysts that develop at the injection site. It works on adult does, but not on fawns. It's not always reliable, and its long-term effectiveness can only be ensured through repeated injections at regular intervals. In a Maryland field study of single-dose injections, 88 percent of vaccinated does were infertile during the first summer after vaccination. During the second summer, that number dropped to 47 percent.[8] In a New Jersey study, those numbers were only 67 percent and 43 percent, respectively.[9]

Earlier studies with captive deer had been more promising. In one study, four of five deer were infertile five years after treatment.[10] In another, six of ten deer were infertile for three years.[11] The difference, researchers speculate, was likely due to better nutrition and hence better immune responses among captive deer. Reporting on the New Jersey study, the authors noted that "severe overbrowsing was evident throughout the study area." The deer in the study were noticeably thin and weighed less than normal, and later necropsies revealed meager fat reserves.[12]

"It is possible," write the authors, "that stronger immune responses (and greater contraceptive efficacy) may have been achieved if study deer had been in better physical condition. As a practical matter, however, most overabundant deer populations that would be candidates for treatment with contraceptive agents would likely have experienced suboptimal nutrition."

Although a single dose of GonaCon costs just fifty dollars, the time and labor associated with delivering that dose brings costs to between five hundred and a thousand dollars per deer.[13] One complication is that deer must first be captured and subdued so they can be injected by hand. The recommended dosage is only 1.0 milliliter, and the EPA spells out injection protocols in great detail. Although darting might undermine the treatment's efficacy even further, there's another more important reason for specifying that GonaCon may only be injected by hand.

A few darts would miss, and others would fall out or be brushed off by deer before delivering their full payload. Since this would be happening at the edge of suburban backyards, sooner or later someone would stumble across a dart, pick it up, and prick a finger. Extremely small doses of GonaCon can cause infertility in human females, and its effects on male deer suggest that it could also cause infertility and various other distressing symptoms in human males.[14] So darting fertile deer with tranquilizers is only the first step. GonaCon must always be injected by hand.

According to the EPA fact sheet, GonaCon is classified as a restricted use pesticide that can only be used by "USDA APHIS Wildlife Services or state wildlife management personnel or persons working under their authority." Its use is restricted to one species: whitetail deer. Required personal protective equipment includes long-sleeved shirt and long pants, gloves and shoes, plus socks. Children aren't allowed in areas where GonaCon is being used, and pregnant women should not be involved in handling or injecting it. Finally, the fact sheet notes, "All women should be aware that accidental self-injection may cause infertility."[15]

The EPA has classified GonaCon as a pesticide, which would seem to officially make whitetail deer pests rather than noble game animals. Should you ever have questions about how to properly use GonaCon, the EPA's fact sheet names an official contact person within the agency. This particular biologist is employed by the Office of Pesticide Programs' Insecticide-Rodenticide branch.

The Urban Battlefield

When nonviolent resistance proves futile, and when it's finally time to declare war on deer, how do we pick our battles? Which weapons do we choose, and what are the rules of engagement?

Some municipalities enlist the help of local hunters using firearms or archery equipment. Others hire professional sharpshooters. More rarely, municipalities resort to "capture and euthanize" tactics. The latter approach is stressful for deer, inefficient for their captors, and expensive for local taxpayers. It's usually only considered in small areas with high deer densities where neither hunting nor sharpshooting is an acceptable solution.

At the far fringes of exurbia, regular hunting seasons go a long way toward keeping deer populations down. But as deer move deeper into the suburbs, hunters can't always follow them. Apart from the practical concerns of gaining permission and finding a place to hunt, hunters using firearms need to comply with certain "minimum distance" laws. In Connecticut, for example, hunting with firearms is prohibited within five hundred feet of buildings occupied by people or domestic animals unless written permission is obtained from the owner. Even when it's possible to hunt safely within those boundaries, it can't happen without permission from the neighbors—*all* the neighbors. When permission isn't forthcoming, that can mean some surprisingly large de facto deer refuges.

It could be worse still. In Illinois the minimum distance is three hundred yards. Even after setting aside the state's four metropolitan Chicago counties, researchers have used geographic information system (GIS) data to calculate that this restriction makes 30.7 percent of the Illinois landscape a no-go zone for deer hunters using firearms.[16] Deer, of course, do not play by the same rules.

These minimum distances are shorter or nonexistent for bowhunters, and out in exurbia they're glad to do their part without any extra encouragement. When deer venture deeper into suburbia, municipalities often establish highly structured "managed hunts." Meanwhile, other jurisdictions just down the road opt for paid sharpshooters. To learn more about which strategy is right for which environments, I talked with two of the country's leading experts.

The first was Dr. Anthony DeNicola, president of the nonprofit White Buffalo, Inc. During the past fifteen years or so, he and his team have removed more than ten thousand deer from American suburbs. On a good night he's personally killed more deer than most hunters will during an entire lifetime. "We have a system and a methodology that we've refined over the years," he told me. "We go in there and have a real impact on the population. We'll also help set up managed bowhunts, but they're less efficient. Plus, they rarely bring populations below fifty per square mile—and even then it's going to require maintenance every year."

In fairness, even White Buffalo's sharpshooters usually need a return visit every two or three years. DeNicola has compared his work to mowing the lawn; it's not something that can be done only once. He and his team are good at what they do, and it's an art and science involving far more than just marksmanship. Their general process, however, is fairly straightforward. They place bait ahead of time, give deer time to find the bait sites and begin visiting them every night, and then return to shoot at night from vehicles or from elevated stands. In states where their possession is legal, they use suppressed rifles. Sharpshooters target each group's dominant doe first, and then shoot the others if they stick around. They only take head shots, and they pass on shots that are less than a sure thing.

"This isn't about fair chase," says DeNicola. "A humane kill is more important. We're trying to meet management goals. This isn't hunting, and isn't fun. It's a job that needs to be done."

I also talked with Dr. Gino D'Angelo, a wildlife biologist with the Pennsylvania office of USDA-APHIS Wildlife Services. At any one time he's managing around twenty deer-removal projects around the state. Although some are at airports or in agricultural areas, most are in suburban settings that range from small communities in the Poconos to parks and green spaces a short distance from downtown Philadelphia. He told me the reasons communities choose one option over the other can be as much social as spatial.

"Our first recommendation is almost always hunting," he said, "and managed hunts are well received in some communities—elsewhere, maybe less so. And for a truly urban situation, sharpshooting is the way to go. We're shooting at night during the winter months when people are indoors with their windows closed. They know the job is being done humanely and professionally, and they're able to accept that it needs to be done."

In other communities residents may feel more comfortable with the idea of managed bowhunts. But when both the setting and the deer become a bit too tame, bowhunters themselves can find the situation uncomfortable. "Some of these deer are totally habituated to human presence," D'Angelo told me. "In winter they'll bed down under decks and beside dryer vents. If they've been fed, they'll walk right up to people. It's not the sort of experience most bowhunters are looking for. But once we begin a managed hunt, those deer get educated in a hurry."

DEATH IN THE SHORT GRASS

One city where that's happened is Duluth, Minnesota. Most of Duluth is on a long, meandering hillside overlooking a harbor at the far western end of Lake Superior. Geographically, if not culturally, think of it as a "San Francisco of the North." Not counting its suburbs or the smaller city of Superior, Wisconsin, just across the bay, Duluth has a population of about eighty-seven thousand. Add in its suburbs, and the number increases to 115,000. At times the city seems to have almost that many deer.

They've invaded for the usual reasons: food, shelter, and an escape from predators. Hunters and homeowners on the city's outskirts have spotted coyotes, wolves, bobcats, bears, and at least one cougar. These are not crackpots mistaking housecats for cougars or coyotes for wolves. Their sightings are the real thing, and many have been corroborated by trailcam photos.

Deer in these neighborhoods are nervous. I'm guessing a few suburbanites are too. They're probably not terribly excited about suggestions from anti-hunters that we reduce populations of locally overabundant deer with increased numbers of nonhuman predators like wolves and cougars. And in Duluth that idea doesn't seem to be working so well anyway.

At first it was fun to see so many deer. It always is. But eventually, apart from damage to the city's forests and parks from overbrowsing, the citizens of Duluth began to complain of more traffic accidents, more damage to gardens and landscaping, and whole herds of deer that had moved into backyards and refused to leave. The city's first step was to totally ban recreational feeding. But even without all that corn to lure them in, deer were still overrunning Duluth.

To learn more about how the problem is being solved (or at least managed so it won't become even worse), I talked with Phil Lockett, president of the Arrowhead Bowhunter's Alliance (ABA). The redundant-sounding name of this organization has to do with northeastern Minnesota's pointy shape on the map. In tourist brochures and local weather reports, it's known as "The Arrowhead." And the ABA truly is an alliance—not just among bowhunters but bowhunters, the city, and nearly all its citizens.

Phil explained that Duluth has large green spaces around its perimeter and more that run right through the city. Belts of green follow contour lines along the hillside, and these strips are in turn connected by corridors on either side of small streams running downhill toward the lake. On these public-land greenways, there's plenty of daytime cover and easy nighttime access to backyard browse. The terrain is perfect deer habitat; it also makes for plenty of good hunting spots on public land.

Private landowners can also contact the ABA if they'd like a hunter stationed right on their property. Pretty much every day throughout fall and early winter, Phil fields calls and e-mails from people who want a hunter to come take care of the half-dozen deer in their backyard. Rather than "not in my back yard," it's "*please* in my back yard." Phil or one of the other ABA board members checks out the site to see if it can be hunted safely. If it can, they may send a hunter over the very next day. Some spots, however, just aren't suitable.

Phil explained that other areas qualify, but just barely. They're deer havens, but borderline shooting zones. Typically they're only an acre or two in size and within a short distance of a busy street or highway. Board members choose very carefully the hunters they'll send to these "hot spots." They don't just want hunters who can shoot accurately. They want hunters who will know when to not shoot at all.

When I later saw just how small some of these hot spots are, it opened my eyes to the lethality and effectiveness of modern bowhunting equipment. Here in Duluth nearly all these deer are down within thirty yards. Most don't make it nearly that far. Patient hunters often kill more than one deer in a single encounter. They wait silently, shoot again, and wait once more. Within minutes, as many as three deer might be down in one lawn or vacant lot, and all within a fifty-foot radius.

On rare occasions wounded deer do make it out of sight and require tracking. Hunters first notify the police and then a board member. Minutes later, experienced trackers are there to help. The ABA reminds its hunters repeatedly that one bad shot, one PR disaster, could jeopardize the entire program. Every fall it does get a few calls or e-mails from property owners who were the first to discover a dead deer in their backyard. But considering the number of hunters out there and the number of deer they're removing, the ABA's record is quite good.

Almost four hundred hunters sign up for the program each year, and together they remove around six hundred deer from within the city limits.

In some parts of the city, they take over forty deer per square mile, but even then it's probably less than 50 percent of the total. Phil emphasized that this program is about reducing the population, not waiting for a trophy buck. Hunters are required to shoot at least one antlerless deer first. A few manage to shoot four or five does a year. If some are fawns, so much the better.

The program is highly regimented and incredibly well organized. ABA members use a sophisticated website to coordinate assigned locations and report deer they've taken throughout the season. The hunt is governed by several pages of city ordinances, eleven pages of ABA rules, and all the usual state hunting regulations.[17]

Still, to make sure everyone remembers the rules and procedures, all hunters are required to attend the annual orientation. It's absolutely mandatory, even for those returning from last year. If you don't show up, you won't hunt.

Just to be invited, hunters must first attend a safety course and pass a proficiency test requiring them to put four of five arrows into a 6.25-inch circle at twenty yards. With a modern compound bow, this is in theory quite easy. In practice, however, it turns out that under pressure, and with a few dozen spectators, some hunters need more practice.

As usual, this year's Orientation Night was scheduled for a weeknight in mid-August. The crowd of nearly four hundred bowhunters assembled in one of the largest auditoriums on the campus of the University of Minnesota–Duluth. Although I did see the camo and stubble I was expecting, I also saw a few suits and ties. Many of these men—plus a couple dozen women—had come here straight from work. A few hunters had brought their children, who for the most part looked rather bored during the presentation. So did many of the adults; it seemed likely that at least half of them were sitting through these same PowerPoint slides for at least the second or third time.

For me it was the very first time. I found fascinating Brian and Phil's reminders to be respectful of private lands, not prune excessively to clear shooting lanes, and avoid confrontations with nonhunters who happened to be enjoying the outdoors in some other way. Dog walking, we were reminded, was not hunter harassment.

Quite often, I later learned, hikers, runners, and mountain bikers pass within yards of these hunters' treestands without ever knowing they're there. On warm September afternoons, young couples out for a picnic in the woods have hurriedly spread their blankets and never known they were being watched from above. At times this has led to loud throat clearing and much awkwardness.

Less happily, Phil mentioned toward the end of his presentation that hunters should once again be on the lookout for blue tarps and other signs of homeless encampments. Every fall, local outreach workers ask ABA members to help pinpoint these spots and pass along what they've seen. Once they know where campers are, they can make contact, get acquainted, offer a pair of warm socks, and pitch the advantages of coming to an indoor shelter when temperatures plummet in November.

At the end of the presentation, hunters formed small groups so they could receive their location assignments. Although especially popular areas require a lottery system, most assignments were quite simple and involved very little fuss or negotiation. For the sake of convenience, nearly all hunters request a spot somewhere in their own neighborhood.

As for me, I was fully oriented and ready to hunt.

Two months later I was back to learn firsthand what the urban bowhunting experience was all about. I'd arranged to head up a tree with Phil Mannon, another member of the ABA board. While working at a full-time construction job and helping coordinate the program for nearly four hundred other hunters, he somehow manages to get out in the woods fairly often himself.

Our plan was to meet at an intersection a mile or so from the spot where we'd be hunting. Phil arrived at 4:15 p.m., right on schedule. We shook hands, chatted for a moment, and headed up the road. I expected to follow him into a turnout beside some park or remnant scrap of land owned by the city. Instead we pulled into a driveway and parked beside the homeowner's garage.

"He's in on the deal," said Phil. "I used to park over by the street, but I could swear the deer were starting to recognize my truck. They knew it meant trouble. So the guy said we could just park right here as long as we don't block his garage door."

Already this year Phil had taken two deer from this three-acre patch of woods. One was a small doe; the other was a large buck he'd just arrowed the week before. When Phil showed me the picture on his phone, the animal's thick neck, broad nose, and cowlike ears reminded me of the trophy deer I'd seen in Buffalo County. He told me his freezer was almost full, but that he could still use one more deer. It would be a long time until next September.

Just before meeting Phil, I'd changed into my hunting clothes while parked in a vacant lot down the street. He was still working on that, and stole a quick glance over his shoulder to make sure no cars were approaching. "Sometimes it gets a little tricky when you're hunting in town," he said. "Almost wish I had a minivan with tinted windows for times like this."

"Fortunately," I said, looking off toward the woods, "there's not much traffic out here. Can't hear anyone coming. You should be OK for now."

"Just wait an hour or so" he said. "This street will be like a freeway. Everyone's going to be on his way home. This is commuter heaven out here."

Phil told me this neighborhood was also deer heaven, and that these deer are fully habituated to traffic and human activity. And when he said they'd learned to associate his truck with danger, he wasn't kidding. These deer know what's normal and what's not. They know there's nothing to fear from a homeowner raking leaves, mowing the lawn, or walking the dog. When Duluth's urban hunt began a decade ago, they were just as naïve about pickups and camo-clad hunters tiptoeing through the woods. They've learned.

Before we headed into the woods, it was time for a brief lesson on treestand safety. Phil gave me one of his safety harnesses to put on. It was his rarely used backup, and it took us a moment to figure it out and get everything untwisted. But eventually I had it on with all the straps going where they should—around my waist, around my shoulders, and tightly encircling each thigh. I was buckled in and ready to go.

Phil shouldered his camo daypack and picked up his bow. We crossed the driveway, slipped behind the garage, and began tiptoeing through the woods. It didn't take long to reach our stand; I'd estimate that we hiked around fifty yards.

Once I became accustomed to my perch twenty feet up an aspen, it was comfortable enough. The breeze was cool but not yet cold, the gentle swaying of the tree was soothing, and I actually began to nod off a few times. Now I understood how so many treestand accidents occur when hunters fall asleep. Each time I started to nod off, however, I was awakened by my chin hitting my sternum rather than by my weight hitting the end of the safety tether.

As the late-afternoon wind grew stronger, our aspen swayed a bit more wildly than I'd have preferred. I hoped it was solid enough, even at this height, to hold the two of us. It was a long ways down. But I did finally get some relief from that itch right between my shoulder blades, the one I'd been unable to scratch for the last hour. At the next gust of wind, I leaned back against the tree. As it flexed, I felt the bark slide up and down along the bumps of my spine. There. Better.

Phil was above me and on the other side of the same tree. When I looked up, I saw only his ankles and the soles of his boots. His bow, an arrow already nocked, hung at the ready. That was about all I saw when I looked up. Everywhere else, however, there was plenty to see. We were in the center of a hidden three-acre valley, with a busy road behind us and houses on three sides. In between, this small, unnoticed patch of woods was laced with well-traveled deer trails leading off in every direction.

We were strategically positioned over a busy intersection on one of Duluth's deer highways—a network of trails that let deer traverse these neighborhoods silently and invisibly. All across America, unseen deer travel through other suburbs. Even if we never see them, they see us. The deer are out there.

Many of them survive by becoming nocturnal commuter deer. They bed down during the day, rarely moving beyond the boundaries of these safe havens. Then at dusk they emerge like vampires to visit backyard feeders, plunder gardens, and nibble landscaping in suburban backyards that are sometimes blocks from the nearest cover. At dawn, as the alarm clocks of human commuters awaken them with crackling traffic reports, these deer are already home and resting safely in their beds.

Although relatively new to deer and deer hunting, I'm already developing an instinct for terrain. It's a fascinating puzzle, a spatial problem really. And here, from my perch twenty feet up this swaying aspen, I could study the curves of the land and imagine the most likely hidden bedding spots, wintertime browsing areas, and optimum travel routes. I could visualize exactly how deer would use this space.

Even here, deer have the same needs—food, water, shelter, safe cover, and secure routes between them all. Layer these patterns over the human patterns of suburbia, and they fit together perfectly. I'd read the papers in which biologists analyzed these patterns with mathematical precision. Now, from my current vantage point in this elevated treestand, I could see them.

In my mind's eye I saw all these things. But I saw no deer. Just at dusk I was pretty sure I heard one behind us somewhere. The wind had slowed, then stopped. The woods were still. I heard slow, tentative footsteps through dry leaves. From the corner of my eye, I saw Phil reaching for his bow. Things were about to get interesting.

A few seconds later, however, an amateur suburban lumberjack stepped out into his backyard, revved up his chainsaw, and began felling storm-damaged trees less than sixty yards away. One tree, from the sounds of it a fairly large one, landed on the metal roof of his garage. We heard cursing. I heard Phil snickering softly above me, and I barely managed to stifle my own laugh. The deer were gone, and darkness was descending. It was time for us to descend too.

Later, in a whispered conversation beside Phil's truck, he told me he had indeed seen a deer. It was still out of range, but heading our direction right about when the guy next door pulled the starter cord on his chainsaw. Phil wasn't surprised when the deer arrived, and he knew more were on the way. It turned out that, as much as I thought I was becoming attuned to the ways of deer, I had much to learn about what to watch for when hunting in an urban environment.

"Remember when the wind was dying down," Phil asked, "and it was getting still again? We heard that guy about a block away yelling 'Get out of here!' He was yelling at the deer in his yard. They were on the way."

Here are a couple more urban hunting tips I learned that night: If you hear a dog barking in the next block, it could be barking at deer. Don't worry.

The dog hasn't scared them off. It never does. They're on the way. And just at dusk, at that magic moment when deer are especially likely to be moving, watch for motion-sensing floodlights in nearby backyards. If the lights switch on, and if they're getting closer, be ready. Deer are on the way.

A week later I was ready to give it another try. Last week was out in the suburbs. Tonight I'd be hunting with ABA board member Brian Borkholder in an urban hot spot three blocks from downtown. As we drove farther into the city, he told me there's been very little opposition to the hunt during the decade since it began.

"In the very beginning," he said, "there was one guy who'd been baiting deer in his back yard and illegally shooting them inside the city limits. His neighbors all knew about it. The guy was worried that 'his' deer would become more wary and that other people would be shooting them. But you'd never know that from all his letters to the editor. You'd think he was from the local People for the Ethical Treatment of Animals chapter. He was probably the one person most outspoken against the hunt. But there weren't many others, and we had strong support from the community."

Brian told me ABA hunters aren't allowed to bait, and the city now has an ordinance that prohibits recreational feeding within the city limits. "But it still happens," he said. "People say, 'You can't tell me what to do on my own property!' The thing is, those deer aren't their property. But they don't get that."

Brian said hunters know exactly where homeowners are feeding deer, even if they can't actually see the feeder from beyond the property line. Feeding influences deer movements, and savvy hunters position their treestands over trails leading to and from the feeder. Every time they shoot a deer, there's further confirmation. And here I learned a new euphemism for "field-dressing," which is itself a euphemism: "unzipping." "In certain parts of town," Brian told me, "every time you unzip a deer, you'll find corn in its stomach."

He described an encounter he'd had the year before with one of these suburban nature lovers: "There's a couple living out on the edge of town but still within the city limits. They feed deer three thousand pounds a month, year-round. The feed mill delivers it in bulk, and everyone knows about it. One of our hunters wounded a deer, and I helped trail it to their place. We knocked on the door and asked permission to go find the deer. The guy hesitated and looked a little sheepish. He said he and his wife fed the deer. We told him we knew, but we didn't care about that right now. So he said, sure, we could look for the wounded deer. But he told us to leave our bows in the truck. He didn't want anyone killing their pet deer."

"Those were his exact words," Brian said. "He said 'our pet deer.' Tells you a lot about how some people view wildlife."

Next Brian told me a story that reinforced the level of public support for the program. He'd just locked his truck and was getting ready to step into the woods. There he was, standing on the sidewalk in his camo, holding his bow with a quiver full of arrows tipped with razor-sharp broadheads. "Along comes this little old lady in tennis shoes," he said. "Literally. White hair, looked to be in her eighties. She was walking her dog. I braced myself for whatever she was going to say. But she just said hello and remarked on what a beautiful fall day it was, and I agreed.

"Then she asked me if I was one of those bowhunters shooting the deer. I took a deep breath and I said, 'Why, yes, ma'am, I am.' She waved her cane toward the deer trail leading into the woods and said, 'Good! Well, enough chitchat. You get in the woods and kill those motherfuckers.'

"I said 'Yes, ma'am!' and I headed for my treestand. Who knows? Maybe the deer had been hitting her hostas pretty hard. Or maybe one of her kids got one with a car the week before. You just never know."

As Brian drove farther into town, I asked for his opinion on the pros and cons of managed bowhunts versus hired sharpshooters. He told me one big advantage of the Duluth model is cost. "We remove over six hundred deer a year," he said. "If you hired sharpshooters at a hundred bucks a deer, that would add up to sixty thousand dollars. But cities pay by the hour or the day, not by the deer. Sharpshooting ends up costing them at least four hundred dollars per deer.[18] So figure an easy $240,000 a year."

In contrast, he explained, the city of Duluth issues participating hunters a permit that costs twenty dollars. It then reimburses board members for their expenses, and that's it. Every year the city comes out a couple thousand dollars ahead.

I asked Brian about the claim that professional sharpshooters are more effective than volunteer bowhunters. In theory that approach makes it possible to remove more deer before survivors become educated and wary. Then it won't be necessary to continue year after year.

"That's an easy claim to make," he told me. "But we wouldn't do any better shooting deer over bait piles with suppressed rifles. We'd still need to shoot more deer every year. And if we waited two or three years, the job would just be tougher next time around. You've seen the terrain we have here. We'll never get every single deer. And every year more filter in from the outskirts."

Just then we rounded a bend in Skyline Drive and saw the city and harbor spread out before us. The open expanse of Lake Superior stretched eastward, all the way to the horizon. "Shooting deer in Duluth," Brian said, "is like going down to Lake Superior and scooping out a cupful of water. More water will fill that hole. It's the same with deer. All we can do is keep the numbers under control. If we do that, we've at least helped restore a little balance."

We were now driving through a hillside neighborhood filled with invisible deer and nearly invisible money. As we turned onto a smaller side street, we drove by homes that appeared quite modest. Most were on the street's downhill side. Short, mostly empty driveways led to closed garage doors. Front yards were tiny or nonexistent, and windows were few. I was pretty sure, though, that the sides of these houses overlooking the harbor and the lake would be different. That's where the windows, balconies, and deer would be.

When we pulled in at the home of Peter and Sally Sneve, Peter was just leaving in his SUV. Phil had told me Peter was a retired investor of some sort, and he looked to be in his late seventies or early eighties. The three of us chatted for a moment, and he wished us luck. We parked in the Sneves' driveway and began descending the dozen or so concrete steps beside their house. There, I saw the first of several shrubs wrapped in wire mesh to protect them from deer.

Around the corner, and there was our ground blind, staked out and ready for us. Since leaving the truck we'd hiked a total of perhaps fifty feet. The blind was a typical design: a camo cube roughly six feet on a side and five feet tall, with only the slightest bit of peak to its roof. Although its camo fabric didn't seem to blend in very well against the gray metal siding of the Sneves' house, the deer were by now accustomed to its presence.

So it wouldn't be blown away, it was staked down and further anchored with three guy lines. One led to a tent stake sunk into the Sneves' lawn, a second to a steel post supporting their balcony, and a third to the compressor of their air-conditioning system. The rear side of the blind was about six inches from the house. This would not be a wilderness experience.

Brian told me the ABA generally requires hunters to use a treestand so they'll be shooting safely toward the ground. This, however, was one of those rare spots with no suitable trees but way too many deer. The Sneves had invited one hunter to come on up and shoot from their balcony, and he did get a doe from that angle. But on a later visit, when Sally quietly slipped him a plate of freshly baked cookies through the sliding glass door, he decided it might be time to return to the ABA's ground blind.

We slipped into the blind and settled in to wait. The lawn was quite small, and beyond it the hillside dropped away steeply. On one side of the lawn were more shrubs wrapped in wire mesh. On the other were a clear shooting lane toward an apple tree nearly stripped clean, a mountain ash still red with berries, and a strip of thick cover along the edge of the Sneves' carefully manicured lawn. I was reminded of *Death in the Long Grass,* Peter Capstick's collection of safari tales from his days as a professional hunter in Africa. This story, however, would be more like *Death in the Short Grass.*

Once or twice I thought I heard a deer approaching from somewhere behind the apple tree. Each time, however, it turned out to be a squirrel. Once we watched a cottontail's slow, intermittent progress across the lawn. I had to ask, but Brian whispered back that he didn't really want to sacrifice a carbon-fiber arrow and an eight-dollar broadhead. That was about it. A quiet night.

Later Brian told me this spot might need to rest for a couple weeks. Another hunter had taken a deer here earlier in the week, and a couple weeks before that Brian had himself shot three in one evening. During the past two seasons, fourteen antlerless deer had fallen to ABA hunters on this one small lawn.

That evening the fifteenth deer never showed up. But from the window of our ground blind, we did have a beautiful view of the harbor and the lake. Below us and just three blocks away were the courthouse, police station, and all of downtown. Beyond were the lift bridge and Canal Park. To our left, out on the lake, a distant freighter was a speck on the horizon. To our right condos, Bayfront Park, more condos, and docks and warehouses sat along the inland side of the harbor. Across the bay was the sprawling city of Superior, Wisconsin. At its far edge a refinery and tank farm glowed warmly in the sunset. Beyond were darkening forests filled with deer.

❦

A couple days later I called the Sneves to hear their story. "When we built this house twenty-eight years ago," Sally told me, "there weren't many deer here. It was an open, grassy area that burned every spring. A few trees here and there, but not all the brush we have now.

"After we built, we put in landscaping and shrubbery, then trees, flowers, and a small garden. And more brush was growing up out beyond the edge of our lawn. I suppose the deer liked that too. So pretty soon they arrived. They'd eat our shrubbery, and then they'd eat our flowers for dessert. You saw the cages around all the bushes. We used to just put them on in the winter. We'd take them off in June and put them back on in the fall. But Peter's eighty-three now, and he has a hard time doing that sort of thing—especially if he has to walk around on the side hill.

"At first," she said, "it was just a few deer. It was fun to see them. But one morning we looked out and saw sixteen deer in our little yard. So we heard about this program, and we decided to give them a call. When Brian came and looked around, he didn't think we had enough space to work with. But he could see there were tons of deer, and eventually we talked them into giving it a try here."

I asked how the neighbors felt about the situation. "I talked with them first," she said, "and they were delighted. All of them. They'd been losing their gardens and their flowerbeds and having all kinds of trouble with the deer. One neighbor was concerned about wounded deer though. I was too. But we've had good hunters here. They've been careful, and it hasn't been a problem.

"I've seen a few deer killed," she said. "I don't like to see it, but you know, I don't like to see them killed on the street either. We see them dead all the time on 7th Street, and this summer we saw a fawn that someone hit on Mesaba. That's a main road, and the driver would have been going fast. It could have been a serious crash. And who knows? Maybe it was.

"And late winter last year, some driver hit a deer that came down into our yard. It died over in the grass at the edge of our lawn. At first we didn't even know it was there. But then the crows started circling. The deer was already frozen, and we could see that its leg was all smashed up. We called Brian, and he came and took it away. It wasn't even a deer from their hunt. Awfully nice of him.

"I know the deer were here first," she said, "and civilization is making its way into their territory. But there are plenty of woods around us they could be in. They don't all have to be here in the city. I hate to infringe on nature, but sixteen deer standing around in our yard all day is just too much. There has to be some kind of balance."

Our Mission: Restoring Balance

Those are the first words you'll see on the website of the Fairfield County Deer Management Alliance.[19] More specifically, its mission is to "foster an informed and collaborative approach to reducing the region's over-abundant deer population . . . thereby reducing the herd's impact on ecological integrity, public health, road safety, quality of life and our stretched local economies." Although it's a model other communities would do well to emulate, the deer have not yet surrendered.

Fairfield County is located northeast of New York City and New York's Westchester County, and it's just across the sound from Long Island. One of the most affluent counties in the United States, this corner of Connecticut is today the suburban home of many commuters, hedge fund managers, and deer. It has deer densities of more than sixty-four per square mile, and its citizens are suffering consequences far more serious than browse lines, landscaping bills, or crumpled fenders.

If you haven't already guessed what I mean, the answer lies a bit farther to the east, in Connecticut's New London County—specifically in the towns of Lyme and Old Lyme. I suspect the residents of Lyme have decidedly mixed feelings about their town being the namesake of a debili-tating, crippling disease that can be fatal when left untreated. Meanwhile, the citizens of Fairfield County have actually been hit even harder by Lyme disease—and also by babesiosis, ehrlichiosis, and a dozen more tick-borne diseases whose host must feed on a large mammal during part of its life cycle. That large mammal is almost always a deer or a human.

When I talked with Alliance chairman Dave Streit, he told me that 94 percent of the adult deer ticks tested in Fairfield County have fed on deer, and that depending on the sample, 40 to 75 percent of them are car-rying Lyme disease and at least one other coinfection. "Our communities have been devastated by these diseases," he said. "We have people sick, pets dying, and kids that can't function in school."

He told me that everyone in Fairfield County lives with the constant awareness that their risk is huge. Lyme tests aren't 100 percent reliable, and just living here puts patients in a high-risk category. As a result, he said, many doctors are prescribing the antibiotic doxycycline on the basis of symptoms alone.

Streit explained that there's a close correlation between deer num-bers and Lyme infection rates, and that epidemiologists have found that restoring deer numbers to ten or twelve per square mile reduces both tick numbers and the incidence of Lyme infection among humans by over 90 percent. No other measures have that same effect. But reducing deer numbers this dramatically isn't easy, and Streit is pretty sure hunting isn't the answer.

"We don't feel recreational hunting will ever make a material differ-ence," he said. "If anything, hunters are an obstacle. I don't know of any deer-hunting organization that wants to restore deer numbers to our goal of ten to twelve per square mile."

Streit believes the problem's root causes run deep, all the way to DEEP—that's the state's Department of Energy and Environmental Protection. "If you think about it," he said, "DEEP is doing more to pro-tect animals than humans. Virtually all the government's regulations are there to protect deer, not humans—and often at the expense of protect-ing humans. Sure, wearing orange makes hunters safer. But nearly all the other laws are there to protect deer.

"Start with deer season," he said. "The whole idea of having one is to protect deer and maintain their population. Yes, you can harvest them three and a half months of the year. But the other eight and half months, you can't. So now you have a creature that poses a significant health risk to humans, and the government is forcing you to give it protection on your property for most of the year. If it flies through your windshield, it's yours. You get to keep it. But if you shoot it on your property out of season, you go to jail.

"If I have an infestation of cockroaches or rats," Streit said, "I'm allowed to address that. But deer are different. I can't touch them. Even during deer season, I have to pay the government for a special license so I can solve the problem." If Streit and his neighbors no longer seem to love the deer quite as much as they once did, perhaps it's for good reason. And by now most of them are ready to do whatever it takes.

Even as hunting is allowed on more of Fairfield County's open spaces, smaller backyards require different solutions. Connecticut now has one ready. Called Public Act 03-192, it lets any municipality, homeowner organization, or nonprofit landholding organization apply for a special DEEP permit that allows the lethal removal of deer at any time (except Sundays), any place, and by any method "consistent with wildlife management principles." Mostly this will mean professional sharpshooting. If applicants can demonstrate that deer are a severe nuisance or causing ecological damage, the rest is paperwork.

When I asked Streit what he'd tell his counterparts in other communities with too many deer, he had this advice: "First," he said, "don't try to organize from the top down. Instead get people involved and build support that's real and deep. One of our towns, for example, has a program called 'Be Safe Redding' that encourages people to allow deer management on their property. It's achieving that objective, but it's also getting people writing letters to town officials and to DEEP.

"Public officials," Streit said, "can be good at letting you use up your time and energy. Then they'll pat you on the head and do nothing. Don't let that happen. Build your contact database of e-mails, addresses, and phone numbers. Get people involved. They become your army. They'll help you disseminate information and keep up the pressure. Once people have the facts and the information, they tend to make the right decision. Without grassroots support the politicians won't make a move, and hunters will oppose your efforts at every turn."

Streit emphasized, though, that the Alliance isn't interested in totally eliminating deer from southwestern Connecticut. It just wants to restore deer numbers to historic levels—the levels they were at before Lyme disease became an epidemic. "All we want to do," he said, "is restore balance."

CHAPTER 10

Beyond the City Limits

Mysteriously, after fifty years in the deer business, I've never been accused by a hunter of underestimating the deer population or over-estimating the wolf population.
—Keith McCaffery, Wisconsin DNR

"When my phone rings and it's from outside the building," says Minnesota Big Game Coordinator Lou Cornicelli, "I know it will be one of three calls. Someone will be complaining about too many deer, not enough deer, or the wrong kind of deer. In one morning I might get all three calls, and all from the same area. And you know what? None of those people are wrong."

To learn more about deer management out beyond the city limits, I talked with the lead deer managers in half a dozen of America's top deer states. Although the details vary, all of them face the same issues. They don't have easy jobs, and the toughest part of the job isn't managing deer. It's managing people.

Within the profession you're likely to hear phrases like "human dimensions of wildlife management" and "good governance." Deer managers of the future will need to understand both biology and sociology (and maybe a little political science too), and Cornicelli is already there. "I'm a classically trained wildlife biologist," he said, "but my PhD was in the social aspects of deer management. And let me tell you, that's a big part of the job."

No matter how well trained the professionals are, they get plenty of advice from us amateurs. "You need a thick skin," Cornicelli told me, "and this job isn't for everyone. But that's what happens when you're managing a species that matters to people."

DEER WARS

To some of us, whitetail deer are a species that matters just a little too much. Although love and obsession don't always equal learning and observation, don't tell that to the obsessed. Regional outdoor magazines regularly publish letters questioning deer managers' intelligence, integrity, and parentage. Some have faced crowds of angry protesters, received death threats, and even worn bulletproof vests to public listening sessions. One was Gary Alt, who was Pennsylvania's lead deer manager during its "deer wars" of the early 2000s.

In his book *Deer Wars: Science, Tradition, and the Battle Over Managing Whitetails in Pennsylvania*, Bob Frye describes how heated the debate had become: "Law enforcement officials within the Game Commission persuaded him to begin wearing a bulletproof vest to his lectures. Armed officers accompanied him to each event and suggested that he always have an escape route from the stage to an exit should things turn violent. Alt, though, went out of his way to talk to hunters, always staying as long as it took for every single sportsman to get all of his questions answered."[1]

As you might guess from the title of Frye's book, Pennsylvania's deer wars were all about the collision of science and tradition. As in much of America, deer were nearly eliminated from the Pennsylvania landscape around the turn of the last century. Seasons were shortened, and for decades hunters were only allowed to shoot bucks. Over time they came to believe it just wasn't manly to shoot does. And besides, it was just plain wrong. Always was, always would be. Eventually, however, these sacrosanct traditions would long outlive their usefulness.

In a familiar story, Pennsylvania now had a new problem. It now had far more deer than the land could support. The forest was suffering, and the deer themselves were suffering. The science was solid, and the solution was obvious: It was time to shoot more deer and different deer. Hunters would now be allowed and even encouraged to shoot does. Some were delighted at the opportunity to shoot more deer. Others were not. They threatened, quite literally, to shoot the messenger.

I recently talked with Chris Rosenberry, Pennsylvania's current deer manager. He tells me the state's deer wars are pretty much over, and most hunters have accepted a new structure that includes generous numbers of doe permits. In urban parts of the state where deer numbers are especially high, these permits are available in unlimited numbers. Elsewhere, each year's allocation of doe permits is adjusted to match population goals. Every year they sell out completely.

Meanwhile, other states continue to fight deer wars of their own. Only a few states with large numbers of deer have managed to avoid these conflicts, and all of them have one thing in common: At some point early in the twentieth century, they experienced such a precipitous decline in deer numbers that hunting seasons were closed altogether. In practice it didn't take such drastic measures to prevent hunters from shooting more deer. There simply were none left to shoot.

Ohio is a good example. "We totally lost our deer herd," says DNR Deer Project Leader Mike Tonkovich, "and that gave us a chance to start fresh. Other states saw huge declines around that same period, but not total extirpation. Here in Ohio we had no deer left. None."

Ohio took a break from deer hunting for nineteen years. Its next open season was in 1943, and by 1947 the herd had rebounded enough so that either-sex hunts were held in some parts of the state. No one complained. After deer hunting had ceased for an entire generation, old traditions were broken and new ones could begin.

Out beyond the city limits, however, some states' deer wars continue to be fought over questions that might seem academic to most of us. They're simple questions with no simple answers: How many deer is too many? How many is too few? How many deer, and precisely which deer, should hunters be shooting? What are our priorities, and what trade-offs are we prepared to make? How should we make these decisions? And most of all . . . who gets to make them?

HOW MANY IS TOO MANY?

As is so often the case, the answer to this question depends on whom you ask. For the beginning deer hunter, and sometimes even the experienced one, the phrase "overabundant deer" remains a puzzling oxymoron that simply does not compute. A botanist or ecologist, on the other hand, would remind us that it definitely is possible to have too many deer, and that all our decisions involve zero-sum choices. If we manage for more deer, we manage for less of everything else. When we purposefully manipulate the population levels of a single species, especially this one, it means we're tampering with every other moving part of entire ecosystems all across the landscape.

Although these decisions are based on sound science, hard data, and public input, a lot of the public input comes from hunters who are unconvinced about the science and the data. For one thing they're pretty sure scientists don't know how to count deer. Over the years, however, retired Wisconsin deer biologist Keith McCaffery has noticed an inexplicable pattern. "After fifty years in the deer business," he said, "I've never been accused by a hunter of underestimating the deer population or overestimating the wolf population. Go figure.

"And after all those years of supposedly harvesting too many deer," he said, "we certainly should have run out by now. Similarly, all those hunters who write letters to the editor saying they're going to boycott the DNR and not buy a hunting license next year? If they all followed through on their threats, the woods would be pretty quiet on opening morning. But somehow neither of those things has happened."

Without going into the technical details of how biologists count deer and estimate populations, let's just say the process is based on solid science and calculations that, if not simple, are at least fairly straightforward. State wildlife agencies can indeed estimate deer populations with a fair degree of precision. In the end, however, the numbers may not be worth arguing over.

Brent Rudolph, director of the Michigan DNR's Deer and Elk Program, explained it to me like this: "If we knew exactly how many deer are killed and exactly how many are left, it still wouldn't end the controversy. We'd still have to figure out what the right number is, and we'd still have to watch for trends. Plus, when deer populations do fall, they can bounce back even faster. So in the end, watching the habitat and understanding people's expectations are both more important than knowing the exact number of deer out there in the woods." (Rudolph, by the way, is another deer manager who did his doctoral work studying the job's sociological and political aspects.)

More often than not, habitat limitations and human expectations point toward two very different population goals. Indeed, biologists often speak of a "nutritional" or "biological" carrying capacity (BCC) and a "social" or "cultural" carrying capacity (CCC). Simply defined, BCC is the maximum number of deer the land can support without a precipitous decline in the health of the habitat or the deer themselves. The land's CCC is the maximum number of deer local humans are willing to tolerate.

In practice neither measure is so simple. Although biological tipping points do exist, most transitions are gradual. Long before deer approach the land's theoretical BCC, they've begun to have adverse effects on their habitat. Plants they find especially delicious are already gone, the forest understory is disappearing, and songbird populations are in decline. By the time they reach and surpass the habitat's BCC, only the most browse-resistant seedlings remain. At BCC deer are at their most numerous, but they're already suffering nutritionally. There are more of them, but each individual is smaller and less healthy. As the deer pass their BCC, they eat the remaining browse until there's none left at all. Then they starve.

What's more, neither BCC nor CCC is a universal constant. Just as each local habitat is able to support a different number of deer per square mile, each person—and collectively, sometimes, each suburb—is able to tolerate a different number of deer. In America's suburbs and exurbs, deer often reach cultural limits long before they've approached biological ones. Even when frustrated homeowners have herds of sixteen deer refusing to leave their backyards, their neighbors' gardens and shrubs might still be available tonight as a deer's midnight snack. If not, there's still plenty of corn in a backyard feeder two doors down.

Increasingly frequent deer-vehicle crashes are another factor that limits our appetite for high deer populations. There seems to be no truth, however, to the urban legend that insurance companies have secretly influenced state wildlife agencies to keep deer numbers low. Just for the record, I made sure to ask about this conspiracy theory every time I talked with a lead deer manager from one of these agencies. They all laughed. All but one told me that during their entire career they'd never once been contacted by anyone from the insurance industry. Nor had they heard of that happening to anyone else within their agency.

For a moment I became quite excited when one state's top deer manager finally answered yes to this question. This would be a scoop. His explanation, however, was a bit of a letdown: "Actually," he told me, "I did once hear from someone in the insurance industry. But it was earlier in my career, maybe twenty years ago. I was a warden out in the field, and an insurance agent asked if I could swing by the body shop to verify that those were deer hairs caught in the crumpled fender of a policyholder's truck. They were."

There's culture, and then there's biology. Out beyond the city limits, botanists, foresters, birders, and wildflower lovers might wish for deer numbers that are well below BCC. So would some hunters. They know that when deer are fewer in number, each individual animal will be healthier, better nourished, and more likely to fill a freezer or carry trophy-class antlers. Other hunters, however, simply want to see more deer every time they step into the woods. They'd only be satisfied with deer populations that are well above BCC.

So how many deer *do* belong out on the landscape? No matter how accurately we're able to estimate deer populations, and no matter how closely we monitor their ecological impacts, we'll rarely be in total agreement on the answer to this simplest question of all. It depends on where, and it depends on whom you ask.

WHICH DEER SHOULD WE SHOOT?

The answer to this question isn't simple either. But one thing is certain: "None of the above" is not the right answer. Wildlife managers occasionally get helpful advice from armchair naturalists and anti-hunters who believe it's wrong to shoot any deer. After watching so many deer line up at their backyard feeder, they're experts too. But whether we like it or not, GonaCon and cervid sterilizations will not make hunters obsolete anytime soon.

Cultural carrying capacity in the suburbs of Connecticut is certainly a factor to consider. But let's also consider biological carrying capacity, and for that matter the health and welfare of deer themselves—all of them, not just the one individual deer at the edge of your lawn. It's a beautiful animal you'd hate to see harmed. But consider, too, all the other deer, waiting unseen just beyond the edge of the woods. Now consider their unborn descendants, whose arrival is imminent.

Deer population dynamics is a complex subject, but the short version is that deer are good at two things: eating and reproducing. They've evolved a physiology and social structure that allow them to quickly populate large areas with large numbers of deer. Doe fawns are fertile during their first autumn, and many of them give birth to fawns of their own the following spring. From then on, given adequate nutrition, they'll conceive one to three fawns nearly every year. Meanwhile, deer also have a social structure that encourages new generations to disperse, explore, and colonize.[2]

Deer coevolved with large numbers of predators, most of which they've outlasted by millions of years. Due to human influence, the four-legged predators that remain are now few in number. In much of North America, deer populations are limited only by disease, starvation, and hunting.

Left unchecked, populations increase rapidly until deer have dramatically degraded their habitat. Then they slowly starve. A few years later their population rebounds and the cycle begins anew. Standing back to watch is not a good option, and doing nothing is not a kindness.

I'm not here to defend hunting, and I'm not sure it needs defending. If someone wants to hunt squirrels or quail, their pastime is harmless enough. They'll get fresh air, exercise, and the occasional small dinner. But strictly from an ecological standpoint, deer hunting matters in a way that no other North American hunting does.

It's true that black bears are sometimes locally overabundant, and that elk, moose, and Canada geese have all become a nuisance in certain suburbs. Snow geese, given an extra nutritional boost when they forage in American grain fields, are experiencing a population boom with serious ecological consequences for their nesting grounds in the Arctic. In all these cases hunting is part of the solution. None of these problems compare, however, to those posed by overabundant deer. Nor are we likely anytime soon to be overrun by hordes of squirrels wreaking ecological havoc across an entire landscape. Deer are different.

So "none of the above" is not a good answer to the question of which deer should be harvested. In most of North America, neither is "only bucks." But where deer numbers are unusually low, a bucks-only regimen can still make sense. In a few states hunters even face antler point restrictions (APRs) that limit them to bucks whose antlers have a minimum number of points. Although this lowers hunters' odds even further, it does reduce the harvest and give more small bucks a chance to grow into big ones.

One state with APRs is Vermont, where outdoor writer Chuck Wooster recently speculated on the possibility of some unintended genetic consequences: "Antler size is partially hereditary. Some bucks grow bigger antlers than others. . . . Your average yearling is protected while your above-average yearling is legal." Wooster then quotes an unnamed Fish and Wildlife official who acknowledges that this sort of unnatural selection is likely to backfire and eventually lead to more bucks with smaller antlers.[3]

Or maybe not. Elsewhere, hunters who control large tracts of land have done just the opposite, attempting to grow "quality" deer with large antlers by culling the bucks with inferior ones. Except in very rare circumstances, however, this approach isn't advocated by the QDMA, as studies have shown it to have little effect on free-ranging populations.[4] Part of the reason is that antler growth is also related to such variables as age, nutrition, injury, and stress. The largest antlers of all are grown by well-fed captive bucks raised in a stress-free environment. Let's remember, too, that heritable genes for large antlers aren't just passed along by bucks; they come from both the paternal and maternal sides. On deer farms breeders maintain careful pedigrees for both bucks and does, and both are individually identified with microchips or large plastic ear tags.

In the wild APRs are most useful as an indirect incentive for hunters to shoot more does. When both bucks and does are fair game, and when tradition-minded hunters aren't allowed to shoot a yearling buck, they could be more likely to settle for a doe. Minnesota Big Game Coordinator Lou Cornicelli told me that once a state with too many deer has issued large numbers of doe permits, APRs are one of the few tools left in the deer manager's toolbox. There are also, he explained, two others:

"Separate early antlerless seasons have an additive effect but low partici-pation rates. Here in Minnesota it's only 15 percent. And while it's not always popular, earn-a-buck has the greatest impact of all."

(Earn-a-buck regimens, sometimes abbreviated EAB, require hunt-ers to shoot a doe before they're eligible to shoot a buck. States only impose them in areas where deer populations are especially high, and in some states hunters can save their EAB certificate and use it the follow-ing year. But because EAB rules force hunters to do something they'd rather not, they tend to be unpopular. Alert game wardens have often caught hunters registering roadkill does—or even registering the same doe in different locations under half a dozen names. Cornicelli told me Minnesota hunters' support for EAB was "OK, but not great." Next door in Wisconsin, the state legislature recently mandated that the DNR no longer be allowed to use EAB incentives.)

"So putting more pressure on does," Cornicelli said, "is the real reason for APRs. It protects the antlered males, but that's only a by-product." Cornicelli also told me, and his counterparts in other states agreed, that longer seasons aren't the answer either. "The vast majority of hunters only shoot one deer—that's if they get even one. And the rare hunters who want two or three aren't going to easily be nudged up to three or four. No matter how long the season is, it won't make that much of a difference."

＊＊＊

Although the QDMA joins wildlife agencies in encouraging hunters to harvest the appropriate number of antlerless deer to balance deer herds, CEO Brian Murphy told me 1999 was the first year in modern history that American hunters shot more antlerless deer than antlered bucks. Despite having made great progress over the past two decades, deer man-agers in some states are still trying in vain to get hunters to shoot more deer—and especially more of those sacred does.

To old-timers who still believe that it's impossible to ever have too many deer and that real men only shoot bucks, there's only one thing worse than being told to go ahead and shoot more does. Here it comes. I'm about to go where most biologists fear to tread. How about shooting more fawns?

Seriously. It turns out there are times and places when hunters should do just that. What's more, there are no sound biological reasons they shouldn't. Any stigma attached to shooting fawns from the previous spring is cultural, not rational.

For the moment, try not to think of Bambi and Faline. Newborn fawns grow rapidly, lose their spots in late summer, and have turned into a very different animal by the time hunting season rolls around. By October or November, a doe born the previous spring weighs fifty to seventy-five pounds. A buck fawn weighs eighty to one hundred pounds, as much as many adult does. Even if each fawn yields slightly less venison, it's likely to be more tender, high-quality meat. Those harvested earlier in the fall taste a lot like veal—but from the forest rather than from a pen.

Deer hunters are already shooting a fair number of fawns. They just don't call them that. To avoid using the F-word, they tend to call them "button bucks," "small does," or "yearlings." (Technically, however, they won't be yearlings for another year.) Wisconsin's numbers are probably fairly typical: Fawns make up roughly 40 percent of the antlerless harvest, with the other 60 percent being adult does. Doe fawns make up around 18 percent of the antlerless harvest, buck fawns around 22 percent.[5] (Bucks don't grow antlers until their second summer, and are thus classified as "antlerless" during their first autumn.)

While some fawns are admittedly rather naïve, most are quite wary. And since they're more likely to be traveling with other deer as part of a social group, hunters can usually only shoot them by simultaneously deceiving three or four older, more sophisticated deer. Still, many hunters see shooting younger deer as less of an accomplishment—and just plain wrong. Even if they wouldn't be embarrassed about shooting young-of-the-year squirrels or pheasants, deer are different.

There's no sound biological reason for these beliefs, and wildlife biologist John Ozoga makes a strong case for harvesting more whitetail fawns—especially in the northern part of their range. Having spent more than thirty years studying deer in Upper Michigan, he probably has more firsthand knowledge of starving, winter-stressed deer than just about anyone.

In peer-reviewed journals and in articles published by the QDMA and *Deer and Deer Hunting,* he explains that in northern states where winters are harsh, a large percentage of fawns don't survive their first year.[6] They have minimal fat reserves, and being smaller they have more surface area in proportion to their body mass. As a result, they lose heat more quickly than would a larger deer. Ozoga believes the critical threshold for fawns to be somewhere between seventy-seven and eight-eight pounds.

Fawns are also less able to push through deep snow or reach an overhead browse line. When there's a limited food source, adult deer may push them away. For all these reasons, a fawn shot during hunting season may not have made it to the following spring anyway. Ozoga describes two especially tough winters in the 1990s when an estimated 310,000 whitetails died in Upper Michigan. Over 50 percent of them were fawns. "During more moderate winters," he writes, "fawns represent 80 to 90 percent of total winter mortality."

Here's one more factor to consider: Even if they haven't just come through an especially harsh winter, doe fawns have a much lower pregnancy rate. Depending on nutrition, climate, and other factors, it can vary locally from 0 to 60 percent. By comparison, adult does have an 80 to 90 percent chance of being pregnant—often with twins or triplets. So if a hunter wants to shoot a doe but have less impact on the deer population, the best way to do that is to shoot a doe fawn.

For tradition-minded trophy hunters, however, the worst offence of all is to shoot a buck fawn. They believe your button buck—so-called because during its first autumn it has small, button-size nubs where its antlers will eventually grow—would have been their monster buck three or four years from now. But even if these young bucks make it through their first winter, they may not make it through their second and third autumn. Most don't. Despite carrying more modest antlers, these bucks fall to hunters in the largest numbers. They never have a chance to grow old, grow exceptionally massive antlers, and end up on the wall of some lucky hunter.

If they do, that lucky hunter is probably going to be someone else. Even for those who own hundreds of acres, it's difficult to stockpile trophy bucks. Every spring yearling bucks disperse into new territories. If they're still not ready to go when younger siblings arrive, their mothers push them away. Over the summer and fall, they disperse even farther. It's nature's way of maintaining genetic diversity and colonizing new habitat.

WHO GETS TO DECIDE?

Whitetail deer are one of the most charismatic of all megafauna. They're also North American hunters' favorite big game animal. In fact, given a decline in small game hunting that's happening even faster than the decline in overall hunter participation rates, deer are now North American hunters' favorite quarry, period. If the questions we've been exploring are controversial, it's because so many of us care so much about deer. Whether we hunt them or just watch them, they've gained our love and obsession like no other animal.

It's no surprise, then, that whitetail deer are by far the most studied animal in the woods. That trend is only accelerating. Ecologist Stephen Webb recently counted 1,980 peer-reviewed papers published between 1900 and 1984, 3,260 between 1985 and 2010, and 601 more between 2006 and 2010.[7] He believes this acceleration is due in part to the fact that new technologies like remotely triggered cameras, GPS and GIS systems, and various types of DNA analysis are helping scientists gain new insights into topics that include spatial ecology, landscape ecology, and molecular genetics. Meanwhile, access to new levels of computing power is allowing them to analyze massive amounts of data and find patterns and meaning in the numbers.

Scientists know a lot about deer. Deer managers working for state agencies base their recommendations on the best available science, and most are themselves highly trained wildlife biologists. They also, however, base their recommendations on public input. To a degree, that's appropriate. After all, there is that public trust doctrine. The states—and in Canada, the provinces—are only holding deer in public trust for us. These deer are our deer, and every one of us deserves a say in what happens to them.

Very little public input is offered in the form of tentative suggestions. Although they're careful never to use it in public, wildlife biologists and deer managers have a highly technical term for the instant experts who are constantly second-guessing them: "barstool biologists." These hunters—and nearly all of them are hunters—are convinced they know far more about deer than the scientists do. After all, they spend their time up in a treestand rather than up in an ivory tower. Out in the woods we often find a pronounced Lake Wobegon effect: Every hunter's marksmanship, woodsmanship, and knowledge of deer are above average, and every hunter knows more about deer than any scientist.

Helpful politicians add another level of complexity, and their involvement is unavoidable. Deer managers, after all, must often manage deer through legislated adjustments to hunting regulations and harvest quotas. But to get elected in the first place, candidates for state legislative bodies need to show hunters they're on their side. Believing voters who hunt tend to skew conservative, Republican candidates are especially unlikely to profess in public their fervent belief in evolution, anthropogenic climate change, or the knowledge, intelligence, and integrity of PhD deer biologists.

In all fairness, however, many state legislatures have demonstrated broad bipartisan support for the barstool biologist. In late 2011, for example, a Pennsylvania legislator introduce a bill that would have taken most deer management decisions from the Game Commission and put them in the hands of a bipartisan Antlerless Deer Harvest Committee. The committee's nonexpert political appointees would then decide, among other things, how many doe permits should be issued in each wildlife management unit. A total of twenty-six legislators signed on as cosponsors—ten Republicans and sixteen Democrats.

In an interview with *Pennsylvania Outdoor News,* one of the bill's Democratic cosponsors said, "I question some of the Game Commission biologists' findings, and I think hunters are a better indicator of our deer herd. I've had enough experience hunting to make judgments about the deer herd. I'd like to decrease the slaughter of does. . . . The thrill of the hunt is seeing game, and there has been an overkill of deer."[8] The same bill, however, would have also required the Game Commission to manage deer by "maximizing the sustainable harvest." This is not a term used by scientists; nor was it defined in the legislation. Currently the bill seems likely to expire in committee.

One might easily view stories like these as part of broader societal trends having to do with political pandering, scientific illiteracy, and a mistrust of science and experts in general—especially when it comes to subjects like evolution, climate change, or deer management. There is, however, a slightly more charitable explanation. Here's how Wisconsin hunter and outdoor writer Chris Larsen explained it: "Suppose I'm some guy who doesn't believe in global warming. It's something a scientist is saying, and I've never been to the North Pole to see the ice melting. Whether it's true or not, I can't see it with my own eyes.

"But I can go out in the woods," he said, "and see that there are no deer. So here's what's really going on. Take Wisconsin, for example. During the archery season we have at most two hundred thousand bowhunters out there—but not all on the same day. It's spread out over months. All of them are scent-aware, and they're putting a lot of effort into not being detected. Later, when the gun season starts, things are different. Now this isn't true for everyone, but gun hunters tend to be more casual in their approach. This is the only hunting most of them do all year.

"So suddenly one morning the woods are inundated with six hundred thousand smelly hunters slamming truck doors and crashing around in the brush. What do you *think* the deer are going to do? They're instantly on high alert. They go back in the brush and lock down. For the rest of the season, they're not going to move any more than they have to—especially not during daylight hours. So most hunters don't see what the biologist or the early-season bowhunter does. That guy in the tavern who hasn't seen any deer is telling the truth. People want to be successful. If they're not, they look for a reason—and maybe even someone to blame."

UNCONTROLLED VARIABLES

Deer managers face myriad challenges, complications, and uncontrolled variables. In the South unprecedented drought and high temperatures leave deer herds decimated. In the North long, cold winters are followed by April, that cruelest month when emaciated bucks fail to arise from their beds and gaunt does survive by reabsorbing their fetal fawns. Perhaps next winter will be warmer, drier, and shorter—a short-term blessing but a long-term challenge when a surfeit of survivors are left standing in the springtime sun.

Or maybe next winter will arrive early, in the form of a blizzard on the opening morning of deer season. If the Bengals, Lions, Packers, or Vikings play on Sunday afternoon, the deer in those states will get even more of a lucky break. The same would not be true, however, in Connecticut, Delaware, Maine, Maryland, Massachusetts, New Jersey, North Carolina, Pennsylvania, South Carolina, Virginia, or West Virginia. It remains illegal in these eleven states to hunt deer on the Sabbath. Nearly all eleven are also blessed with overabundant deer, and the simple step of legalizing Sunday hunting could go a long way toward bringing their deer populations under control.

Just before the 2011 deer season, an outbreak of epizootic hemorrhagic disease (EHD), more commonly known as "blue tongue," swept through western North Dakota and left so few deer alive that the Game and Fish Department suspended the sale of hunting licenses in that part of the state. The department even offered to send refunds to hunters—but only if their requests were postmarked by the day before hunting season. Meanwhile, in fifteen states and two Canadian provinces, deer managers are keeping a close watch on outbreaks of CWD, the cervid version of mad cow disease.

Despite complications like these, deer managers' greatest challenges tend to involve "human dimensions" and issues of "good governance." Dealing effectively with these challenges requires a certain sort of perspective, one summed up by Pennsylvania's Chris Rosenberry: "Deer management is data driven, but it's also goal driven. The public has given us those goals, and it's my job to help meet them. I don't get to make a single decision. I make recommendations."

Michigan's Brent Rudolph made a similar distinction, and without prompting used those same two words. "Elected officials," he said, "are accountable to the public. The electorate elects them to make decisions on their behalf. As deer managers we're technically trained civil servants who provide those officials with the best available data. We make very few decisions, but lots of recommendations."

Although this definitely isn't a job for the timid, wise deer managers pick their battles carefully. "You won't last long," said Minnesota's Lou Cornicelli, "if you flop on every sword that's waved in front of you." But when the time comes, Cornicelli and his counterparts in other states are ready with the facts. "These debates can be highly charged," he told me, "and sometimes you're testifying against what a legislator may have heard elsewhere. But our role is to present the facts as we see them, along with plenty of supporting data. I get accused all the time of not being truthful. I just tell people they're free to look at my data any time."

SHEEPFEST

A good example of Cornicelli's data-driven approach is his agency's landmark 2008 study of how lead gets into venison. For years evidence had been piling up that bullet fragments in gutpiles might be poisoning condors, eagles, and other scavengers. Now new concerns were being raised about human health, and it was beginning to look as though dust-size particles might be traveling farther on impact than previously suspected. These fragments were tiny but still large enough to show up on X-rays and CT scans of steaks, roasts, and burger.

Although other studies had been published earlier, the issue first gained widespread attention in March 2008 when North Dakota physician William Cornatzer scanned ninety-five one-pound packages of ground venison from local food banks. He found traces of lead in fifty-three of them.[9] Because he was on the board of a raptor conservation organization called the Peregrine Fund, some hunters doubted his motives and objectivity. Critics argued, too, that whatever medical training Dr. Cornatzer may have had, he was a dermatologist, not a toxicologist.

Potentially at risk, however, were public health, hunter participation levels, and donation programs that every year provide hungry Americans with 2.6 million pounds of lean, high-protein venison.[10] Conventional wisdom held that any dangers could be eliminated by trimming away the visibly damaged meat immediately adjacent to the wound channel. (It's something you'd want to do anyway; this meat, usually only a few ounces' worth, has been pulverized and jellied in a way that does not look appetizing.) Some of the lead Cornatzer and others were discovering could have simply ended up in ground venison when butchers didn't trim carefully enough. But what if there were another explanation?

To find out, Cornicelli and DNR biologist Marrett Grund began planning an experiment of their own. There was no time for delay; they wanted to be ready with preliminary results well before the 2008 gun deer season. They decided to test five different rifle bullets, including a non-toxic all-copper design. In addition, they'd test heavier, slower projectiles of the type used in muzzleloaders and shotguns. To make the test more meaningful, they'd fire each bullet design at ten targets (except for the two muzzleloader bullets, which were only fired at six targets each). They already had a head start with eight deer that had been shot in April and stored in a freezer. For the remaining seventy-two test subjects, they'd have to settle for previously euthanized sheep. Being anatomically similar and about the same size, sheep seemed like a good stand-in.

Methodically, Cornicelli, Grund, and a half-dozen others set to work. First they used straps to suspend each sheep carcass in front of a backstop fifty yards away. Then, shooting over a chronograph that recorded each bullet's velocity, they fired a shot into each sheep, right behind its shoulder. Then it was time for the next sheep. And the next. At intervals they paused to dig bullets out of their backstop, a box filled with sand. Later, back at the lab, they'd carefully weigh each recovered bullet. Meanwhile, a constant parade of sheep carcasses was being shuttled back and forth from cold storage to the shooting range and back again. All this took place over two long, grueling days in the summer of 2008.

Over the next few weeks, veterinarians back at the lab took X-rays, made various measurements, and collected tissue samples for further analysis. The verdict: Two designs, one of them the all-copper bullet, fragmented very little and left no lead. One type of muzzleloader bullet left only three fragments, all of which remained within an inch of the wound channel. All the other bullet types left lead fragments that varied in number, on average, from 34 to 141. Fragments were found at an average maximum distance of six to eleven inches from the wound channel. One fragment was found fourteen inches from the wound channel.[11]

"We learned a lot about bullet performance," Cornicelli said, "and we were surprised at how far those fragments did travel. But everyone evaluates risk differently. One segment of the public thinks the tiniest trace of lead is bad. At the other end of the spectrum, you have people who think it should be a dietary supplement. So our goal wasn't to tell people what to do—just what to expect. We give them the facts, and they can decide what to do with those facts.

"And let me tell you," he added, "that experiment wasn't nearly as much fun as you might think. We made bad jokes and called it 'Sheepfest,' but it was no party. It was two long, hot summer days. The deerflies were biting us, the dead sheep stank, and the guns kicked hard. But we learned a lot."

When you're a data-driven deer manager, it's all in a day's work.

CHAPTER 11

Toward a Balance Restored

We humans are the only species with the power to destroy the earth as we know it. The birds have no such power, nor do the insects, nor does any mammal. Yet if we have the capacity to destroy the earth, so, too, do we have the capacity to protect it.
—HIS HOLINESS THE FOURTEENTH DALAI LAMA OF TIBET

With great power comes great responsibility.
—ATTRIBUTED VARIOUSLY TO SPIDER-MAN, HIS UNCLE BEN, AND VOLTAIRE

By now you've come to know our deer a little better. You've met those who love and covet them beyond all reason, and you've even met a few of the truly obsessed. All these stories have consequences for us, our deer, entire ecosystems, and the very landscape itself.

The briefest glimpse inside America's deer-industrial complex reveals countless examples of the hard work and entrepreneurial spirit that made America great. It also reveals other aspects of our national character. Some of us seek new challenges, and some of us seek new shortcuts. Still, deer hunting remains a great American tradition enjoyed by rich and poor alike—for now. And whether you hunt or not, these deer are still your deer—for now.

As I described the changing gear, tactics, and values of today's deer hunters, I didn't give away any secrets a nonhunting city dweller couldn't have learned in seconds after visiting a few stores or websites—or, for that matter, by simply cruising a newsstand, browsing a new corner of the bookstore, or pausing for a moment at one of those hunting channels most of us surf right on past. The story was there all along, just waiting to be told. I've only held up a mirror. If hunters don't like everything they see, then maybe it's time to think about why that is and what should be done about it.

I met many wonderful people in Buffalo County, and I can only admire their dedication. Few will ever know how hard they work to provide their clients such unparalleled experiences and hunting opportunities. This brand of trophy hunting also occurs elsewhere around the country, and it's a subculture that's foreign even to most deer hunters. It's in some ways similar to the hunting scene one might encounter in certain European countries. For those who can afford to hunt Buffalo County, I don't begrudge them these experiences. But is this the future of all American deer hunting? I hope not. And by the way, these deer are *not* your deer. Not unless you bring a very fat checkbook.

You've met feeders, baiters, and foodplotters, and you've learned why feeding deer recreationally isn't such a harmless pastime after all. Supplemental feeding, which has now become the norm in many southern states, raises questions of its own. When does feeding become farming, and when do *our* deer become *your* cattle? Food plots, as different as they may feel from a pile of corn dumped out on the ground, raise the same fundamental questions. When seed companies, implement dealers, magazine articles, and the titles of how-to books promise we'll be able to "grow" better deer with bigger antlers, are we still hunting deer? Or merely farming them?

Venison is delicious, and Americans eat around three million pounds of it every year. What's more, this delicacy matters all out of proportion to the portions on those lucky hunters' plates. Although nonhunters may feel ambivalent about the whole idea of hunting, there is that survey telling us 85 percent of Americans still approve of hunting for meat. And if hunting is our best hope for restoring a balance we've disrupted, then it's vital that the majority of nonhunting Americans continue to support it—or to at least tolerate it. Those "hunting for meat" numbers are the real reason deer meat still matters.

To hungry hunters and vegan wildlife watchers alike, the phrase "overabundant deer" can seem an oxymoron. Both want to see more deer every time they look out their back window, walk their back forty, or go for a run in their local park. If you're one of them, by now you'll better understand why it's definitely possible to have too many deer. The next time you're out in the woods, you'll recognize those sharp, clearly defined browse lines for exactly what are.

Dr. Timothy Nuttle, the ecologist you met earlier, has this to say about how we perceive deer: "Most people, whether they hunt or not, see large numbers of deer out in the woods and think it's a measure of how healthy that ecosystem is. It is, but in exactly the opposite way they think. A forest with too many deer is not a healthy forest." If we couldn't care less about seedlings, saplings, or sapsuckers, then we should at least care about the deer themselves. Says Nuttle about what inevitably happens when deer become hyperabundant, "Just because we're not shooting them doesn't mean we're not killing them. And just because we're not shooting them doesn't mean they're not suffering."

Deer reproduce rapidly, and their populations are not self-regulating. As much as some of us might wish otherwise, GonaCon and other contraceptives will never be an effective tool for managing deer on a landscape level—or even, for that matter, in a single, sprawling suburb. It's impossible to repeatedly, right on schedule, dart, capture, and inject every single doe in a wild, free-roaming population. In just a few short years, one or two wary, elusive, and fertile does will inevitably render the entire effort meaningless.

For the foreseeable future, then, we'll be counting on hunters, and quite possibly fewer of them, to help reduce or at least maintain our present deer populations. But if smaller populations of hunters continue to hope they'll see more deer with less effort, and if politicians continue to give them what they want, then balance will remain elusive.

Meanwhile, even as overabundant deer eat the understory and midstory right out from under our forests, they're also filtering out from the woods every night to visit farm fields. Although I was fascinated to learn what serious deer damage actually looks like out in the field, for me the biggest revelation was that only a tiny percentage of eligible farmers participate in abatement and claims programs. For every farmer who gets a check for those two outer rows of corn that have been devoured by deer, dozens more pick their corn and leave four rows standing for the deer. Love and obsession.

Statistically, car crashes make deer the deadliest animal in North America. That will probably remain true for the foreseeable future. I needn't say a lot more, just this: Don't veer for deer. And in the words of Awesome George, "Cars are like socks. Be ready to change them once in a while." If you ride, wear a helmet.

In America's suburbs and exurbs, balance remains elusive. In the words of Sally Sneve, the homeowner from Minnesota whose tiny lawn has become an official deer removal hot spot, "I know the deer were here first. . . . I hate to infringe on nature, but sixteen deer standing around in our yard all day is just too much. There has to be some kind of balance." She'd get plenty of agreement from her counterparts in Connecticut, where the motto of the Fairfield County Deer Management Alliance is simply: "Our Mission: Restoring Balance."

Meanwhile, out beyond the city limits, the greatest long-term challenge facing deer managers is the prospect of too few hunters pursuing too many deer. Let's remember, too, that these hunter participation trends also have major implications for how we fund state wildlife agencies—and even for how we fund conservation initiatives and environmental protections more broadly. Despite a recent uptick, the long-term trends are not encouraging. As hunter numbers fall and their average age climbs, will a new wave of adult-onset hunters and locavore foodies help swell their dwindling ranks? It's hard to say.

Today the United States has around thirty million deer and 13.7 million hunters. If current trends continue, it's quite possible that forty years from now we'll have a population of four hundred million humans, forty million deer, and fewer than four million hunters. And what if hunter numbers dip even lower, say to four hundred thousand? Then what? Either way, no matter how much these hunters and their families enjoy venison, in the fall of 2052, they'll have a tough time putting a dent in our nation's deer herd.

Some have suggested increased incentives and more structured opportunities for deer donations. Already, however, nearly every state in

Deerland has some sort of donation program in place. Some, like the relatively friction-free programs in Wisconsin and Iowa, facilitate the donation of thousands of deer per year at no cost to the hunter. Typically one dollar from every hunting license is earmarked for a fund used to reimburse participating processors seventy-five dollars per deer, and the ground venison is then distributed to food banks.

Currently New Jersey, Connecticut, Georgia, Minnesota, Missouri, Pennsylvania, Tennessee, and Texas require hunters to pay for all or part of the processing fee, and hence tend to have lower participation rates. In much of the United States and Canada, private and faith-based charities like Farmers and Hunters Feeding the Hungry (FHFH) help take up the slack, and in 2008 Nebraska launched its Nebraska Deer Exchange, which is essentially a matchmaking website for hunters and the hungry. Although on rare occasions participating hunters have paid for processing, it's usually the recipients' responsibility. This seems likely to reduce participation among financially strapped recipients who are truly "hungriest." Since the program began, however, participants have exchanged enough deer to add up to an estimated twenty-five tons of venison.[1]

One recent paper proposed another, more radical solution. Its title is "Regulated Commercial Harvest to Manage Overabundant White-Tailed Deer: An Idea to Consider?" In its introduction the authors write, "Objective assessments . . . suggest that we are victims of our own success and perhaps constrained by paradigms and philosophies that rightly achieved prominence when protection and recovery of deer populations were the most imperative goals. . . . We assert that management paradigms must expand to accommodate new realities."[2]

The next three headings in their paper are revealing: "The Developed Landscape Conundrum," "Limitations of Current Control Methods," and "Regulated Commercial Deer Harvest—Another Tool in the Toolbox." Their argument is carefully reasoned and laid out in great detail. They even suggest a list of qualifications that might be required of someone seeking a commercial deer harvester license (CDHL). One by one, they thoroughly address a long list of expected concerns and objections. By the end of their paper, they've begun mapping out a blueprint for how one of these programs might work.

When I talked with two of the paper's coauthors, David Drake of the University of Wisconsin and Scott E. Hygnstrom of the University of Nebraska, the first thing they wanted to emphasize is the "regulated" part of their idea. This would be very different from the totally unregulated harvest of the eighteenth and nineteenth centuries. They also emphasized that they're not trying to make recreational hunters obsolete. The programs they envision would simply be "one more tool in the deer manager's toolbox."

A key tenet of the North American Model of Wildlife Conservation, let alone any number of state and federal laws, is that wildlife shall not be sold commercially. "But if you think about it," Drake reminded me, "we already have exceptions. What about furbearers? And some fish, even freshwater fish, can be sold commercially. In a sense, they're wildlife too. But somehow our culture sees deer differently."

Both Drake and Hygnstrom acknowledged that the idea of a commercial deer harvest is likely to be controversial among hunters and nonhunters alike. But if it's an idea whose time hasn't yet come, then that time may be approaching fast.

Precedents abound. We hear much about the illegal trade in African "bush meat," and Britain and several Western European countries do allow the sale of legally harvested wild game. Worldwide, however, the only wild animals now harvested legally for their meat on a commercial scale are kangaroos. In recent years annual quotas have ranged from four to seven million, which is in the same neighborhood as the six million or so deer that hunters harvest every year in the United States. Kangaroo meat is sold in most Australian grocery stores, and it's also exported to Great Britain and several European countries. It's quite lean and healthy, and I'm told it tastes a lot like venison.

True, not all Australians are proud of their country's kangaroo industry. Nor would most Americans be delighted at the prospect of legalized market hunting for deer. This could be one more difficult decision we'll need to make on the basis of sound science. The parallels, in any case, are remarkable. Australia has from thirty-five to fifty million kangaroos, with locally overabundant populations creating serious ecological problems. Like our deer, they're often a nuisance in suburbs and exurbs. Kangaroo-vehicle crashes are as frequent as our deer crashes. And although there's also amateur kangaroo hunting in Australia, the amateurs aren't nearly numerous enough to keep up with the kangaroo population. That's where the professional market hunters come in.

And what of the American amateurs who are still hunting deer a generation from now? Who will they be, and where will they hunt?

Just across the road from where I sit right now are thousands of acres of public land, all of it open to hunting. Down the road in either direction are thousands more. For four months of the year, were I so inclined, I could stop writing a little early every afternoon, reach for a rifle, shotgun, or bow, and then step across the road and into the woods to look for dinner on public land. Although I'd admittedly return empty-handed most days, the opportunity alone is something I shouldn't take for granted. In much of America, especially in eastern states where whitetails are most numerous, there's very little public hunting land. Private land open to hunting is even harder to find, and access often comes with a daily, weekly, or yearly price tag. Increasingly, hunting is becoming a pastime of the wealthy.

I've also seen another vision of the future, one I find vaguely disturbing for other reasons. It's one I glimpsed back in Duluth, Minnesota. There, I tagged along with hunters participating in the city's managed bowhunt. I also talked with several more. Invariably, even though it may mean hunting a three-acre patch of woods out behind someone's garage, these hunters feel incredibly fortunate to have a hunting opportunity so close to home. For most of them, it's the only way they can leave work on a weekday afternoon and still manage to squeeze in a couple hours of hunting before darkness falls. There's no competition for a spot; locations are assigned or carefully coordinated and traded among hunters. When hunted, these deer are as wild and wary as any. The challenge is here, and so are the deer.

When researchers surveyed bowhunters participating in similar programs in Westchester County, New York, and Fairfield County, Connecticut, they found three long-term threats to the programs' sustainability: First, 78 percent of the respondents were over forty. Second, the opportunity to hunt previously unhunted land was cited as a primary incentive for participating in the program, but it was an incentive that by its nature would be transitory. Third, hunter effort was likely to decline as deer populations decline.[3] In other words, if the programs work too well, they may stop working. Balance. Still, 71 percent of respondents "reported that their enjoyment had increased since first joining a program, and satisfaction was not linked to harvest opportunity or success."

One hunter in Duluth did tell me, however, that every now and then he still needs to get out for a more normal, big-woods hunting experience. On the weekends, when he has more time, he heads for one of his other stands where he'll find more solitude. I expected him to describe some location an hour or more from the city, perhaps a mile from the nearest dirt road out in one of the area's many county, state, and national forests. But no. His "big woods" spots are still within Duluth's managed hunt zone, and technically they're still within the city limits. Like most American cities, Duluth and its suburbs sprawl out beyond the horizon and fade into exurbs whose fingers reach even farther into adjacent forests and farmland. They're a perfect home for deer.

If deer have adapted to this new habitat, so has a new breed of hunter. Even when cities don't conduct a structured, managed bowhunt like the one in Duluth, their suburbs and exurbs are providing new opportunities for deer hunters who don't necessarily demand a wilderness experience. Although firearms aren't usually allowed in these new hot spots, quite often archery equipment is. So are crossbows.

Neighborhoods like these typically have much higher deer densities than the "big woods," and hunters are even discovering they're a good place to bag a trophy buck. In their 2011 book, *Bowhunting Whitetails the Eberhart Way*, John and Chris Eberhart include an entire chapter titled "Suburbs and Exurbs."[4] It opens with these words: "Like it or not, hunting in suburbs and exurbs is going to play a big role in the future of bowhunting. If you aren't hunting areas such as this already, you probably will be in the future. These areas sometimes provide tremendous hunting, but they also have potential for personal and political conflict. Knowing how to handle the situation is very important for hunting success, avoiding conflict, and retaining your hunting permission." The Eberharts then go on to share what they've learned about "handling the situation."

As I write these words, 2052 is only forty years away. Looking back, it's been thirty-five years since *Deer and Deer Hunting* magazine, which now has almost a quarter million readers, began in 1977 as a ten-page typewritten newsletter distributed to a couple dozen members of the Stump Sitters Whitetail Study Group. It's been forty-five years since the printing and mailing of my yellowed 1967 Herter's catalog that includes none of the must-have digital deer gear today's hunters order over the Internet from their phones and computers. Although bowhunting's popularity has skyrocketed in just the past twenty years, the first compound bows began appearing around forty years ago. The Pope and Young Club was founded fifty years ago. The year 2052 isn't so far away after all.

The technology, culture, and values of American deer hunters are all changing faster with every passing year. As you've seen, they've changed radically during just the past decade or two. That will remain true in the next decade, and in all the decades that follow. Meanwhile we'll continue to search for balance. Hunters of the year 2052, however many of them remain, will still complain of too few deer. Just down the road, ecologists will still measure the ailing health of a forest with too many deer.

It was only last year that Dr. Timothy Nuttle and his collaborators published their paper "Legacy of Top-down Herbivore Pressure Ricochets Back Up Multiple Trophic Levels in Forest Canopies over 30 Years." If we or our grandchildren visit their study sites forty years from now, we'll still be able to detect the legacy of that one single decade with way too many deer. Whatever songbirds we hear or don't hear during that visit, and whatever plants and trees we see or don't see, chances are good we'll see deer. The only question is how many.

The sites are scattered across one small corner of a national forest in northwestern Pennsylvania. Meanwhile, all across dozens of other states, we've altered entire landscapes in ways that benefit deer. We've removed predators that once kept their numbers in check. In vast, sprawling suburbs and exurbs, we've even given them refuge from human predators. We've disrupted a balance that will not be easy to restore.

When I talked with Nuttle, he cautioned me against using the word "balance" as often as I do. He told me that even if I mean balance—as do the Fairfield County Deer Management Alliance and that homeowner we met in Duluth—in the sense of making trade-offs and compromises, the word tends to reinforce certain misconceptions about "the balance of nature." He reminded me that if equilibrium and stasis exist in nature, they're rare, momentary, and fleeting.

Most ecologists, he told me, no longer believe in the classic concept of a steady-state "climax forest." Even without storms, fires, or loggers to open a large clearing, smaller ones still appear whenever a single tree falls in the forest—even when there's no one there to hear it fall. Something new will grow in that clearing. It might be the same kind of tree, or it might not be. If enough deer are present, it probably won't be.

"In nature," Nuttle said, "there's no balance and there's no fulcrum. There's only harmony." He reminded me that the natural world is always changing, and that on this continent most of what we view as "nature" is far less pristine than we imagine it to be. I suppose he's right. We've burned, logged, plowed, paved, and tampered. There's no single perfect natural state to which we can return. But if we can't go back, we can at least move forward in harmony with nature—and perhaps even in harmony with deer.

What changes will the next forty years bring? I can only guess. In 2052 someone else will write the sequel to this story. But I do know this: By mid-century America will be a different place. At the very least it will be warmer, tamer, and more crowded.

Meanwhile, all across a changing American landscape, one thing will remain constant: The deer will be here, living among us. We'll be living among them. And our relationship will not be simple.

Further Reading

Cerulli, Tovar. *The Mindful Carnivore: A Vegetarian's Hunt for Sustenance.* New York: Pegasus Books, 2012.

DeNicola, Anthony J., et al. *Managing White-Tailed Deer in Suburban Environments: A Technical Guide.* A Publication of Cornell Cooperative Extension, The Wildlife Society, and the Northeast Wildlife Damage Research and Outreach Cooperative, 2000 (available free online from a variety of sources).

Dizard, Jan. *Going Wild: Hunting, Animal Rights, and the Contested Meaning of Nature.* Amherst, Mass.: University of Massachusetts Press, 1999.

Frye, Bob. *Deer Wars: Science, Tradition, and the Battle Over Managing Whitetails in Pennsylvania.* University Park, Penn.: Penn State University Press, 2006.

Halls, Lowell K. (ed.). *White-Tailed Deer Ecology and Management.* Harrisburg, Penn.: Stackpole Books, 1984.

Hewitt, David G. (ed.). *Biology and Management of White-Tailed Deer.* Boca Raton, Fla.: CRC Press, 2011.

Latham, Roger Earl, et al. *Managing White-tailed Deer in Forest Habitat from an Ecosystem Perspective: A Pennsylvania Case Study.* Audubon Pennsylvania and the Pennsylvania Habitat Alliance, 2005 (available free online from a variety of sources).

McCaulou, Lily Raff. *Call of the Mild: Learning to Hunt My Own Dinner.* New York: Grand Central Publishing, 2012.

Nelson, Richard. *Heart and Blood: Living with Deer in America.* New York: Random House, 1997.

Willging, Robert. *On the Hunt: The History of Deer Hunting in Wisconsin.* Madison, Wis.: Wisconsin Historical Society Press, 2008.

Finally, these three titles will be helpful if you find yourself inspired by that "Deer DIY" passage:

Burch, Monte. *Field Dressing and Butchering Deer: Step-by-Step Instructions, from Field to Table.* Guilford, Conn.: Lyons Press, 2007.

Fromm, Eric, and Al Cambronne. *Gut It. Cut It. Cook It: The Deer Hunter's Guide to Processing and Preparing Venison.* Iola, Wis.: Krause Publications, 2009.

Shaw, Hank. *Hunt, Gather, Cook: Finding the Forgotten Feast.* New York: Rodale Books, 2011.

Notes

I. Love and Obsession

Chapter One: Darwin's Deer

1. "when he is mounted and armed with the bolas." Darwin, Charles. *The Voyage of the* Beagle. 1839. Chapter 3, from an entry dated July 26, 1832.

2. "escaped or were released unintentionally." For more on the various species of free-ranging deer in Britain, visit the British Deer Society at www.bds.org.uk or The Deer Initiative at www.thedeerinitiative.co.uk.

3. "maybe even save a few motorists' lives." For more on the center and its mission, visit www.deerstudy.com.

4. "that weigh nearly a ton." Heffelfinger, James R. "Taxonomy, Evolutionary History, and Distribution," pp. 3–39 in Hewitt, David G., editor, *Biology and Management of White-Tailed Deer*. Boca Raton, Fla.: CRC Press, 2011. (Additional references to this work will be noted as "Hewitt.")

5. "fossil record tells only part of the story." Heffelfinger in Hewitt, p. 11.

6. "just south of the Arctic Circle." Heffelfinger in Hewitt, p. 18.

7. "at least sixteen here in the United States." Baker, Rollin H. "Origin, Classification, and Distribution," pp. 1–18, in Lowell K Halls, Richard E. McCabe, and Laurence R. Jahn, editors, *White-Tailed Deer Ecology and Management*. Mechanicsburg, Penn.: Stackpole Books, 1984. (Additional references to this work will be noted as "Halls.")

8. "and Georgia (1,058)." Heffelfinger in Hewitt, p. 12.

9. "entered into the record books anytime soon." Heffelfinger in Hewitt, p. 21.

10. "a new version called Hollofil II." See www.dupont.com.

11. "up to sixty feet of small and large intestine." Ditchkoff, Stephen S. "Anatomy and Physiology," in Hewitt, pp. 43–73.

12. "the Florida Keys, Cuba, and the Virgin Islands." Hefflefinger in Hewitt, p. 20.

13. "humans fewer than five million." Carpenter, Tom. "Why the Whitetail Nose Knows." *Outdoor Life,* November 2011.

14. "larger olfactory bulbs than ours does.""Why the Whitetail Nose Knows."

15. "through a full 180 degrees." Bishop, Phillip. "The Ears Have It." *Deer and Deer Hunting,* October 2008.

16. "in a full 360 degrees." Ditchkoff in Hewitt, p. 63.

17. "in near total darkness." Ditchkoff in Hewitt, p. 63.

18. "wavelength of blaze orange." Bishop, Phillip. "Understanding Deer Vision." *Deer and Deer Hunting,* September 2008.

19. "excites our red-sensing cones." Jacobs, G. H., J. F. Deegan II, J. Neitz, B. P. Murphy, K. V. Miller, and R. L. Marchinton. "Electrophysiological Measurements of Spectral Mechanisms in the Retinas of Two Cervids: White-tailed Deer (*Odocoileus virginianus*) and Fallow Deer (*Dama dama*)." *Journal of Applied Physiology A.* 174: 551–57, 1994.

20. "80 to 90 percent of the casualties are fawns." Ozoga, John J. *John Ozoga's Whitetail Intrigue: Scientific Insights for White-Tailed Deer Hunters.* Iola, Wis.: Krause Publications, 2000.

21. "vehicle collisions 24 percent." Jacques, Christopher N., et al. "Evaluating Survival and Cause-Specific Mortality in Adult and Fawn White-tailed Deer in Northern and East-central Wisconsin." Available online from the Wisconsin DNR at dnr.wi.gov.

22. "or are discovered by predators." Marchington, R. Larry, and David H. Hirth. "Behavior," in Halls, pp. 129–68. For graphic photos of these deer mishaps, see pp. 166 and 167.

23. "appear to be unaffected by it." Campbell, Tyler A., and Kurt C. VerCauteren. "Diseases and Parasites," in Hewitt, pp. 219–49.

24. "possibly much longer." Campbell and VerCauteren in Hewitt, p.233.

25. "tonsils, eyes, or lymph tissues." See, for example, the hunter brochure from Wisconsin's Department of Agriculture, Trade and Consumer Protection at http://datcp.wi.gov/. The same brochure has been adopted by a number of other deer-hunting states and is available on their respective websites.

26. "highly artificial laboratory conditions." Belay, Ermias D., et al. "Chronic Wasting Disease and Potential Transmission to Humans."

Emerging Infectious Diseases, Vol. 10, No. 6, June 2004. Available online from the Centers for Disease Control and Prevention at www.cdc.gov.

27. "eradicating deer from infected areas." From an overview at the Chronic Wasting Disease Alliance, an invaluable online clearinghouse of CWD information. See www.cwd-info.org.

28. "lived to be twenty years old." Sauer, Peggy R. "Physical Characteristics," in Halls, pp. 73–90. See p. 90.

29. "rather than a perfect circle." DeYoung, Charles A. "Population Dynamics," in Hewitt, pp. 147–80.

30. "compared to 46 to 70 percent of yearling bucks." DeYoung in Hewitt, p. 155.

31. "unlocks the whole stalemate." For examples, visit YouTube and search for "deer tangled locked antlers."

32. "cowards, shirkers, and abstainers." Geist, Valerius. *Whitetail Tracks: The Deer's History and Impact in North America*. Iola, Wis.: Krause Publications, 2001. See chapter 7.

Chapter Two: Inside America's Deer-Industrial Complex

1. "expenditures increased a full 30 percent." All figures from the US Fish and Wildlife Service's *2011 National Survey of Fishing, Hunting, and Wildlife-Associated Recreation*. Available online from www.fws.gov.

2. "Colgate-Palmolive, Medtronic, and Southwest Airlines." Based on figures from the 2012 Fortune 500; see www.fortune.com.

3. "from gifts and furnishings." All figures from Cabela's 2011 Annual Report. Cabela's Inc., Sidney, Nebraska. For current figures, see www.cabelas.com.

4. "clothing intended specifically for fishing." Cabela's fall 2011 master catalog. Cabela's Inc., Sidney, Nebraska. See also www.cabelas.com.

5. "intensively manage their property." McKean, Andrew. "The Whitetail Depression." *Outdoor Life*, September 2011.

6. "watch for its antler-and-camo logo." See www.realtree.com.

7. "about 175 companies in seventeen countries" See www.bonnier.com.

8. "to stroll by your deer stand." For a more detailed explanation of the QDMA philosophy, see www.qdma.com.

9. "was eclipsed a few days before the end of December." Cratty, Carol. *USA Today*, December 27, 2011. Figures reported by FBI are based on

data from its National Instant Criminal Background Check (NICS). Unfortunately, since Apple rarely shares detailed sales figures, the "more guns than iPads" meme is difficult to verify.

10. "during its three-day estrous cycle." Bestul, Scott. "Mr. Doe Pee." *Field and Stream*, August 2006.

11. "and Alaska have banned them outright." For a July 2012 news story about the announcement, visit the Alaska Department of Fish and Game website: www.adfg.alaska.gov.

12. "over six hundred thousand dollars in appearance fees." McKean, Andrew. "On the Record." *Outdoor Life*, May 2010.

13. "one hundred thousand dollars, two hundred thousand, or even more." Personal communication from Buffalo County Realtors Stu Hagen, Gordy Weiss, and Tom Fedie.

14. "purchase around 87 percent of them." All statistics from the US Fish and Wildlife Service. Details and current numbers available at www.fws.gov.

15. "purchase, restoration, and protection of wildlife habitat." US Fish and Wildlife Service.

16. "a perpetual battle to keep that access." In response to a December 21, 2011, blog post by Chad Love at www.fieldandstream.com.

17. "71.8 million wildlife watchers spent fifty-five billion dollars." US Fish and Wildlife Service, *2011 National Survey of Fishing, Hunting, and Wildlife-Associated Recreation.* Available online at www.fws.gov.

18. "the North American Model of Wildlife Conservation." For a more detailed explanation of the model, see the TWS website: www.wildlife.org.

Chapter Three: The Deer of Buffalo County

1. "all of Canada's provinces combined." Overall records are kept by Boone and Crockett; see www.boone-crockett.org. Separate archery-only records are kept by Pope and Young; see www.pope-young.org. In both cases the entries from Buffalo County, Wisconsin, fill several pages.

2. "land values increased nearly fivefold." Personal communication from Buffalo County Realtors Stu Hagen, Gordy Weiss, and Tom Fedie.

Chapter Four: Feeders, Baiters, and Plotters

1. *"Please Don't Feed the Deer."* All these publications are available online from the respective agencies and were a key source for many of the basic facts and ideas in this passage.

2. "hunker down near warm dryer vents." Personal communication from Gino D'Angelo, USDA-APHIS Wildlife Services.

3. "generalized weakness may also be seen." The Michigan Department of Natural Resources provides an excellent overview of acidosis and enterotoxemia on its Corn Toxicity page at www.michigan.gov.

4. "in wildlife, domestic animals, and humans." The Wildlife Society. *Baiting and Supplemental Feeding of Game Wildlife Species.* Technical Review 06–1, December 2006. Available at www.wildlife.org.

5. "can contain up to 300 ppb." CPG Sec. 683. "100 Action Levels for Aflatoxins in Animal Feeds." See www.fda.gov.

6. "contained over 300 ppb." Texas Parks and Wildlife Department. Test samples reinforce concern over aflatoxin in deer corn. News release, September 7, 1998.

7. "7.5 times what's allowed for most other livestock." Fischer, J. R., A. V. Jain, D. A. Shipes, and J. S. Osborne. "Aflatoxin Contamination of Corn Used as Bait for Deer in the Southeastern United States." *Journal of Wildlife Diseases* 31: 570–72, 1995.

8. "or unfair advantage over the animal." For more detailed rules that support these general principles, see www.pope-young.org.

9. *"decides to leave before the warden arrives."* Fleener, Jason. "The Great De-bait." *Wisconsin Natural Resources,* February 2009.

10. "hunter effort per deer was 6 percent less." Ruth, C. R., Jr., and Derrell A. Shipes. "Potential Negative Effects on Regional White-tailed Deer Harvest Rates in South Carolina: A State with Conflicting Baiting Laws." *Annual Meeting Southeast Deer Study Group* 28: 18, 2005.

11. *"and inevitably toward the European system."* McCaffery, Keith. Book Reviews. *Journal of Wildlife Management,* Vol. 69, No. 4 (October 2005), p. 1,753.

12. "take the wild out of hunting?" Duke, Oak. "Food Plots Change Deer Hunting: They Take the Wild Out." *Wellsville Daily,* August 19, 2011.

Chapter Five: Venison: The Other Red Meat

1. "same impact as an arrow from a modern compound bow." For more on the surprising sophistication and effectiveness of this ancient weapon system, see the website of Bob Perkins (aka "Atlatl Bob") at www.atlatl .com. See also the World Atlatl Association's site: www.worldatlatl.org.

2. "with knives, hatchets, and clubs." McCabe, Richard E., and Thomas R. McCabe. "Of Slings and Arrows: An Historical Retrospective," in Halls, pp. 19–72. See especially the table on pp. 42–47.

3. "and thirteen fish species." McCabe and McCabe in Halls, p. 28.

4. "no mention of turkey—only venison." Winslow, Edward. From a letter dated December 21, 1621, and later reprinted in the pamphlet *Mourt's Relation* (1622).

5. "enjoyed during the months before and after." Bradford, William. *History of Plymouth Plantation by William Bradford, the Second Governor of Plymouth* (Boston, 1856).

6. "and oftentimes so take them." McCabe and McCabe in Halls, p. 43. It's impossible to overstate the debt modern scholars and deer aficionados owe these authors. Never before or since has anyone brought together in one place so much information about the historical role of American deer, venison, and buckskin. The authors relied on literally hundreds of secondary and primary sources, among them sales records, bills of lading, and contemporaneous eyewitness accounts.

7. "serveable and vsefull for cloathing." McCabe and McCabe in Halls, p. 61.

8. "and 1921 in Ontario." McCabe and McCabe in Halls, p. 71

9. "from Pensacola, Florida, and Mobile, Alabama." McCabe and McCabe in Halls, p. 26.

10. "went for $1.50 in Michigan." McCabe and McCabe in Halls, p. 63.

11. "for the purpose of making candles." McCabe and McCabe in Halls, p. 63.

12. "trout and venison are a drug on the market." McCabe and McCabe in Halls, p. 67.

13. "over six tons of dressed deer carcasses by rail." McCabe and McCabe in Halls, p. 26.

14. "over six million deer." Addendum to the US Fish and Wildlife

Service's *2006 National Survey of Fishing, Hunting, and Wildlife-Associated Recreation*. Available online from www.fws.gov.

15. "not including shipping and handling." Based on author's 2012 online survey.

16. "a retail value of seventy-nine billion dollars." Figures are for 2011; see www.usda.gov.

17. "approved of 'hunting for meat.'" "Americans' Attitudes Toward Hunting, Fishing and Target Shooting 2011. A survey by Duda, Mark Damian, Martin F. Jones, and Andrea Criscione of Responsive Management in Harrisburg, VA"; www.responsivemanagement.com. Commissioned by the National Shooting Sports Foundation; press release available at www .nssf.org.

18. "a dish fit for a king." Deuteronomy 14:5 and 1 Kings 4:23.

II. CONSEQUENCES

Chapter Six: Why the Mountain Fears Its Deer

1. "207 in Kansas City." Bullers, Finn. "Hordes of Deer Threaten Shawnee Mission Park. *Kansas City Star*, December 28, 2008.

2. "241 in Philadelphia." Wood, Anthony R. "'Lethal Reduction' Culls Valley Forge Deer by 70 percent." *Philadelphia Inquirer*, April 25, 2012.

3. "300 in parts of New Jersey." Terusso, Julia. "Union, Essex County Hunts Aim to Control Deer Population in Suburban Areas." *Star-Ledger*, January 8, 2012.

4. "400 in Washington, D.C." Brown, Emma. "Fairfax County Opens Parks to Bowhunters for Deer Culling." *Washington Post*, September 4, 2011.

5. "between 20 and 40 deer per square mile." deCalesta, David S. "Effect of White-tailed Deer on Songbirds within Managed Forests in Pennsylvania." *Journal of Wildlife Management*, 58: 711–18, 1994.

6. "Multiple Trophic Levels in Forest Canopies over 30 Years." Nuttle, Timothy, et al. "Legacy of Top-down Herbivore Pressure Ricochets Back Up Multiple Trophic Levels in Forest Canopies over 30 Years." *Ecosphere*, an open-access journal of the Ecological Society of America. January 2011. See www.esajournals.com.

Chapter Seven: We Get the Leftovers

1. "calculated deer-related losses at $2,443 per acre." Drake, David, and John Grande. "Assessment of Wildlife Depredation to Agricultural Crops in New Jersey." *Journal of Extension,* Vol. 40, No. 1, February 2002.

2. "impacting their ability to reduce deer numbers." New Jersey Agricultural Station. 1998. "Are White-Tailed Deer Affecting Agriculture in New Jersey?" Available at www.rutgers.edu.

3. "deer had damaged twenty acres." Miller, Craig A., et al. 2003. *Perceptions of Wildlife Crop Damage and Depredation among Agricultural Producers in Illinois.* A study prepared for the state of Illinois (project no. W-112-R-11). Available at www.illinois.edu.

4. "53 percent indicated the damage exceeded their tolerance." Conover, M. R. "Perceptions of American Agricultural Producers about Wildlife on Their Farms and Ranches." *Wildlife Society Bulletin* 26(3): 597–604, 1998.

5. "76 percent of its appraised losses." Detailed statistics and more information about how the program works are available online from the Wisconsin Department of Natural Resources (WI DNR).

6. "The state's record, set in 2000, was 615,293 deer." All figures from the WI DNR. See dnr.wi.gov.

7. "20 percent remaining for human consumption." USDA. 2011. *Crop Production and Supply/Demand Report.* See www.usda.gov.

8. "neither ethanol nor biodiesel would be profitable." Congressional Budget Office. 2010. *Using Biofuel Tax Credits to Achieve Energy and Environmental Policy Goals.* See www.cbo.gov.

9. "may actually take more energy to produce than it yields at the pump." As noted, this question remains a matter of some debate. Although more optimistic industry sources claim energy return ratios as high as 2:1, studies like the 2003 and 2005 analyses by Cornell's David Pimental and Tad Patzek found that ethanol production took 1.3 times more fossil energy than the ethanol produced. See *Natural Resources Research,* Vol. 14, No. 1, March 2005, DOI: 10.1007/s11053-005-4679-9. In their 2007 paper *Ethanol: A Look Ahead* (MIT Publication No. LFEE 2007-002 RP), MIT researchers Tiffany A. Groode and John B. Heywood used a model that

incorporates a range of values for each key variable; it found that most scenarios for corn ethanol returned a value close to 1:1. Both papers are available online.

Chapter Eight: The Deadliest Animal in North America
1. "insurance payouts of over $3.8 billion." Sloan, Allan. "Deer Overpopulation Taking Economic Toll." *Washington Post*, November 1, 2010.
2. "a complete lack of control comparisons." Knapp, Keith K., et al. 2004. *Deer-Vehicle Crash Countermeasure Toolbox: A Decision and Choice Resource.* A paper completed as part of the Deer-Vehicle Crash Information Clearinghouse Initiation Project for the Wisconsin Department of Transportation. Available at www.deercrash.org. (Additional references to this work will be noted as "Knapp.")
3. "no discernible reduction in deer crashes." Insurance Institute for Highway Safety. "Deer, Moose Collisions with Motor Vehicles Peak in Spring and Fall." *Status Report*, Vol. 28, No. 4, April 3, 1993.
4. "who responded to a newspaper ad." Tracy, T. *A Program to Reduce Collisions with Animals.* Final Report to California Office of Traffic Safety for Project RS0110. Modoc County Road Department, Alturas, California, February 2003.
5. "actually better off without the whistles." Romin, L. A., and L. B. Dalton. "Lack of Response by Mule Deer to Wildlife Warning Whistles." *Wildlife Society Bulletin*, Vol. 20, No. 4, 1992, pp. 382–84.
6. "was 'totally lost' in the noise produced by a typical vehicle at forty miles per hour." Scheifele, M. P., D. G. Browning, and L. M. Collins-Scheifele. "Analysis and Effectiveness of 'Deer Whistles' for Motor Vehicles: Frequencies, Levels, and Animal Threshold Responses." *Acoustics Research Letters Online*, Vol. 4, No. 3, July 2003, pp. 71–76.
7. "deer approaching the roadway will be more visible." Knapp, pp. 119–39.
8. "the results were mixed." Knapp, pp. 74–87.

Chapter Nine: Invasion of the Suburban Cervids
1. "dozens have been posted on YouTube." For examples, visit YouTube and search for "deer crash security camera."

2. "safer travel routes between food, water, and cover." Gorham, Dawn A., and William F. Porter. "Examining the Potential of Community Design to Limit Human Conflict with White-Tailed Deer." *Wildlife Society Bulletin,* September 2011, pp. 201–08.
3. "that results from extreme exertion." DeNicola, Anthony J., et al., 2000. *Managing White-Tailed Deer in Suburban Environments: A Technical Guide,* p. 25. A publication of Cornell Cooperative Extension, The Wildlife Society, and the Northeast Wildlife Damage Research and Outreach Cooperative (available online from a variety of sources). (Additional references to this work will be noted as "DeNicola.")
4. "had cost $431 to capture and relocate." O'Bryan, M. K., and D. R. McCullough. "Survival of Black-tailed Deer Following Relocation in California." *Journal of Wildlife Management* 49: 115–19, 1985.
5. "reported costs per deer of $400 to $2,931." DeNicola, p. 25. Based on figures from one 1984 study and three 1995 studies. For reasons noted in the text, few translocation projects have been conducted since then.
6. "not an effective means of controlling deer populations." See, for example, DeNicola, p. 29. See also Bowman, Jacob L. 2011. "Managing White-tailed Deer: Exurban, Suburban, and Urban Environments," in Hewitt, pp. 599–620.
7. "it cost around a thousand dollars per deer." Boulanger, Jason R., et al. "Sterilization as an Alternative Deer Control Technique: A Review." *Human-Wildlife Interactions* 6(2), Fall 2012.
8. "that number dropped to 47 percent." Gionfriddo, James P., et al. "Field Test of a Single-Injection Gonadotrophin-releasing Hormone Immunocontraceptive Vaccine in Female White-tailed Deer." *Wildlife Research* 36(3): 177–84, 2009.
9. "67 percent and 43 percent, respectively." Gionfriddo, James P., et al. "Efficacy of GnRH Immunocontraception of Wild White-Tailed Deer in New Jersey." *Wildlife Society Bulletin,* September 2011, pp. 142–48. (Additional references to this work will be noted as "Gionfriddo et al.")
10. "infertile five years after treatment." Milles, Lowell A., et al. "The Single-shot GnRH Immunocontraceptive Vaccine (GonaCon) in White-tailed Deer: Comparison of Several GnRH Preparations." *American Journal of Reproductive Immunology* 60: 214-223, 2008.

11. "infertile for three years." Perry, K. R., et al. "Mycobacterium Avium: Is It an Essential Ingredient for a Single-shot Immunocontraceptive Vaccine?" *Proceedings of the Vertebrate Pest Conference* 23: 253–56, 2008.

12. "necropsies revealed meager fat reserves." Gionfriddo et al.

13. "between five hundred and a thousand dollars per deer." See, for example, www.usda.gov and www.deeralliance.com.

14. "distressing symptoms in human males." Gionfriddo et al.

15. "accidental self-injection may cause infertility." See www.epa.gov.

16. "a no-go zone for deer hunters using firearms." Storm, Daniel J., et al. "Deer-Human Conflict and Hunter Access in an Exurban Landscape." *Human-Wildlife Interactions* 1(1): 53–59, Spring 2007.

17. "and all the usual state hunting regulations." For details on city ordinances and ABA rules, visit www.bowhuntersalliance.org.

18. "at least four hundred dollars per deer." This figure, while perhaps on the low side, is generally congruent with rates quoted by sources like USDA-APHIS and Anthony DeNicola of White Buffalo, Inc. Costs per deer sometimes end up being over twice this amount, and contracts from private firms typically include charges for the consultation, planning, and pre-implementation work that takes place before the shooting even begins. Other clauses specify early termination costs and hourly or daily rates for court testimony, delays caused by temporary injunctions or animal rights protests, etc. Additional costs to municipalities can include meat processing costs for food bank donation, extra law enforcement costs in the event of protests, and legal costs when projects face lawsuits from animal rights activists.

19. "the Fairfield County Deer Management Alliance." See www.deer alliance.com.

Chapter Ten: Beyond the City Limits

1. Frye, Bob. *Deer Wars: Science, Tradition, and the Battle Over Managing Whitetails in Pennsylvania.* University Park, Penn.: Penn State University Press, 2006.

2. "encourages new generations to disperse, explore, and colonize." For a more detailed discussion of deer population dynamics and how deer use the landscape, see chapters 5 and 6 in Hewitt.

3. "lead to more bucks with smaller antlers." Wooster, Chuck. "Are Vermont's Deer Losing Their Antlers?" *Northern Woodlands*, November 2011.

4. "little effect on free-ranging populations." The Quality Deer Management Association. "Is Culling Necessary?" *The QDMA 2011 Whitetail Report*. Available from the QDMA at www.qdma.com. See also Webb, Stephen L., et al. "Effects of Selective Harvest on Antler Size in White-Tailed Deer: A Modeling Approach." *Journal of Wildlife Management*, September 2011, pp. 48–56.

5. "buck fawns around 22 percent." Figures from WI DNR. See dnr.wi .gov.

6. "don't survive their first year." From Ozoga's article "Fawn Harvesting— A Logical Alternative for Northern Range," available at www.qdma.com. Ozoga has also popularized his research by writing articles appearing in magazines like *Deer and Deer Hunting* and by writing several books. See, for example, *John Ozoga's Whitetail Intrigue: Scientific Insights for White-Tailed Deer Hunters*. Iola, Wis.: Krause Publications, 2000.

7. "and 601 more between 2006 and 2010." Webb, Stephen L. "Review of Biology and Management of White-Tailed Deer." *Journal of Wildlife Management*, September 2011, pp. 220–21.

8. "there has been an overkill of deer." Nale, Mark. "Reaction Mixed to Doe Panel Bill." *Pennsylvania Outdoor News*, January 5, 2012.

9. "traces of lead in fifty-three of them." Macpherson, James. "Warnings of Lead in Venison Irk Hunters." *USA Today*, March 29, 2008.

10. "2.6 million pounds of lean, high-protein venison." Avery, D., and R. T. Watson. "Distribution of Venison to Humanitarian Organizations in the USA and Canada, in R. T. Watson, M. Fuller, M. Pokras, and W. G. Hunt, editors, *Ingestion of Lead from Spent Ammunition: Implications for Wildlife and Humans*. The Peregrine Fund, Boise, Idaho (DOI 10.4080/ ilsa.2009.0114). By conducting its own survey of venison donation organizations, the National Rifle Association has arrived at similar numbers. See www.nra.org.

11. "fourteen inches from the wound channel." Grund, M. D., et al. "Bullet Fragmentation and Lead Deposition in White-tailed Deer and Domestic Sheep." *Human-Wildlife Interactions* 4(2): 257–65, Fall 2010. Their paper

is also available, along with summaries, photos, and related information, from the Minnesota DNR's website: www.dnr.state.mn.us.

Chapter Eleven: Toward a Balance Restored

1. "an estimated twenty-five tons of venison." Hildreth, Aaron M., et al. "The Nebraska Deer Exchange: A Novel Program for Donating Harvested Deer." *Wildlife Society Bulletin,* September 2011, pp. 195–200. Most recent figures by personal communication with Kurt C. VerCauteren, one of the paper's coauthors.

2. "must expand to accommodate new realities." VerCauteren, Kurt C., et al. "Regulated Commercial Harvest to Manage Overabundant White-Tailed Deer: An Idea to Consider?" *Wildlife Society Bulletin,* September 2011, pp. 185–94.

3. "hunter effort was likely to decline as deer populations decline." Weckel, Mark, et al. "The Sustainability of Controlled Archery Programs: The Motivation and Satisfaction of Suburban Hunters." *Wildlife Society Bulletin,* September 2011, pp. 330–37.

4. "an entire chapter titled 'Suburbs and Exurbs.'" Eberhart, John and Chris. *Bowhunting Whitetails the Eberhart Way.* Mechanicsburg, Penn.: Stackpole Books, 2011.

Acknowledgments

As I researched this story, I encountered a great many people who gave generously of their time and knowledge. Because this book couldn't be any longer, I wasn't able to tell all of their stories. This doesn't mean, however, that their contributions weren't valuable.

As I began my chapter "Darwin's Deer," I was able to gain a more global perspective with the help of Robin Gill, Emma Goldberg, and Ralph Harmer of the Forest Ungulate Research Network (FURN). For an update on how the deer are doing in Charles Darwin's old neighborhood, I'd like to thank Jeanette Lawton of the Deer Study & Resource Centre in Stoke-on-Trent. Closer to home, I'd like to thank Keith McCaffery of the Wisconsin Department of Natural Resources (DNR) and Arizona biologist and writer Jim Heffelfinger, author of *Deer of the Southwest*.

For unique insights that helped me better understand America's deer-industrial complex, I'd like to especially thank Brian Murphy, CEO of the Quality Deer Management Association, and Jeff Davis, editor of the Whitetails Unlimited magazine *Quality Whitetails*. Theirs are the world's two largest conservation and hunting organizations devoted specifically to deer, and both provided information and insights that proved invaluable. For on-target background about the world of bowhunting, I'd like to thank Paul Korn of A1 Archery; Glenn and Kevin Hisey of the Pope and Young Club; and Bob Ohm, Ron Cormier, and Corrine Yohann at Mathews, Inc.

In Buffalo County I'd like to thank Todd Mau and Kris Johansen of the USDA's National Resources Conservation Service (NRCS) for sharing the bedrock-simple secret behind all those trophy antlers—and also for explaining the far less simple story of what that secret has meant for the people of Buffalo County. I'd also like to thank Realtors Gordy Weiss,

Tom Fedie, and most of all Stu Hagen. No one else knows as much as they do about Buffalo County's deer-driven real estate market. I'd also like to thank Stu's neighbor, farmer and hunter Dave Linse, for helping me better understand the past, present, and future of deer hunting in Buffalo County. I thank County Clerk Roxann Halverson for her anecdotes about long-distance plat book sales. Ted Marum showed me what it takes to make good hunting land great. Finally, for a better understanding of how hard outfitters work and what really goes on behind the scenes, I'd like to thank Scott Kirkpatrick, owner of Buffalo County Outfitters; Tom Indrebo, owner of Bluff Country Outfitters; and Butch Fox, owner of Bluff Bucks Outfitters.

Several people went out of their way to help me gain a deeper understanding for the "Feeders, Baiters, and Plotters" chapter. Among them were Warden Lance Burns of the Wisconsin DNR, Pat Rantala of Country's Garden Center, Tim Bauer of Deer Creek Seed, and Paul Korn of A1 Archery. I'd also like to thank Austin Delano of Biologic and Steve Scott of the Whitetail Institute. Theirs are two of the largest food plot companies in the business, and it was great to get their insiders' views and perspectives.

For their gracious hospitality, a fascinating look behind the scenes, and even some helpful tips on disassembling deer more efficiently, I'd like to thank Rob, Laura, Clyde, and Carol Hursh, plus the whole extended Hursh family and all the employees at Hursh Meat Processing. Thanks to Betty and Dan Wilkens for hosting Deer Day at their farm, and to Linda Bylander and Lou Cornicelli of the Minnesota DNR for allowing me to attend and visit with participants. For further insights about the growing phenomenon of adult-onset hunting, I'd like to thank author Tovar Cerulli and also hunting and shooting instructor Erik Jensen.

For help with my initial research for the chapter "Why the Mountain Fears Its Deer," I'd like to thank Wisconsin DNR biologists Greg Kessler and Fred Strand. Greg's tours of deer-nibbled areas within the Brule River State Forest and the Bayfield County Forest were especially enlightening. For an eye-opening look at deer impacts like nothing I'd ever seen, I'd like to thank Tom Rooney of Wright State University and also the members of Dairymen's. For further insights and field experiences, I thank Tim

Nuttle at Indiana University of Pennsylvania; Craig Golembiewski of the Douglas County Forestry Department; Doug Thorburn of Nelson, British Columbia; and Rob Bryan of Forestsynthesis, Inc.

For big-picture background on the "We Get the Leftovers" chapter, I'd like to thank Brad Koele of the Wisconsin DNR, Cindy Blonk of Burnett County, and Robert Willging of USDA-APHIS. I'd especially like to thank Chad Alberg and Eric Fromm, also of USDA-APHIS. They patiently answered my incessant questions while still managing to keep moving, keep measuring, and accurately appraise the deer damage in several large cornfields and bean fields. Both are truly outstanding in their fields. For the ag tag hunt scene that opened this chapter, I'd like to thank a certain farmer.

For "The Deadliest Animal in North America," I'd like to thank Dan Rogers and his sister, Kathy Moe, for their hospitality, candor, and willingness to tell a difficult but important story. I'd also like to thank Awesome George Hertzner of Awesome Auto Body; Tom Brisky, General Manager of Link's Ford; and Trooper Dean Luhman of the Wisconsin State Highway Patrol. Thanks, too, to everyone in the chain of command who helped make possible my ride with Trooper Luhman, including "Car One."

For inside intel on "Invasion of the Suburban Cervids," I'd like to thank Anthony De Nicola of White Buffalo, Inc.; Gino D'Angelo of USDA-APHIS; David Drake of the University of Wisconsin–Madison; Scott Hygnstrom of the University of Nebraska–Lincoln; Philip Lockett, Phil Mannon, and Brian Borkholder of the Arrowhead Bowhunters Alliance; Peter and Sally Sneve of Duluth, Minnesota; David Streit of Connecticut's Fairfield County Deer Management Alliance; and Bill Alexander, author of The $64 Tomato.

For firsthand insights on the challenges of managing whitetail deer out "Beyond the City Limits," I'd like to thank Lou Cornicelli of the Minnesota DNR, Keith McCaffery of the Wisconsin DNR, Brent Rudolph of the Michigan DNR, Mike Tonkovich of the Ohio DNR, Chris Rosenberry of the Pennsylvania Game Commission, Chris Larsen of Foremost Outdoors, and one or two others. You know who you are.

If I've inadvertently left anyone out, I ask their forgiveness. Thanks to all of you for your help.

Thanks to *Deer and Deer Hunting, Meatpaper,* and *Cooking Wild.* In a different form, certain passages in this book first appeared in those publications. Similarly, a far more detailed version of the "Deer DIY" story first appeared in *Gut It. Cut It. Cook It: The Deer Hunter's Guide to Processing and Preparing Venison.* For that reason a special nod is due to Krause Media. I'd like to also thank Eric Fromm, my friend, hunting mentor, and coauthor of *Gut It. Cut It. Cook It.* His insights and encouragement helped me begin following this particular deer trail. Thanks, too, to Tovar Cerulli, author of *The Mindful Carnivore: A Vegetarian's Hunt for Sustenance.* My discussions with Tovar and with visitors to his blog were tremendously helpful as I thought through certain passages having to do with the meaning of shooting one's dinner.

For reading and providing helpful feedback on early revisions and key passages, I'd like to thank Brian Murphy, Tim Nuttle, Tom Rooney, Dave Streit, and Bob Willging. If this story still contains errors of fact or omission, they're solely my own.

At Lyons I'd like to thank the stellar editorial team of Janice Goldklang, David Legere, Devin O'Hara, and Paulette Baker. Their constructive feedback and helpful suggestions have made this a far better book than it otherwise would have been. I'd also like to thank Publicist Jessica DeFranco for all the hard work she did to help spread the word about *Deerland.*

I'd especially like to thank Laurie Abkemeier of DeFiore and Company for her wise counsel, tireless advocacy, and patient guidance as she led me through the literary labyrinth. She has been truly wonderful to work with, and I feel tremendously fortunate to have her for an agent.

Finally, I'd like to thank my wife, Jean, for her support and forbearance during this long project. She has listened patiently to way too many deer stories, and somehow continues to smile at my predictable toast . . .

Here's to the deer!

About the Author

Al Cambronne is a freelance writer and photographer. He is the coauthor of *Gut It, Cut It, Cook It*. A graduate of the University of Wisconsin–River Falls, he lives with his wife in northern Wisconsin.

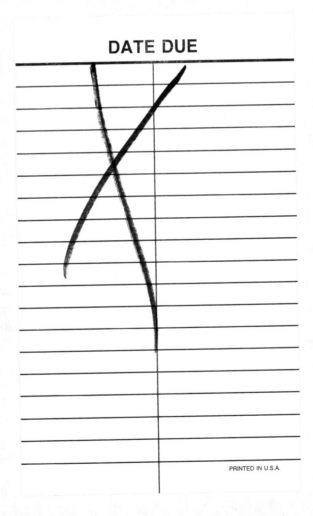